FOOD LOVERS'
GUIDE TO
NASHVILLE

FOOD LOVERS' SERIES

FOOD LOVERS'
GUIDE TO
NASHVILLE

The Best Restaurants, Markets & Local Culinary Offerings

1st Edition

Jennifer Justus

Guilford, Connecticut

Editor: Kevin Sirois
Project Editors: Heather Santiago and Lauren Brancato
Layout Artist: Melissa Evarts
Text Design: Sheryl Kober
Illustrations by Jill Butler with additional art by Carleen Moira Powell and MaryAnn Dubé
Map: Alena Pearce © Morris Book Publishing, LLC

ISBN 978-0-7627-8154-6

Printed in the United States of America
10 9 8 7 6 5 4 3

All the information in this guidebook is subject to change. We recommend that you call ahead to obtain current information before traveling.

Contents

About the Author

Jennifer Justus writes about food and life for *The Tennessean*.

Raised at the table of a meat-and-three, Jennifer later received her formal food training at Boston University, where she created her own food-writing curriculum with courses in both journalism and gastronomy, a cultural study of food founded by Julia Child and Jacques Pépin.

Prior to journalism, Jennifer worked in qualitative research studying the emotional connections we make with food. She spent hours in the kitchens of home cooks looking for the reasons behind the comfort in a pot of chili, and she conducted deprivation studies with teenagers across the country to understand the craving for a slice of pepperoni pie.

Jennifer's work has been featured in Volumes 5 and 6 of *Cornbread Nation: The Best of Southern Food Writing* and in *Alimentum* literary food journal. She has written for *Southern Living, Food Network* magazine, the *Boston Herald,* and the *Boston Globe,* among other publications, and she has been a speaker at the Southern Food Writing Conference during the International Biscuit Festival. She blogs at *A Nasty Bite,* anastybite.blogspot.com, an expression her grandmother gave to a simple meal.

Acknowledgments

To the chefs and restaurateurs, thank you for your hard work and creativity in keeping Music City well-fed and inspired. I love showing you off.

To my parents, thank you for always believing in me—even when I wrote badly about peas in the second grade.

To my editor, Kevin Sirois, thank you for giving me the opportunity to write about the city I love, and thank you for your kind, supportive words.

Thank you to my Tennessean family—Linda Zettler and Jessica Bliss especially.

Thank you to Ellen Margulies, Thomas Williams, John Egerton. Thank you to my friends Jaime Miller and Ann Manning and to Jamie Justus, who truly knows what this work means to me.

And to my favorite dining companion, Tony, thank you for keeping me laughing and inspired. Because even though you took me to City House on our first date, you had me at the hot sauce challenge.

Introduction

Just a couple years after moving to Nashville, I had a friend visit from London, and I couldn't decide where to take him.

Should we go to City House where R.E.M. and Bill Clinton have dined? Or honky-tonking on Lower Broad? I wanted him to eat turnip greens at Arnold's Country Kitchen, a classic Nashville meat-and-three, but I also wanted him to hear our Grammy-winning symphony. I was torn between hip sake cocktails at Virago or hipster PBRs at Red Door East. In the end I realized it's not one side of Nashville I wanted him to experience, it was the spectrum. Because as they say in the music business, this town's got range.

I like to believe that Nashvillians have a special appreciation and pride in both the low and high culture of our place—the mix of divey, soulful magic and innovative new South that make our city great. It's a variety that shows up in our music, for sure, but also in our food.

Take the Nashville-style hot chicken at The Catbird Seat, for example. The Catbird Seat isn't just one of the hottest restaurants in town—it's one of the hottest in the country, making *GQ* magazine's recent top 10 list. Even with a seven-course tasting beginning at $100 per person,

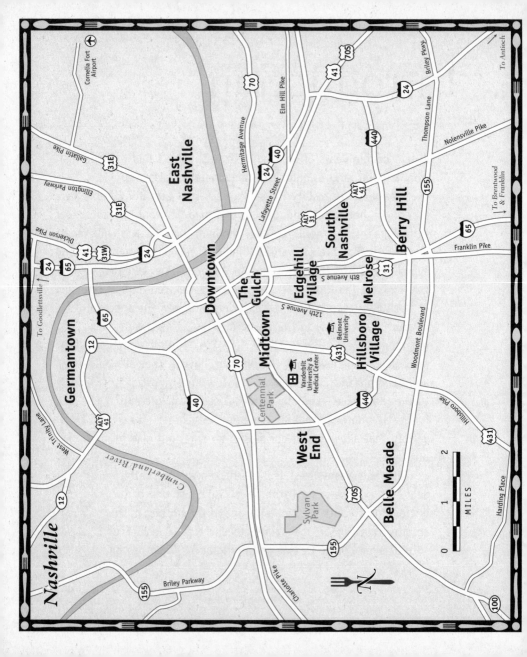

reservations stay booked for the creations of chefs Josh Habiger (stints at Alinea and CRAFT) and Erik Anderson (Noma and The French Laundry). As an homage to a gritty Nashville experience, though, the restaurant sometimes serves its own version of hot chicken. At traditional hot chicken joints,
the chicken is fried in cast-iron skillets and served on grease-soaked white bread. At The Catbird Seat it's a square of crispy chicken skin no bigger than a business card, dusted with spice, topped with white bread puree and sprinkled with dill-pickle salt.

"I think it's important as a chef to know about every type of food you can," Habiger said, "to just soak up."

So just as Nashville attracts creative musicians of all types (who just might be filling your wine glass at dinner), Music City also has been drawing creative cuisines, too. The hot chicken and meat-and-threes live on with a strong legacy, but so do farm-to-table restaurants, celebrating our agrarian roots in new ways, as well as innovative restaurants, heralding the new American South.

How to Use This Book

I like to geek out on travel planning when I head to a new city, so I organize the restaurants I'd like to hit up by area of town. That way if I'm craving a particular kind of food—or if I find a restaurant unexpectedly closed—I can make a quick Plan B. No disappointments. No wasting time. No bad decisions. Given that philosophy, I'm hoping the organization of this book by area of town will be helpful to you.

Within each chapter, you'll find establishments listed alphabetically under the following:

Foodie Faves

This section includes any restaurant worth a visit, from longstanding favorite holes in the wall, to the hottest chef-driven destinations.

Landmarks

These are the establishments that have been around for ages, or that are reliable legends. Either way, the Nashville food scene wouldn't be the same without them.

Meat-and-Threes

It's been said we have more meat-and-threes in Nashville than any other Southern city. I'm sure there are folks from other Southern cities who would argue. But there's no sense fighting over fried chicken, I say, and these spots simply warrant their own section on soulfulness alone.

Specialty Stores, Markets & Producers

These sections list the artisan chocolate makers, bakers, coffee shops, and farmers' markets of an area.

Recipes

At the back of the book, some of the best chefs in town have offered recipes to help you take a bit of Nashville back to your home kitchen, from favorite dishes like the Celery & Blue Cheese Soup at The Yellow Porch to Nashville-style hot chicken, legendary meat-and-three fare, chefs' specialties, and the favorite dishes these pros like to make at home.

Price Code

Each restaurant listing comes with a price code to indicate cost of a single entree. The code works like this:

$	**Less than $10**
$$	**$10 to $20**
$$$	**$20 to $30**
$$$$	**$30 to $40**

Keeping Up with Food News

In 2012, *Bon Appétit* magazine called Music City the "Tastiest Town in the South." Musician (and Nashville resident) Dan Auerbach of The Black Keys helped our cause when he bragged on Music City's fresh Mexican food at Mas Tacos Por Favor, the pizza at City House, and the whole hog barbecue from Martin's Bar-B-Que Joint. And while we were pleased to have the national recognition, my reaction to the *Bon*

MEAT-AND-THREES

It's been said that Nashville has more meat-and-threes than most other Southern cities. But no one can seem to figure out why.

I've asked the question many times of those who run these popular country-cooking restaurants where you can get a plate lunch of one meat (fried chicken or roast beef, maybe) and three or more sides (typically mac and cheese, turnip greens, squash casserole, green beans). Reasons vary on the topic. We're a town that's long been wrapped up in a working-man's culture, especially given our musical roots. We're also a town plopped among farmland where the ingredients of a meat-and-three grow. And even Southern Foodways Alliance director and acclaimed food writer John T. Edge once raised the theory in his book *Southern Belly* that maybe it's because we're a country-come-to-town kind of place. I liked the theory. But then John Egerton, another great food writer and author from Nashville, shot a hole in his argument citing the country folk who made their way to work the coal mines of Birmingham, Alabama.

No matter the theory, I just hope we keep it up. For the finest of plate lunches—like at James Beard award–winning **Arnold's Country Kitchen** (p. 177) or **The Pie Wagon** (p. 136), which dates back to the 1920s—see the Meat-and-Threes sections under the neighborhoods in this book.

Appétit story was the same as when, a few months earlier, *Rolling Stone* named Nashville as the best live music scene—well, yeah.

Local chefs have been receiving James Beard Foundation recognition, new restaurants have been putting down roots, creative wine dinners and happy hour specials help keep us entertained. Local independent restaurants have been bravely throwing open their doors—and filling seats—in Nashville despite a tough economy. And while we had just a handful of food trucks in 2010, about 40 roll onto the streets these days handing burgers, *banh mi* sandwiches, and fish tacos out their windows.

With so much happening, I'm thankful to have other food lovers in town for consulting. More than 100 people blog about food in Music City, organizing Food Blogger Bake Sales for Flood Relief (after Nashville's flood of 2010), holding regular meet-ups, and even sponsoring the first Food Blog Forum Nashville in 2011, which hosted bloggers both locally and from outside the city.

The food community in Nashville is just that—a community. We learn from one another by tasting and tweeting and sharing our tales of burger quests and favorite brunch spots. And as long evidenced by strangers becoming friends over a meal or family members reconnecting at the table, if anything can get a group to come together, it's food.

Publications

Alimentum, alimentumjournal.com. Though this literary journal about all things food features pieces from writers from across the country, it's based in Music City. So we're claiming it. This site includes only the best in food prose in the form of poetry, fiction, nonfiction, and Q&As with writers like Amanda Hesser of *Food52,* and John T. Edge, a columnist for the *New York Times* and director of the Southern Foodways Alliance.

The City Paper, nashvillecitypaper.com. This weekly news publication is owned by SouthComm Inc., the company that also publishes the weekly alternative paper the *Nashville Scene.* Online and in the print version of this glossy pub, you'll find restaurant news from veteran music food writer Dana Kopp Franklin.

Entree, facebook.com/entreenashville; entreenashville.posterous .com. This free bimonthly magazine is available at coffee shops, grocery stores, bars, and more, for "all things food" in Nashville. Issues have included chef spotlights, feature stories on topics like the competition barbecue circuit or the growing food truck culture, as well as reviews and recipes.

Local Table, localtable.net. This free monthly publication is the resource for farms, farmers' markets, community-supported agriculture programs, wineries, and artisan retailers in the area. Featured stories might focus on the health benefits of eggs or a guide to winter squashes, as well as profiles of local food heroes, including chefs, farmers, or food advocacy proponents. Online you'll find recipes, video chats with farmers, and blogs, including one by founder and publisher Lisa Shively. I often refer to the magazine's seasonal produce chart to know what's growing in Middle Tennessee at a certain month of year.

Nashville Business Journal, bizjournals.com/nashville. Though you won't find restaurant reviews or lifestyle stories in this weekly business-focused newspaper, it offers coverage of the local restaurant industry, including local chains like O'Charley's and Cracker Barrel, as well as independent restaurant development, openings, and closings.

Nashville Lifestyles magazine, nashvillelifestyles.com. This glossy magazine owned by Gannett hits newsstands monthly. The magazine's Taste section often includes profiles and roundups of restaurants in categories such as best brunches or best Italian restaurants. The big keeper for food lovers, though, is the Restaurants issue printed each year in April, often with features from local food writer Stephanie Stewart, local author and veteran food critic Kay West, former *Tennessean* food critic and author Jim Myers, author and Nashville Scene blogger Chris Chamberlain, and me.

Nashville Post, nashvillepost.com. This bimonthly business magazine also owned by SouthComm includes food business and restaurant news from Dana Kopp Franklin.

Nashville Scene, nashvillescene.com. The weekly alternative paper of Nashville collects its food news online in the *Bites* blog.

Dana Kopp Franklin edits the blog and posts about restaurant openings, closings, and other happenings. Local author Chris Chamberlain often writes posts covering wine and new restaurants. The *Scene* also welcomes writers from off the food beat who comment on dining experiences or offer product reviews, often with a humorous touch. The *Scene*'s restaurant reviews, which appear in print version as well as online, are written by Carrington Fox, a veteran and pro food critic.

The Tennessean, tennessean.com. Nashville's daily newspaper, a Gannett publication, has a food section called Taste that runs on Wednesday. It often includes a Chef du Jour column as well as a Front Burner section with local food happenings and tidbits. The featured articles include profiles of home cooks, recipes, trend stories, a column by author Tammy Algood, articles by guest bloggers, and 101 Minutes, a series about local restaurants. A 5 to Try restaurant feature as well as local craft-beer news runs on Friday. Nancy Vienneau, a trained chef, former restaurateur, and blogger at *Good Food Matters* (nancyvienneau.com), writes restaurant reviews that run on Sunday, covering establishments from food trucks and meat-and-threes to higher-end restaurants. Wine news also runs on Sunday. All food coverage also can be found at the Taste section online.

Local Food Blogs

Nashville's food blogging community is more than 100 strong, and you can visit **Nashville Food Bloggers** (nashvillefoodbloggers.com) to keep up with events and peruse the list of members and their blogs. The group organizes meet-ups and events like food truck festivals. And in 2011, a handful of local bloggers put together Food Blog Forum Nashville, hosting about 100 participants from the Middle Tennessee area and beyond.

East Nashville with Love, eastnashvillewithlove.com. Longtime music editor (and awesome drummer) Nicole Keiper keeps this blog about her neighborhood and culinary hot spot East Nashville. While the blog covers all things entertainment, Nicole has her finger on the pulse of the culinary scene, giving first impressions of new restaurants and news about openings, closings, and special promotions.

eat. drink. smile., eat-drink-smile.com. Beth Sachan chronicles her adventures dining out in Nashville, shopping for products, attending events, and cooking at home. Outside of her blog, Beth works in marketing for the iconic Goo Goo Cluster, a 100-year-old candy bar founded in Nashville.

Nashville Restaurants, nashvillerestaurants.blogspot.com. This husband-and-wife team—a vegetarian and a meat eater—have reviewed hundreds of budget-friendly restaurants on their site since 2007, from traditional Mexican eateries to barbecue and pizza joints. I like that the pair focuses on affordable restaurants and offers different perspectives on the food.

Vivek's Epicurean Adventures, viveksepicureanadventures.com. Walk into a happening food event in Nashville—whether it be a chef's book signing, the Night Market at the Nashville Farmers' Market, a food truck meet-up or the debut of a restaurant's sea-sonal menu—and you'll probably spot Vivek Surti. He blogs about his experiences at restaurants as well as his own kitchen, where he has chronicled a year-long charcuterie contest. Vivek also hosts a local supper club.

Several Nashville food bloggers focus more on cooking at home than dining out (although there's crossover, naturally). A few of the most popular, and my favorites, include the following.

Erin's Food Files, erinsfoodfiles.com. This television editor by day blogs about her adventures in the kitchen (and at restaurants) during her time off. She does most of her cooking on the weekends, but even with her busy schedule she posts regularly, and I have never seen a photo of hers that didn't make me want to eat my computer screen.

Ezra Pound Cake, ezrapoundcake.com. Rebecca Crump's cleverly named blog combines the names of modernist poet Ezra Pound with pound cake. It's a nod to her background as an English major and writer, and the time she spent as a professional baker. Her blog has gained a large following for her witty writing and accessible recipes.

La Aguacate, laaguacate.com. When blogger Annakate Tefft studied abroad in Spain, her friends gave her the nickname La Aguacate, or "the Avocado," because her name sounded similar to the Spanish name for the fruit. Hence the name of her blog, which chronicles her adventures in the kitchen and at local restaurants. Annakate works in public relations for *Alimentum* literary journal. She also works with Just a Pinch, a national online recipe club based in Franklin, Tennessee.

Lesley Eats, lesleyeats.com. While there are other blogs in Nashville suited for people with allergies or certain culinary and lifestyle preferences, *Lesley Eats* focuses on vegetarian cooking and eating around Nashville, proving that living without meat is anything but boring.

Life a la Mode, lifealamode.com/blog. Tabitha Ong Tune makes *macarons*, which is impressive in itself. But she's also a social media guru who blogs about her experiences both at restaurants and baking at home.

Love & Olive Oil, loveandoliveoil.com. Lindsay Landis and her husband, Taylor, started *Love & Olive Oil* in 2007, and Lindsay is the brains behind one of the first Nashville food blogger events. After the Nashville flood of 2010, she organized the Nashville Food Blogger Bake Sale, which raised money for flood relief. Lindsay also helped organize Food Blog Forum Nashville. In December 2011, Lindsay organized a Food Blogger Bake Sale that attracted more than 620 participants from across the country (and even a few from other parts of the world) to bake and exchange more than 22,000 cookies. Lindsay also has written *The Cookie Dough Lover's Cookbook*.

So, How's It Taste, sohowsittaste.com. This blogger once had to beg her college roommate to make her a grilled cheese. That's how little she cooked. But you'd hardly know it from the photos and recipes you'll find on her blog these days. The food lover posts everything from salads and sandwiches to cakes and madeleines, as well accounts of her trips to restaurants. And, yes, you might find a grilled cheese—but a more sophisticated version with honey, figs, and goat cheese spread onto cinnamon raisin bread.

Festivals & Events

January

Restaurant Week, nashvilleoriginals.com. For two weeks out of every year (one week in January and another in September), diners can catch special deals and prix-fixe menus

priced to match the year ($20.12 in 2012, for example). The event is sponsored by Nashville Originals, a group of local independent restaurants.

February

Our Kids Soup Sunday, ourkidscenter.com. Chilly weather in February is suited for soup, so Our Kids, an organization helping child victims of sexual abuse, has held this fund-raiser during the winter month for nearly 20 years. Chefs from about 50 local restaurants compete by making creative soups like the Coconut and Sweet Plantain Soup with Caribbean Crab from **1808 Grille** (p. 215). Warning: Pace yourself.

March

Cupcake-palooza, facebook.com/cupcakepaloozabenefit. A benefit for Books from Birth of Middle Tennessee, Cupcake-palooza gives attendees the chance to sample from thousands of mini cupcakes from some of the most popular bakeries in town such as **The Cupcake Collection** (p. 155), **Sweet Stash** (p. 161), and **The Painted Cupcake** (p. 119), as well as home bakers.

East Nashville Beer Festival, eastnashvillebeerfest.com. Maybe it's the beer or the beer-loving neighborhood (or both), but this festival sells out quickly every year. And by quickly, I mean the day tickets go up for grabs. It's a new festival, too, having its first run in 2011. You'll find mostly craft beer for sampling, like Left Hand Brewing and Lazy Magnolia, but there are food vendors and food trucks, too.

April

Dining Out for Life, diningoutforlife.com/nashville. For more than 10 years, Dining Out for Life has helped raise millions for AIDS-related service organizations. To participate, diners just make a reservation at participating restaurants, and restaurateurs give a percentage of sales (each restaurant publicizes the percentage it chooses) to the organization.

Iron Fork Chef Competition, nashvillescene.com. *The Nashville Scene* sponsors this *Iron Chef*–style throwdown among five local chefs in town each year. Attendees have access to samples, drinks, and the action.

May

Generous Helpings, secondharvestmidtn.org. This is a food event you don't want to miss. Many of Nashville's best independent restaurants serve tasting-size portions of their appetizers, entrees, and desserts to benefit Second Harvest Food Bank of Middle Tennessee. The event takes place at the Nashville Farmers' Market.

Savor Nashville, nashvillelifestyles.com. Sponsored by *Nashville Lifestyles* magazine, this two-day event has featured star chefs from both local restaurants and outside the city for cook-offs and dinners.

June

Nissan Taste of Music City, tasteofmusiccity.com. One of the largest food events of the year, this festival takes over parts of downtown with booths offering everything from food you might find at a state fair to stellar barbecue, samples from some of Nashville's favorite restaurants, and Goo Goo Cluster candy bars. There's a Kids' Zone and Beer Garden, too, though obviously not in the same area.

Nourish Nashville, nourishnashville.com. What began as a flood relief dinner raising more than $70,000 in 2010 has morphed into this event for The Nashville Food Project, a food advocacy group serving hot nutritious meals to Nashville's poor. The event typically features a team of celebrity chefs from throughout the South who come together to offer their talents to our town.

Purity Miss Martha's Ice Cream Crankin' Social, marthaobryan.org. A gigantic ice-cream social held on the lawn of the First Presbyterian Church, Miss Martha's gives visitors a chance to sample from hundreds of gallons of homemade ice-cream flavors. The winning ice cream at this tasting will become an official Purity flavor the following year. Proceeds benefit the Martha O'Bryan Center, an organization to help people in poverty transform their lives through work and education.

July

L'Ete du Vin/Nashville Wine Auction, nashvillewineauction .com. Since it began in 1980 as a way to celebrate wine and raise money for cancer research, this event has become the largest one-day wine auction outside California. It includes a Vintner's Tasting plus a silent auction, and then a live auction with dinner followed by an after party and a late-night dessert buffet. Guests of honor have included Jean-Charles Cazes of Chateau Lynch Bages and Dennis Cakebread of Cakebread Cellars.

MAFIAoZA's Music City Brewer's Festival, musiccitybrewers fest.com. Held in downtown Nashville near the Country Music Hall of Fame, the Brewer's Festival has been drawing beer makers with their samples, from Brooklyn Brewing and Lazy Magnolia to Harpoon, Abita, and even Pabst Blue Ribbon. To keep lines manage-able, the festival has two sessions: noon and 6 p.m. (the later session is preferable due to its cooler temperatures). Though the focus is on the beer, you'll find food, too, from local restaurants that in past years have included **12th South Taproom** (p. 199) and Jim 'N Nick's BBQ. And of course, you'll find pizza from **MAFIAoZA's** (p. 202), too.

Music City Hot Chicken Festival, hotchickenfestival.com. Cofounded by former Nashville mayor (and hot chicken fanatic) Bill Purcell, this festival that began in 2007 swells every year. Amateur cooks can enter the hot chicken contest, or tasters can just visit East Park in East Nashville to sample hot chicken, listen to live music, or visit the locally brewed **Yazoo** (p. 264) beer tent.

Share Our Strength Tasteful Pursuit Dinner, shareourstrength.org. James Beard award–nominated chef Tyler Brown of The Hermitage Hotel's **Capitol Grille** (p. 28) is the host of this annual dinner to raise money to end child hunger. It features an all-star cast of chefs—both local and from out of town—for a multicourse dinner.

Soul Food Festival, ilovesoulfood.com. George Clinton and Parliament Funkadelic headlined this festival at Riverfront Park downtown in 2011, so yeah, it's a big deal. The traveling festival is based in Oklahoma, but it brings together local communities to enjoy soul food and live music.

August

Music City Festival & BBQ Championship, musiccitybbqfestival.com. This two-day festival along the riverfront downtown includes a professional and amateur competition with more than $25,000 in prizes. The festival is sanctioned by both the Memphis Barbecue Network and the Kansas City Barbecue Society. Though festivalgoers can't sample competing teams' barbecue, there are plenty of barbecue vendors as well as live music to keep you entertained.

Tomato Art Fest, tomatoartfest.com. What began as a small neighborhood art festival with a tomato theme has grown into one of the largest festivals in the city. The art component remains strong, but in funky East Nashville, a lot more tomato  kookiness has been added. Drink a Bloody Mary while watching the Second Line parade, or visit rows of vendors including BLT makers and tomato-themed bake sales benefiting the **Nashville Farmers' Market** (p. 145). Those with a competitive streak can enter the tomato-themed cooking contest, too.

September

Music City Southern Hot Wing Festival, musiccitywingfest .com. Hosted at Walk of Fame Park near the Country Music Hall of Fame, this event includes both a wing-cooking contest and a wing-eating contest. The festival benefits the Ronald McDonald House Charities of Nashville.

Southern Artisan Cheese Festival, thebloomy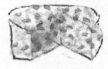
rind.blogspot.com. Kathleen Cotter, a local chee-
semonger with **The Bloomy Rind** (p. 99), put
together the first-ever Southern Artisan Cheese
Festival in 2011. The festival takes places at the **Nashville
Farmers' Market** (p. 145) and includes samples of handcrafted
cheese and cheese-tasting accoutrements such as crackers and jams
from some of the best artisans across the South. There's beer and
wine, too, from local breweries and wine shops. A portion of proceeds goes toward a food-related charity.

Wine on the River, wineontheriver.com. It's an opportunity to
sip wines from all over the world—and even locally—from the
Shelby Street Pedestrian Bridge overlooking the Cumberland River
downtown. Several local restaurants offer bites, too. Tickets often
sell out in advance, and proceeds go to Hands On Nashville.

October

Battle of the Food Trucks, foodtrucksnashville.com. There are
about 40 food trucks in Nashville, but rarely do you see so many
of them in one spot. The parking lot of Greer Baseball Stadium
becomes a food court of food trucks with each of them bringing
their A game. Festival attendees help choose the winner by voting
on favorite dishes. Proceeds benefit The Tomorrow Fund at the
Community Foundation of Middle Tennessee.

Biscuits and Bluegrass Fall Festival, lovelesscafe.com. The **Loveless Cafe** (p. 283) hosts this family festival each year at the restaurant with live music and biscuit giveaways throughout the day.

Celebrate Nashville Cultural Festival, celebratenashville.org. It's like a mini romp around the world without leaving Centennial Park. More than 50 cultures share their traditions in music, dancing, and food. You can sample Ethiopian, Venezuelan, Vietnamese, Greek, and Mexican dishes just to name a few. The festival was founded by the Scarritt-Bennett Center, a conference and educational center.

Music and Molasses Arts & Crafts Festival, tnag museum.org/special.html. This festival has celebrated the tradition of making sorghum molasses for two decades. Visitors can watch the process and taste the final product along with barbecue, homemade ice cream, roasted corn, and grilled turkey legs. Other old-time activities include apple butter making, square dancing, quilt making, and blacksmithing.

Nashville Beer Festival, nashvillebeerfestival.com. Sample more than 80 beers at this festival held at Public Square Park downtown. Participants include Abita, French Broad, Guinness, Jolly Pumpkin, Sweetwater, Lazy Magnolia, Brooklyn Brewery, and Flying Dog as well as locals like **Yazoo** (p. 264), **Blackstone** (p. 261), Boscos, and Calfkiller. Oh—and there will be food, too, from a variety of vendors. Proceeds benefit Second Harvest Food Bank of Middle Tennessee.

Oktoberfest/Germantown Street Festival, nashvilleoktober fest.com; historicgermantown.org. Though it's technically two separate festivals, you can hardly tell the difference. Both happen on the same day each year in the streets of the Germantown neighborhood and both involve lots of live music, polka dancing, lederhosen, and beer. Of course German food is available, too.

November

Phoenix Club Taste of Nashville, tasteofnashville.com. Not to be confused with Taste of Music City, this event is held indoors, and the ticket is a bit pricier but with higher-end options. You might sample, for example, the French-influenced food of **Miel** (p. 220) and the sushi of **Virago** (p. 130) as well as drink samples from local breweries and distilleries. Proceeds benefit the Boys & Girls Clubs of Middle Tennessee.

Food Trucks

In just a couple of years, Nashville's food truck culture has taken off, so to speak, from just a handful of trucks to more than 40 hitting the streets these days.

This is a moveable feast, though, with mobile vendors pulling up to business parks for lunch one day, breweries during happy hour on other days, and evening dinner events at farmers' markets. I've listed five favorites below, and I recommend checking out nash foodtrucks.com to see what's new and find out about food truck happenings around town. To track these trucks down, follow them on Facebook or Twitter (handles listed here).

Biscuit Love Truck, @BiscuitLuvTruck. Scratch-made biscuits made even more decadent with toppings that transform them to sandwiches and dessert. Try The Princess, a hot chicken biscuit with house-made pickles and a drizzle of honey, or The Gertie, a biscuit with caramelized banana jam, house-made peanut butter with pretzel crunch, and **Olive & Sinclair** (p. 97) chocolate gravy.

The Cupcake Bus, @cupcaketweets. The mobile version of a family-run cupcake shop in Germantown (see p. 155), this bus spreads happiness in the form of Key lime and red velvet cupcakes.

The Grilled Cheeserie, @grlldcheeserie. You could call it the comfort wagon, as this couple serves up gourmet grilled cheeses in options like The B&B with local buttermilk cheddar, Benton's bacon, orange and apricot marmalade on multigrain. Don't miss the homemade pudding cups—especially the salted caramel pudding.

Mas Tacos Por Favor, @mastacos. With a brick-and-mortar location (see p. 78), this truck doesn't make the rounds like it used to, but that makes it even more of a coup when you find it. Try the tacos, of course, like quinoa and sweet potato, pulled pork, or fried avocado. But I also love the *elote*. See Owner Teresa Mason's recipe for **Chicken Tortilla Soup** on p. 291.

Riffs Fine Street Food, @riffstruck. B. J. Lofback and Carlos Davis, a culinary team from Detroit and Barbados, respectively, bring fresh food with an international flair to the streets. While the menu changes often, you might find *bulgogi*-style pork tacos with ginger-scallion dressing and Asian slaw, for example, or pecan-crusted chicken with orange-basil sauce and roasted vegetables.

Downtown

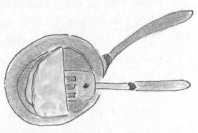

If you stand on the hill beside the Ryman Auditorium—the "Mother Church of Country Music" that now hosts the likes of Merle Haggard to Primus—you can watch as crowds converge on the corner of Lower Broadway and 4th Avenue. Locals in hockey jerseys flood out of Bridgestone Arena where the Nashville Predators play and merge with tourists following the neon lights and live music of the honky-tonks. Downtown office workers dart out of restaurants where they've had after-work drinks, and residents head out of their condos for a late snack or to catch some live music. Downtown makes for a lively cocktail of cowboy boots, stilettos, and sneakers, with the lights and energy of a party gone full tilt—hence the nickname Nashvegas. But it hasn't always been that way. Back in the mid-1970s when the Grand Ole Opry moved from the Ryman to Donelson, some of the honky-tonks were strip clubs. Then in the 1980s developers turned back to downtown, making the riverfront warehouses along 2nd Avenue a destination. The Country Music Hall of Fame and Museum followed in 2001, as did the sophisticated Schermerhorn Symphony Center in 2006. And now with nightlife back in swing, and the massive Music City Center convention space predicted to open in 2013, the food scene downtown has followed the action as it continues to improve. While some of these spots offer a quick midday meal for businesspeople on lunch hour, other restaurants are worth making the trip downtown—with or without the bars and music—for the meal alone.

Foodie Faves

Arpeggio, Schermerhorn Symphony Center, 1 Symphony Place, Nashville, TN 37201; (615) 687-6400; nashvillesymphony.org; American Contemporary; $$$$. It's the type of spread you'd find at a proper wedding reception—soup, salad, main entrees, and desserts. Even the tables with white cloths feel reception-like as they give the room a temporary banquet sort of feel. In a way they are, because this restaurant in the East Lobby of the Schermerhorn Symphony Center only opens before concerts at the hall. You'll find sliced beef tenderloin, as an example, and maple-grilled quail with figs, cherry couscous, and pistachios. There's always a vegetarian offering, too, such as stuffed pastas with tomato ragout. You'd be hard-pressed to find a finer room to dine in than the Schermerhorn, which opened in 2006. It finds its model in many European concert halls built around the late 19th century, with its soothing mint-colored walls and dripping art deco lights. And if you're the type to be racing toward shows in the nick of time, then dining inside the building guarantees you'll have a fine bite and drink—and still make curtain. Reservations preferred.

Capitol Grille, The Hermitage Hotel, 231 6th Ave. North, Nashville, TN 37201; (615) 345-7116; capitolgrillenashville.com; Contemporary Southern; $$$. Sometimes restaurants inside hotels serve as not much more than a convenient means of sustenance. But the Capitol Grille at the historic Hermitage Hotel is a destination unto itself. From the lobby, you'll descend a wide staircase into the lush dining room with warm golden light and cushy chairs. A two-time James Beard award nominee, Executive Chef Tyler Brown can often be found at the restaurant's period garden at Glen Leven, a partnership with the Land Trust for Tennessee, where he raises rows of heirloom vegetables and heritage beef for a menu that's seasonal, local, and sophisticated Southern. You might find an heirloom white-bean soup with collard greens, sorghum, and lemon crème fraîche, or an a la carte selection that include  house-aged beef with heirloom carrots, turnips with boiled peanuts, or truffled mac and cheese. At lunch look for daily blue-plate specials (meatloaf Monday or chicken and dumplings Friday, for example) or just a bowl of onion bisque, a type of soup that's been on the menu since the hotel opened a century ago. At breakfast, go for the Tennessee Jack Egg Sandwich with Jack Daniel's–infused french toast, fried egg, jowl bacon, and tomato gravy. See Executive Chef Tyler Brown's recipe for **Brunswick Stew** on p. 296.

Chile Burrito, 162 4th Ave. North; Nashville, TN 37219; (615) 248-0025; Mexican; $. This build-your-own burrito place is popular with downtown office workers, hence its lunch-only hours between 10:30 a.m. and 3 p.m. on weekdays. But when you catch them, it's usually bustling and quick. Choose among three tortilla sizes (10, 12, or 15 inch) and then have it stuffed as you wish with pork, steak, chicken, or beef, as well as toppings like fresh serrano peppers, lettuce, onions, sour cream, and either black beans or refried beans; spice them up to the degree you'd like with 5 varieties of fresh salsa, including a mild pico, medium tomato jalapeño, barbecue chipotle, and 2 kinds of hot tomatillo. And, yes, while there are other options on the menu like nachos, salads, quesadillas, and even fish tacos, the burritos are the calling card to this place. Just watch for a heavy hand with the rice. They tend to overstuff the tortillas with starch and rob them of Chile Burrito's other myriad of tasty flavors.

El Rey, 139 2nd Ave. North, Nashville, TN 37201; (615) 726-8862; Mexican; $. There are not a lot of surprises here menuwise, just good ol' Mexican-American favorites in a gazillion combinations, like enchiladas wrapping up shredded chicken, steak, or cheese, and smothered with red or green sauce, along with burritos stuffed with chorizo, beef, and beans, or chile rellenos, tamales, chimichangas, flautas, or maybe just a selection of sizzling fajitas like the *alambre* with steak or chicken with bacon. The room is no-frills, too, with its booths and small bar. But the space is smaller and cozier than many of the larger chain restaurants along 2nd Avenue. And this spot in the middle of a touristy district keeps up with the action by offering awesome prices on its margaritas: The frosty drinks of the lime-and-tequila persuasion will run you just $2.99.

Etch, 303 Demonbreun St., Nashville, TN 37201; (615) 321-6024; facebook.com/etchrestaurant; Contemporary/Eclectic; $$$. When Deb Paquette closed her beloved Zola restaurant off West End in 2010, it ranked as a major food event in town, and I wrote a story for *The Tennessean* on the six degrees of separation of Deb Paquette. The chef who worked at the Bound'ry and other restaurants before opening her own place has worked with—and trained—many other chefs in town. Some of them even call her "mama." So food lovers rejoiced when Paquette announced in 2011 that she would open her own space again in the Encore condominium tower downtown near the Schermerhorn Symphony Center. Paquette graduated from the Culinary Institute of America, but she's known for blending traditional techniques with worldly flair from Morocco and Spain and other regions of the world. Etch, which has an open kitchen as centerpiece, caters to a variety of diners from downtown dwellers to tourists or symphony patrons who stop in for a pre-show snack or post-show dessert.

Fleet Street Pub, 207 Printers Alley, Nashville TN 37219; (615) 200-0782; fleetstreetpub.com; British; $$. Fleet Street Pub with its English-influenced menu and football (soccer) on the telly, seems an unlikely fit wedged among the karaoke and honky-tonks in Printers Alley, the historic former printing and publishing district now lined with bars. But a welcome diversion it is. Take the stairs down to this subterranean space where you might find the Beatles or Led Zeppelin on

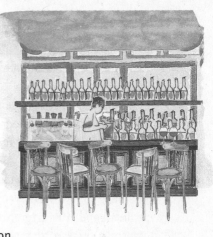

the sound system, darts along the back wall, and locals stopping in for a Stella or a Harp after work. On the menu, there are local twists on British favorites such as the Hatton Cross Hot Hen—a Cornish hen served spicy, inspired by Nashville-style hot chicken. Chef Warren Sanders perfected the Piccadilly fish-and-chips with homemade tartar sauce by studying the technique of English chef Heston Blumenthal. He also offers a St. James Shepherd's Pie with stewed lamb, vegetables, and mashed potatoes and cheese; and a curry dish (a la London's Brick Lane) with jasmine rice and chutney. Also not to be missed are the Tower Hill Devils on Horseback: spiced dates stuffed with stilton, wrapped with bacon, and served with cider-vinegar syrup.

400 Degrees, 319 Peabody St., Nashville TN 37210; (615) 244-4467; 400degreeshotchicken.com; Hot Chicken; $. This is one of

Nashville's main hot chicken joints, and though the location is not simple to spot, it's definitely worth seeking out. Owner and Nashville native Aqui Simpson learned the art of hot fried chicken by eating at the original **Prince's Hot Chicken Shack** (p. 89) on a very regular basis. But she puts her own (some say a hotter) spin on the bird. Located in a no-frills building off 4th Avenue, you'll likely spot a sign for Quizno's first, but 400 Degrees is in the same brick building. It's a good idea to call ahead; this chicken is made to order. You can choose your level of heat beginning with 0 degrees for fried chicken, 100 degrees for mild, 200 degrees for medium, and 400 degrees for hot. One difference you'll find in Simpson's chicken from the competition is that the chicken here is deep-fried rather than fried in a skillet. Daily sides include potato salad, coleslaw, and crinkle-cut fries dusted with paprika.

Frist Center Cafe, 919 Broadway, Nashville, TN 37203; (615) 244-3340; fristcenter.org/visit/cafe; Cafe; $. Located in the Frist Center for the Visual Arts, a 24,000-square-foot, art deco space for hosting visual art exhibitions, this cafe is tucked along the backside of the complex. The back wall of windows floods the space with natural light and overlooks a courtyard. Even though it's inside a museum, it's casual and reasonably priced (especially as museum

cafes go). Menu items concentrate on daily soups, salads, and sandwiches such as a grilled flank steak panini with horse-radish and rosemary spread, red onions, tomatoes, and mozzarella, or a stilton salad with strawberries, mandarin oranges, walnuts, and strawberry vinaigrette. Even the classics have a bit of a twist, like the chicken salad spiked with dried apricots and cranberries, with the crunch of sunflower seeds and celery, and champagne vinegar and mayo on a croissant. The cafe serves beer and wine as well as a kids' menu with chicken tenders, grilled cheese, and the like. Finally, happy hour applies to desserts—a free cup of coffee with purchase of a sweet treat every day from 2 to 5 p.m.

Koto, 421 Union St., Nashville, TN 37219; (615) 255-8122; koto sushibar.com; Japanese; $$. This is Nashville's oldest sushi restaurant; it originally opened in 1985 in another downtown spot. From the outside, the concrete-columned sliver of a downtown block bedecked with red flags as decoration doesn't seem to hint at what you'll find inside. As you pass over a foyer and into a single but open and tranquil room, couples sip green tea in the booths along the wall or business people gather at lunch. Filling the back corner of the room and sitting catty-corner is the sushi bar under a faux pergola with sushi chef often offering a hello. As for the food, you can either play it safe with a bowl of miso soup, a seaweed salad, and a variety of rolls like spicy tuna. Or go for the chef's choice for several kinds of nigiri and sashimi and perhaps a few rolls too. There's also a hibachi grill for ordering teriyaki dishes. It's a small place, and there will likely be only one server on staff who can handle it with ease.

THE HERMITAGE HOTEL

Gene Autry has stayed here. So have gangsters, actresses, and presidents known as FDR and JFK. Movies and music videos have been filmed between the walls, and even Minnesota Fats, the world's greatest pool player, called it home for several years. Like a lot of locals, he found his way to the daily happy hour at the Oak Bar.

With a past more than 100 years long, it's no wonder that this hotel has seen some history. Named for Andrew Jackson's Hermitage estate, it has been crafted of Italian sienna marble, Russian walnut, and stained glass in the vaulted lobby. The art deco men's room has been called one of the most famous in the country.

For the food lover, The Hermitage Hotel gives us the **Oak Bar** (p. 37) and the **Capitol Grille** (p. 28). Though sitting adjacent to one another at the bottom of a wide staircase leading underground, these two spots essentially offer separate options to dine. The cozy Oak Bar is more casual with snacks like deviled eggs, oysters on the half shell, and the Tennessee Stack burger with two 4-ounce patties of locally raised beef, cheddar, bacon jam, sweet onion, and hot

Manny's House of Pizza, 15 Arcade Building, Nashville, TN 37219; (615) 242-7144; mannyshouseofpizza.com; Pizza; $. Forget warm and fuzzy greetings or plush ambience, this place is just all about good pie. Manny Macca learned to make pizza during his college years while working at a pizza joint in Brooklyn. Years later he moved to Nashville and opened a small storefront painted in the blocked colors of the Italian flag in The Arcade, a covered retail and mustard. The Capitol Grille has a more formal and lush feel with distinguished renditions of Southern favorites. Steaks or trout might be paired with fried green tomatoes and truffle mac and cheese. A version of the sweet onion bisque, served with mini grilled cheese, has been on the menu since the hotel opened.

Famed chef Sean Brock, whom *Bon Appétit* called the greatest chef in the country, held down the kitchen here for years and remains a friend to the city and to current chef Tyler Brown. These days, Brown grows much of the restaurant's food and raises Double H beef at the nearby Glen Leven property, a relationship the hotel shares though the Land Trust for Tennessee. As Brown splits his time between the roles of chef and farmer, he creates a sustainable menu both literally and culturally. He pays homage to the past through the ingredients and through cooking practices, even drawing from his grandmother's recipe box. 231 6th Ave. North, Nashville, TN 37219; thehermitagehotel.com; (615) 244-3121.

restaurant space built in 1903 that bustles with locals during lunch hours. Step to the counter—but best be ready with your order—and choose a thin-crust slice of New York–style pizza or maybe a thicker Sicilian slice. Manny also makes strombolis, calzones, rolls (toppings of choice rolled in pizza dough with cheese and served with marinara dipping sauce), lasagna, spaghetti, subs, and cannoli for dessert. And in addition to making great pizza, he is a smart marketer, too. Look for his daily deals on Twitter (@MannysHOP) and specials geared toward downtown office workers, such as a whole pie to take home.

Merchants, 401 Broadway, Nashville, TN 37219; (615) 254-1892; merchantsrestaurant.com; Contemporary Southern; $$ Downstairs; $$$ Upstairs. A fixture in Nashville since the 1800s, the former Merchants Hotel has hosted the likes of Willie Nelson and Hank Williams. Then after a few wayward years as a bar and not-so-stellar restaurant, it underwent another much-needed makeover when young entrepreneurs and brothers Max and Benjamin Goldberg took over the space. Nowadays it's one of the best spots to dine downtown, offering essentially two restaurants in one. Downstairs, it's a hip, lively bistro with rock and roll on the sound system, black-and-white checkered floors, mirrored walls, and a long curved copper bar where bartenders in suspenders and Chuck Taylors tend to craft cocktails. The menu downstairs includes brisket with cornbread and slaw and lighter bites like fish tacos, as well as snacks of duck-fat "tater tots," fried green tomatoes, and deviled eggs. Upstairs it's more subdued with navy walls, exposed brick, and flickering votives on tables and in the original fireplaces. Dishes there might include osso bucco, trout with lobster mashed potatoes, steaks with a classic iceberg-wedge side, Brussels sprouts braised with stout and bacon, and gnocchi mac and cheese.

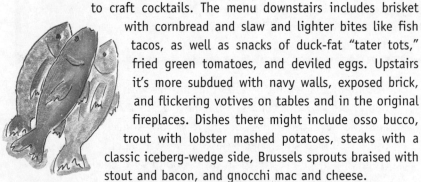

Oak Bar at The Hermitage Hotel, The Hermitage Hotel, 231 6th Ave. North, Nashville, TN 37219; (615) 345-7116; capitolgrille nashville.com; Contemporary Southern; $$. Doormen in top hats at this historic hotel will point you downstairs to the bar, one of my favorites in the city after a day at the art museum or as a civilized spot to kick off an evening of honky-tonking. The daily happy hour is popular with locals, just as it was with Minnesota Fats when he lived at the hotel for several years during the 1980s and early 1990s. Choose from deviled eggs with pickled ramps and *guanciale;* fried green tomatoes and pimiento cheese; or potato chips with buttermilk dip. Items not on the happy hour menu are still reasonably priced and include more of James Beard award–nominated chef Tyler Brown's creativity with the Southern food he grows nearby at the period farm Glen Leven, a hotel partnership with the Land Trust for Tennessee. Look for Chicken Livers in a Jar with kimchi, bacon, and grilled bread; the burger with Glen Leven–raised beef; Brunswick stew with chicken confit and cornbread; and shrimp cocktail with smoked-tomato cocktail sauce and house-made saltines. Before you leave, check out the art deco men's room that's been featured in magazines such as *GQ* (ladies, employees will escort you in for a peek). See Executive Chef Tyler Brown's recipe for **Brunswick Stew** on p. 296.

Pacifica, 506 Church St., Nashville, TN 37219; (615) 252-4077; Pan Asian; $. On the menu at Pacifica, a lunch-and-weekday-only restaurant for office workers, you'll find dishes from China, Vietnam, Japan, and more. Billed as Pan-Asian cuisine, it might seem at first that the options are overwhelming. But the menu at Pacifica isn't overly long and stays on the Americanized side of things with standards like pad thai with bean sprouts, egg, crushed peanut, scallion, and a choice of meat or tofu; *moo goo gai pan* with its classic garlic sauce over chicken, snow peas, water chestnuts, and other vegetables; sweet-and-sour pork, battered and glazed among hunks of pineapple and bell peppers; Tokyo teriyaki, a simple sauce over rice, vegetables, and a choice of meat; and bowls of steaming pho. There are appetizers and soups, too, like lettuce wraps, pot stickers, Vietnamese summer rolls, wonton soup, *tom yum,* and more. Pick up the to-go menu and you'll find it stamped with words *no MSG added* and *fresh and natural,* always a good sign.

Past Perfect, 122 3rd Ave. South, Nashville, TN 37219; (615) 736-7727, pastperfectnashville.com; Pub Food; $$. It's a stone's throw to the honky-tonks, but you'd hardly know it. Quietly tucked away from the madness on 3rd Avenue off Broadway, and just across from the Schermerhorn Symphony Hall, it's a local's place to drink and grab a bite to eat. The long bar along one side of the room gets its glow from votives flickering in oversize beer mugs, but it's certainly not stuffy or too low-key. It's pub-like and open to all with a sound system that might play Pink Floyd, George Thorogood, or Journey. At the bar you'll find a long list of classic cocktails like a Sazerac and sidecar as well as infused liquors and a handful of beers on tap. There's also a cozy but open loftlike room upstairs that makes for good place to eat. Though the menu isn't anything to seek out, it will fill your belly with a plethora of options from a list of bison burgers, wraps, and open-faced, flat-iron steak sandwiches. The owners hang their hat on the meatloaf, a scratch version made with beef and vegetables and topped with Pinot Noir demi-glace alongside mashed potatoes, or you can have it over a bed of spaghetti and topped with marinara.

Piranha's Bar & Grill, 113 2nd Ave. North, Nashville, TN 37201; (615) 248-4375; Sandwiches; $. Never mind that it's downtown Nashville, the specialty here is Pittsburgh-style sandwiches. Rather than serving fries on the side, they come piled on the sandwich like a topping, along with a scoop of homemade slaw. This shop is modeled after the famed Primanti Bros. in Pittsburgh, but it has its own Nashville vibe thanks to its location along 2nd Avenue. The 2-for-1 specials until 7 p.m. during the week draw even locals to the bar. A dark little nook, it has a busy jukebox that's not too loud to talk over, and it's lit outside by neon moons.

When you take a seat at the bar, you'll also have a front-row seat to the sandwich making; the griddle sits behind it in plain view. But just as a warning, these sandwiches are big ol' messy affairs and not for the faint of heart—like the Italian Stallion that piles on capocollo, salami, and all-beef bologna with fries, melty provolone cheese, and cooling slaw.

Prime 108, 1001 Broadway, Nashville, TN 37203; (615) 620-5665; prime108.com; Steak House; $$$$. Train stations can be romantic places full of anticipation and haunted with hellos and goodbyes. And there's something about a train song that fits Nashville. Folks have written a few of them here. So what better place to have a meal than inside the Union Station Hotel, a restored 19th-century train station, with its soaring ceiling. Prime 108, the converted hotel's restaurant, is tucked into a back corner and blends historic stained

glass and stone fireplaces with touches of modern decor and Italian glass chandeliers. Being inside a hotel, this menu has you covered through breakfast, brunch, lunch, and dinner. Highlights include a praline french toast in the earlier hours or omelets with a Sriracha Bloody Mary, or maybe the signature burger for easing into noon. The burger is layered with Berkshire bacon, blue cheese, grilled onion, lettuce, heirloom tomatoes, and house-made pickles with herb fries. For dinner choose from steaks, Niman Ranch lamb, or lobster ravioli. To start or for snacking and sharing before hitting the town, the Tennessee Antipasto has fabulous variety, with Benton's prosciutto, melon, goat cheese, grilled artichoke, stuffed Peppadew, olives, marcona almonds, grapes, and garlic crostini.

Puckett's Grocery & Restaurant, 500 Church St., Nashville, TN 37219; (615) 770-2772; puckettsgrocery.com; Southern; $$. The downtown outpost of this fixture from Leiper's Fork brings a little bit more country to the city. The inside is built with dark wood, and white lights drop in rows from the ceiling as if you're under the stars. There's a stage for live music, and along the edges of the room you'll find cases holding locally made products—chocolate, jams, milk from Hatcher Family Dairy. The menu is as country as cornbread, too—chicken fried steak with pepper gravy, fried chicken, smoked baby back ribs, and even the grilled salmon has a moonshine glaze. There are plate lunches priced like a meat-and-three, and a famous burger, along with a lighter list of entree salads. For those wanting full-on Southern, try the thick-cut smoked bologna sandwich, grilled pimento cheese sandwich, or the Redneck Burrito with pulled pork, baked beans, and slaw wrapped in tortilla. And for a hearty start to the day, choose from pancakes, omelets, french toast, or eggs with country ham, redeye gravy, biscuits, and home fries. Additional brick-and-mortar locations at 120 4th Ave. South, Franklin, TN 37064, (615) 794-5527; and 4142 Old Hillsboro Rd., Leiper's Fork, TN 37064, (615) 794-1308.

Riverfront Tavern, 101 Church St., Nashville, TN 37201; (615) 252-4849; riverfronttavern.com; Pub Food; $. It's really more of a bar than a restaurant, but it's also one of the only spots along 1st Avenue downtown with windows looking out over the Cumberland River. This spot also stays a bit quieter than some of the other bars downtown as it's not in the midst of the action. You'll find more locals here for trivia on Sunday night or just to watch a game or meet friends to drink. And though the menu might not blow your mind, the food still tastes good. The french bread pizzas are a favorite with options such as chicken pesto; the white pizza with just garlic, olive oil, and mozzarella; and traditional pepperoni. The sandwich list is long and includes a popular prime rib sandwich, thinly sliced with a Parmesan-peppercorn sauce and mozzarella.

There's a meatball-Parmesan sandwich, a muffuletta, and many others, from chicken and tuna salads to basic ham and cheese. Downtown workers also pop in for the daily lunch specials such as Cuban sandwich on Monday or salmon sandwich on Friday for $5.95. But if it's the beers you're most interested in, there are more than 20 of those on tap, too.

Roosters Texas Style BBQ, 123 12th Ave. North, Nashville, TN 37203; (615) 770-2880; roostersbbqnashville.com; Barbecue; $$. Owner Rooster Beane swears his barbecue is better than his brother's, Aubrey Bean of Judge Bean's BBQ in Brentwood and The Judge's Vinegarroon in midtown Nashville (Aubrey doesn't use the *e* on his last name). And maybe it's the long-running sibling rivalry that keeps both of them excelling in the barbecue business. Rooster  learned Texas-style barbecue after he signed with the Dallas Cowboys as offensive guard and kicker in 1982. At Rooster's operation near *The Tennessean* offices, he keeps the streets perfumed with smoke. Inside it's brisket, smoked chicken, sausage, steaks, and racks of ribs. And it's all served big like Texas, including the half-pound burger, the convenient Big Roost Tailgate Party with a sampling of the menu to feed 10 to 12 people, and the 72-ounce Big Roost Sirloin featured on The Travel Channel's *Man Versus Food*. For $72 it includes baked potato, salad, and bread, but it's free if you eat it all in under an hour.

Santorini Greek Restaurant, 210 4th Ave., Nashville, TN 37219; (615) 254-4524; Greek; $. You can't miss this mom-and-pop Greek restaurant, painted blue and white on the outside like a tiny Greek isle, among the downtown office buildings. Inside the walls are canary yellow, and the decor is plain, but it does a bustling business at lunch with office workers filing in during their breaks to stand in line at the counter. The menu isn't straight-up Greek, as it mixes words like *gyro* with *fajita* and *Philly steak,* but the crowds love it anyway. The dishes, many of which are pictured in photos along the wall over the counter, include the gyro plate with the shaved marinated lamb, salad, and pita, as well as the chicken fajita plate with grilled chicken, peppers, and onions over salad and served with pita. There's also falafel on the menu as well as hummus, stuffed grape leaves, and tabouli. For dessert, baklava is offered as a choice right next to red velvet cake and Jack Daniel's Chocolate Chip Cake.

The Southern Steak & Oyster, 150 3rd Ave. South, Nashville, TN 37201; (615) 724-1762; thesouthernnashville.com; Southern; $$–$$$. The focal point of this restaurant in the bottom floor of the high-rise Pinnacle building is the open bistro-style bar area that seems to call in guests for a drink and a bite. But this restaurant is open from morning through lunch to late night. Owned by the people behind TomKats Catering, a Nashville-based company that handles meals on movie sets across the country, the menu is whimsical but with sophistication and, of course, a tip of the straw porkpie hat to the South. For brunch try the chocolate chip biscuits with caramelized bananas and whipped cream, or for lunch there's a salad called the Bless Your Heart, one the healthiest offerings on the menu with hearts of romaine, roasted vegetables, pepitas, goat cheese, and balsamic vinaigrette. But there's a hot chicken salad, too, and tons of fun options like the Free Bird (gussied-up cage-free chicken breast), steaks, pork chops, ribs, and pan-fried catfish.

Symphony Cafe, Schermerhorn Symphony Center, 1 Symphony Place, Nashville, TN 37201; (615) 687-6613; nashvillesymphony .org; Cafe; $. Out-of-towners and even locals might not know it's there until they visit the symphony for a show, but this cafe tucked in the West Lobby of the Schermerhorn Symphony Center stays open from 8 a.m. to 2 p.m. every weekday. For breakfast it's a great place to grab a warm cup of Seattle's Best coffee and maybe a Danish or a bagel. There's free Wi-Fi, too, for those needing to plug in. At lunch, the menu keeps it basic with salads and sandwiches such as Black

Forest ham with swiss on a Kaiser roll or a Caprese sandwich on focaccia with fresh mozzarella, arugula, tapenade, basil, balsamic, and tomato. Salads include the cobb of baby organic greens loaded with diced turkey, ham, egg, blue cheese, bacon, and grape tomatoes. The Symphony House also has just greens with tomatoes, cucumbers, carrots, and red cabbage, but you can add chicken or tuna salad to any choice for $2. The cafe also opens 2 hours prior to showtime on nights of performances.

Taste of Italy, 208 4th Ave. North, Nashville, TN 37219; (615) 732-2000; tasteofitaly.us; Italian; $$. No mistaking this place as

Italian themed with its exterior painted the colors of the Italian flag. And though it's on the small side, with orders placed at the counter, the menu is massive. Choose from pizzas, calzones, and strombolis stuffed with ricotta, mozzarella, and provolone or pepperoni, sausage, peppers, and onions, or look to the list of 12-inch subs on freshly baked bread, including meatball, eggplant Parmesan, or even a gyro and rib eye with cheese. Then there's a long list of classic pastas from lasagna, manicotti, fettuccine Alfredo, baked ziti, or spaghetti and meatballs, and even entrees, served with salad and breadsticks, like chicken, veal, or shrimp piccata and chicken Marsala over angel hair, among others. It's one of the few restaurants in the downtown business district that stays open for dinner, too, serving its meals and a plethora of pizza options, from barbecued chicken with bacon to meat lovers' or Tropical Delight with ham and pineapple; delivery and carryout are available to nearby condos. There are additional locations at 575 Stewarts Ferry Pike, Nashville, TN 37214, (615) 732-0200; 132 46th Ave. North, Nashville, TN 37206, (615) 732-0555; 563B S. Water Ave., Gallatin, TN 37066, (615) 230-7827.

Tazza, 510 Church St., Nashville, TN 37219; (615) 742-3223; the tazza.com; Diner; $. Say it's lunchtime on a weekday, and you can't decide what style of food to eat. Or maybe you're traveling with a pack of people with various tastes and you're hoping to please

Homegrown Chains: Oscar's Taco Shop

Atmosphere-wise, this place is pretty basic. But the line spills out the door sometimes as a testament to its popularity. And this is the real deal as far as taco shops go. Oscar and Rocio Ruiz moved to Franklin, Tennessee, from San Diego, where their family, who immigrated to California from Michoacan, Mexico, in the 1970s, has a thriving taco shop. After opening a shop of their own in Franklin first, the Ruiz family now has nine Oscar's Taco Shops in the Middle Tennessee area. While the menu has burritos and quesadillas, enchiladas, nachos, and taco salads, it's really the basic taco wrapped in corn tortilla that you want to go for, with options like *carnitas* or *carne asada* with pico de gallo and guacamole; and the battered and fried flounder with cabbage, pico de gallo, and creamy secret sauce, among others. The original location is at 1511 Columbia Ave., Franklin, TN 37064; (615) 794-5651; oscarstacoshop.com. Additional locations at 4115 Mallory Ln., Franklin, TN 37067, (615) 790-1003; 188 Front St., Westhaven, Franklin, TN 37064, (615) 790-3020; 5300 Nolensville Rd., Nashville, TN 37211, (615) 833-0460; 7177 Nolensville Rd., Nolensville, TN 37135, (615) 776-1361; 530 Church St., Nashville, TN 37243, (615) 251-1507.

them all. Well then, Tazza is the place for you. The list of options here makes a Cheesecake Factory menu look like a flimsy one-page flyer. At my latest count there were nearly 30 appetizers (from nachos to Santa Fe spring rolls and fried asparagus), and nearly 30 salads (from Thai chicken with peanut sauce over romaine to grilled salmon with black olives and chopped eggs, club, and Greek). Then there are burgers, deli sandwiches, a long list of pastas (lobster and shrimp Alfredo, rosemary chicken jumbo ravioli), Louisiana Chicken with Parmesan-crusted chicken, andouille sausage, mushrooms, and roasted red peppers in a spicy sauce), and even a section of Mexican specialties (fajitas, taco salad, enchiladas, fish tacos). But even while its menu is expansive, the space remains cozy with booths and lamp lighting and a second level overlooking the first, loft-style. It's open until 11 p.m. every day, offers online ordering, and delivers, too.

Two Twenty-Two Grill, Country Music Hall of Fame and Museum, 222 5th Ave. South, Nashville, TN 37203; (615) 291-6759; country musichalloffame.org; Contemporary Southern; $$. Even if you don't like country music (and of course not everyone in Nashville does), I bet you'll find plenty to love at the Country Music Hall of Fame and Museum with its educational exhibits that span musical genres and historic tidbits, as well as straight-up juicier ones like Dolly Parton's sparkly clothes and one of Elvis's Cadillacs. The restaurant inside the museum is Two Twenty-Two Grill, named for the building's address, and offers a nice option for lunch or brunch downtown, too. Check the schedule to catch *Cookin' Out Country*—lunch and a live performance cookout-style in the front courtyard. Otherwise the regular menu has plenty of sandwiches, burgers, and plates, such as pulled pork barbecue piled over corn cakes, and other Southern specialties including fried green tomatoes and yam fries with roasted garlic aioli for dipping. At brunch the menu has classics like eggs Benedict and omelets or the decadent chicken biscuit with fried chicken, egg, and gravy as well as the Biscuit Bowl, a humongous scratch biscuit shaped like a bowl and topped with homemade sausage gravy and an egg cooked to order.

Wild Wasabi, 209 10th Ave. South, Nashville, TN 37203; (615) 251-1441; Japanese; $$. This little sushi and hibachi spot sits inside Cummins Station, the industrial-looking redbrick building with a mix of offices and a few restaurants and shops. The historic site is the former Maxwell House Coffee warehouse, constructed in 1902. There aren't too many options for food in the building, and it houses several offices, so Wild Wasabi can be packed during lunch for its sushi buffet with standard rolls like tuna and salmon as well as trendier versions like the That's How We Roll Roll. There's a hibachi grill, too, that serves up teriyaki over rice dishes, as well as a few Korean dishes such as *bulgogi*. And though it bustles during the week, it makes for a quieter spot for dinner and on weekends.

Landmarks

Demos' Restaurant, 300 Commerce, Nashville, TN 37201; (615) 256-4655; demosrestaurants.com; Steak House; $$. It doesn't have a hip sign or a fabulous location, but oftentimes you'll still find a line of visitors forming outside of Demos'. Founder Jim Demos started working for his father at age 9 in the strong tradition of Greek family restaurants in Birmingham. He later landed in Nashville and opened his own restaurant in nearby Murfreesboro in 1989, honing the recipes while his wife, Doris, managed the front of the house. The couple opened their second Demos' downtown Nashville in 1992. The steaks are reasonable and come with a side of spaghetti, choice of soup or salad, and basket of homemade rolls. But the menu goes on and on. There's a spaghetti section, of course, which includes their Mexican sauce of chili, made with extra meat and Mexican spices, ladled over noodles and topped with cheddar cheese, diced fresh onions, bell peppers, tomatoes, sour cream, and jalapeño peppers. Greek-Style Chicken Sauce Spaghetti is another family recipe, with slices of chicken cooked with olive oil, garlic, onions, and tomatoes. There are also meatballs or marinara as well as simple brown butter and garlic sauce, which the menu notes is "the reason Doris married Jim." There are additional locations at 1115 NW Broad St., Murfreesboro, TN 37129, (615) 895-3701; 130 Legends Dr. (US 231, turn at signal #5), Lebanon, TN 37087, (615) 443-4600; 161 Indian Lake Blvd., Hendersonville, TN 37075, (615) 824-9097.

417 Union Restaurant & Bar, 417 Union St., Nashville, TN 37219; (615) 401-7241; 417union.com; Diner; $. The building where this cozy 2-level American diner sits has been gathering the downtown politicians, lawyers, local business people, and tourists since 1932. It offers breakfast all day, 7 days a week, and while some come in for the fresh, fair-traded and organic coffee, others prefer a cold beer or Bloody Mary. The breakfast menu is fairly basic but hot and tasty. Choose your eggs in myriad combinations, with options like house potatoes, toast, grits, french toast, pancakes, bacon, or sausage. For something more substantial there's a list of omelets (veggie, spinach with swiss, Western, and the Blue Ribbon with prime rib, mushrooms, onions, and Gorgonzola). And for specialty pancakes pick from a stack topped with rum- and maple-glazed bananas or a stack with warm fried apples—both finished with whipped cream and butter. For lunch there's a long list of standard sandwiches (hamburger, Reuben, salmon BLT) and salads as well as daily lunch specials such as meatloaf, fried chicken, and barbecue pork chop, with sides like turnip greens, pinto beans, mashed potatoes, green beans, and macaroni and cheese.

Ichiban, 109 2nd Ave. North, Nashville, TN 37201; (615) 244-7900, ichibanusa.com; Japanese; $$. Sitting smack in the middle of 2nd Avenue—the main tourist drag downtown with a Coyote Ugly, Hooters, Hard Rock Cafe, and other American eateries—is Ichiban Japanese Cuisine and Sushi Bar. The name means "number one" or "the best," but the quiet vibe of this place seems much less boastful. There's a small bar for beverages like sake and Kirin just inside the door, and a small sushi bar toward the back of the restaurant. Otherwise it has cozy booths and tables for tucking in for a quieter dinner than you might expect from the outside. The menu here is known as being one of the most authentic in town. While, yes, there are Americanized rolls like the California roll and even the Nashville roll along with several standard teriyaki dishes, Ichiban also serves dinners like sukiyaki (thinly sliced beef and vegetables) as well as *sake onigiri* (rice ball with bonito flakes) and *ume cha* (pickled plum in rice broth).

Jack's Bar-B-Que, 416 Broadway, Nashville, TN 37203; (615) 254-5715, jacksbarbque.com; Barbecue; $. First I should say that a common misconception about Nashville is that we're a big barbecue town. And while we do have some good barbecue, I wouldn't consider it a specialty here like it is in Memphis. That said, if you're looking for a plate of pork, brisket, or ribs, Jack's is among the best. You can also sample different styles, such as Tennessee pork shoulder, Texas beef brisket, Texas sausage, St. Louis–style ribs, and smoked chicken, and 6 award-winning sauces such as a mustard-based Carolina sauce, a sweet and smoky Kansas City style, and a Tennessee white made with horseradish and mayonnaise. But don't expect fancy digs. It's paper plates and tables pushed close together. There also might be a line out the door at the downtown location, but it moves fast, and there's plenty of people watching to keep you busy. Jack's also sits in the heart of the action—literally right among the best honky-tonks of Lower Broad. It even has a neon sign of flying pigs to prove it. There is an additional location

NASHVILLE CITY CLUB

Everyone loves a room with a view, and the **Nashville City Club** certainly offers one from its perch on the 20th floor of the 4th and Church building downtown. Since 1957, the members-only club has provided a more relaxed refuge from the nightlife in downtown Music City. These days, members might take the elevator up for a quiet business lunch or they might visit the bar with its panoramic views before a show at nearby Bridgestone Arena or the Ryman Auditorium. Though it has the old-school feel of a club with the rich wood walls, the people keep it lively, too, and the space also plays hosts to private events and parties. The kitchen prepares elevated Southern cuisine, a term former Executive Chef Toby Willis coined for sophisticated Southern dishes while working at a fine dining restaurant perched on a bluff overlooking the Tennessee River in Alabama. (He also keeps a blog by the same name at elevatedsouthern.wordpress .com). The menu has included Willis's elevated Nashville-style Baked Hot Chicken (see his recipe on p. 298); deviled eggs with candied Benton's bacon; sweet potato ravioli with country ham, bitter greens, zucchini, squash, and brown butter; and cast-iron skillet–seared scallops with swiss chard and Tabasco-soaked cherries. 201 4th Ave. North, Nashville, TN 37219; (615) 244-3693; nashvillecity.com; Contemporary Southern; $$$.

at 334 W. Trinity Ln., Historic Talbots Corner, Nashville, TN 37207; (615) 228-9888.

Sam's Sushi, 200 4th Ave. North, Nashville, TN 37219; (615) 726-1700; Japanese; $. Warning: Don't mention politics or anything else controversial unless you're ready for a lively debate with the owner of this shop. And yes, that's just good manners anywhere. But you best mind your p's and q's in Sam's house, the tiny space run completely by Sam Katakura in the heart of downtown business district. I suspect he's got a softer side, though, maybe slipping the warmth into his famous $1 miso or the to-go boxes he loads with sushi for his regulars. The sushi is good and inexpensive (not a single roll over $4) and the choices aren't too exhaustive, as they can be in some sushi restaurants. There are standards like spicy tuna, salmon and cream cheese, scallop, California crab, and barbecued eel. Just follow his rules and posted wait times and no one will get hurt (and no one will leave hungry either).

Sole Mio, 311 3rd Ave. South, Nashville, TN 37201; (615) 256-4013; solemionash.com; Italian; $$. Giancarlo (Carlo) Agnoletti met his American wife in Italy at a restaurant where he worked as maitre d'. She was visiting from New York, and he said it was like *colpo di fulmine,* a bolt of lightning. The pair married and owned a restaurant together called Pappagallo (or parrot) on the northern Italian coast until moving to Nashville nearly 20 years ago and opening Sole Mio near the Schermerhorn Symphony Center. Though the menu has all the classics with fresh house-made pasta, there's a rack of lamb with rosemary demi-glace, chateaubriand with béarnaise, and the catch of the day as well. For dessert, Agnoletti suggests zabaglione though there's cannoli, tiramisu, and amaretto-soaked chocolate cake layered with chocolate mousse, too. For those headed to the Schermerhorn, check out the Symphony Special—appetizer and entree before the performance, coffee and dessert afterward—or the Business Express Lunch menu for those on the clock.

The Standard at The Smith House, 167 Rosa Parks Blvd., Nashville, TN 37203; (615) 254-1277; smithhousenashville.com; Contemporary Southern; $$$. This 3-story former townhome has been hosting Nashville and its guests since 1840, first as a boarding house, then as the Concordia Society Club, and then the Standard Club in the late 1800s. Underneath the ballroom in the back of the brick townhome, the club erected what's believed to be the first bowling alley in Nashville. Now the tin ceiling remains, along with many other architectural treasures such as refurbished fireplace mantels and a hidden courtyard. Though The Standard still hosts a private club today, it also has a restaurant with a reservation-only dinner. On the menu, you'll find simple but sophisticated dishes with a few nods to the South such as grilled salmon topped with spritely seviche alongside spears of asparagus, roasted chicken and vegetables, and steaks with expertly whipped mashed potatoes and demi-glace, and peach cobbler with ice cream for dessert.

Stock-Yard Restaurant, 901 2nd Ave. North, Nashville, TN 37201; (615) 255-6464; stock-yardrestaurant.com; Steak House;

$$$$. Back in 1924, the Nashville Union Stock-Yard opened as a livestock trading center with corrals of cattle, hogs, and sheep for sale along 2nd Avenue, and offices inside for trading companies. The building also housed a Western Union, saloon, and private gambling room with a 10-foot craps table, and though the stockyards closed in 1974, the building soon reopened as a restaurant. So it's appropriate then that the focus should be meat with all the classics you'd expect from a steak house: filet mignon, porterhouse, bone-in cowboy-cut rib eye, and wet-aged New York strip among others. If you prefer your protein from the sea, there's a lobster tank as well as crab legs, salmon, and tuna steaks. For sides and starters you'll find favorites like the Stock-Yard's mac and cheese or creamed spinach with crispy shallots as well as house-made lobster bisque, oysters Rockefeller, and escargot with herbed butter. Though it can be a touristy destination with plenty of space to host large groups, the Stock-Yard remains a historic and grand place for a meal with its original Italian marble and cherry decor.

Meat-and-Threes

The Copper Kettle, 94 Peabody St., Nashville, TN 37210; (615) 742-5545; copperkettlenashville.com; $. This round building sitting up on Rutledge Hill and looking over the Cumberland River has a bit of a spaceship feel on the outside, but the food and vibe inside are comfortable enough to send you into a post–Thanksgiving dinner nap. Line up at the steam table and take a tray for loading up with fried chicken on Monday or meatloaf on Tuesday and pot roast on Thursday with turnip greens, jalapeño cheese grits, sweet potato casserole, fried okra, and black-eyed peas. There are plenty of other menu items, too, such as the inventive wraps including turkey and dressing with cranberry mayo; the pimento cheese wrap with tomatoes, cucumbers, bell peppers, green onions, and baby greens; or the ahi tuna wrap with sesame-seared fish, Asian slaw, wasabi mayo, and miso dressing. For a lighter bite, this place has fabulous salads, too, like Caribbean jerk mahimahi over spinach with blueberries, shredded coconut, peanuts, pineapple, fresh mango salsa, and Key lime vinaigrette. Visit also for the Sunday brunch buffet at just $16.25 per person; it includes omelets to order, eggs Benedict, biscuits and gravy, smoked salmon, fruit, and fresh pastries. Additional location at 4004 Granny White Pike, Nashville, TN 37204; (615) 383-7242.

Katie's Meat-n-Three, 10 Arcade, Nashville, TN 37219; (615) 256-1055; $. This meat-and-three is located inside The Arcade, a covered strip of businesses that stays busy with downtown office workers at lunch. It's not a spacious place, though there is an upstairs room for seating, and it has a cafeteria feel. But as far as meat-and-threes go, that can be a good thing. The cooks here load up to-go boxes for patrons with the option of eating inside the restaurant, eating at tables along the inside of The Arcade, or enjoying lunch back at the office desk. You'll find fried chicken on the menu every day along with fried fish, turnip greens, mac and cheese, green beans, mashed potatoes, and slaw. Otherwise look for the plate of the day, such as meatloaf and pork chops on Monday, salmon croquettes on Tuesday, and chicken and dumplings on Thursday. For dessert, check out the old-school Coca-Cola cake as well as banana pudding.

Varallo's Chile Parlor & Restaurant, 239 4th Ave. North, Nashville, TN 37219; (615) 256-1907; varallos.com; $. This small, no-frills spot claims to be Nashville's oldest restaurant, having been opened in 1907 by Frank Varallo Sr., a traveling violinist from Viggiano, Italy. The restaurant is still in the family today, with Todd Varrallo the fourth generation to run it. The space has a few rows of tables with red-and-white checked tablecloths, and though it has daily plate lunches like a meat-and-three, the menu item that made it legendary is chili. You can order just a warm, spicy bowl in regular or king size (which is only $4.55) or the Chile Three Way that includes spaghetti and a tamale. As for the plate lunches, take Wednesday for example, when you could choose fried catfish, meatloaf, barbecue pork, country-fried steak with turnip greens, mashed potatoes, green beans, stewed apples, creamed corn, and macaroni and cheese. Varallo's serves breakfast as well, with pancakes the main draw, but there are eggs and omelets to order as well as grab-and-go biscuit sandwiches like country ham, chicken biscuits, or biscuits with egg.

Specialty Stores, Markets & Producers

Bang Candy Company, 1300 Clinton St., Nashville, TN 37203; (615) 587-4819; bangcandycompany.com. When owner Sarah Souther relocated to Nashville from Tipperary, Ireland, we gained a creative force in Music City. She has taught yoga at the Nashville Ballet, she worked as an assistant to famed musician Buddy Miller, and she makes art with silk. But the single mother really hit her stride when she had the idea to make gourmet marshmallows. They come in flavors like toasted coconut (with one square corner dipped in Belgian chocolate), as well as Chocolate Chile, Espresso, Rose Cardamom, or Orange-Ginger-Cinnamon. Sarah started her operation by placing her cleverly packaged products at retail locations and selling from a food cart, but now she has a shop of her own in Marathon Village, where she teaches classes and serves lunch and early dinner, including homemade soups and panini such as the Bulletproof with rosemary, ham, and cheddar. You'll find the marshmallows, too, of course (and hot chocolate!). But in addition to those sweets, Sarah also makes flavored syrups in interesting flavors like habanero-lime for adding to soda or Prosecco.

Crema, 15 Hermitage Ave., Nashville, TN 37204; (615) 255-8311; crema-coffee.com. One of the hippest coffee-shop hangs in Nashville also happens to have some of the most expertly brewed cups of espresso and coffee. Perched on Rutledge Hill overlooking the Cumberland River, this is the downtown spot for coffee geeks

Goo Goo Clusters

It's been called the first candy bar ever to incorporate multiple ingredients, and the Goo Goo has been a Southern icon as a sponsor on the **Grand Ole Opry** (p. 275), noted in films such as Robert Altman's *Nashville,* and even an answer on *Jeopardy!* And in 2012 it celebrated a 100-year anniversary. But after a century, we're lucky to still find Goo Goos on the shelves. The chocolate-covered clusters of nuts, caramel, and marshmallow nougat were created in 1912 over a copper kettle at Standard Candy Company on Clark and 1st Avenues in Nashville. Hand-dipped in chocolate at first and sold without wrappers from under glass candy counters at drugstores, they later were hand-wrapped in tinfoil until the advent of automated manufacturing. But after years of sluggish sales, Standard Candy Co. of Nashville had started to focus on other areas of its business. At least until about 2010 when they hired Lance Paine to completely overhaul the product—adding real nuts instead of wheat-germ nuggets, adding better quality chocolate, changing manufacture method, and updating the packaging.

These days, Goo Goos have made a comeback with the makeover, and when the Nashville Sounds baseball team hits a home run off the GOO GOO GONE sign in the outfield, everyone in the crowd gets a candy bar.

to get their caffeine, and it starts with small-batch roasted beans and regular cuppings (tastings) by staff. The shop does much of its own roasting and holds classes with partner Beve Brew Methods throughout the year on topics such as siphon brewing, single-cup pour-over brewing, and more for a price that often includes a bag of coffee. As for menu items, one of the shop's favorite offerings is the Cuban, a blend of espresso, sweetened condensed milk, and steamed milk. Many of the baked goods, including scones and coffee cakes, come from **Sweet 16th Bakery** (p. 101) across the river in East Nashville. Also, for a savory snack, don't miss the Cremarito, a tortilla stuffed with red-skin and sweet potatoes, herbs, and cheese.

✓ **Diana's Sweet Shoppe,** 318 Broadway, Nashville TN 37201; (615) 242-5397; dianasnash ville.com. You have Gibson Guitar to thank for this one, though you'd hardly ever know it from looking. The company dismantled a defunct yet beloved candy shop originally built in 1926 in Port Huron, Michigan, and moved it to Nashville, and then rebuilt it on Lower Broad, keeping the name and old-fashioned interior intact. Walk through the front door, and it's a rainbow of old-fashioned candies that

you'll see first—slabs of fudge behind a glass counter on one side and glass bowls filled with jelly beans and sugar-covered Gummi drops, and taffies. Also look for logs of old-time Bit-O-Honeys. You'll also find bars of local **Olive & Sinclair** (p. 97) chocolate. The back part of the room is a diner and soda shop with three-cheese grilled cheese and cup of soup, meatloaf sandwich on white bread, and tuna melt with cheddar on sourdough, among other classic sandwiches and salads. As for desserts, this is the place to go banana split or in winter, Diana's homemade hot chocolate.

Mike's Ice Cream, 208 Broadway, Nashville, TN 37201; (615) 742-6453; mikesicecream.com. In the warmer months, this spot is like the cooling station for tourists hanging around the Lower Broad honky-tonks and shops. And those who can't find a chair inside spill out onto the street with their cones of oatmeal cookie dough, Nutter Butter, Tennessee fudge, and horchata flavors. Mike Duguay makes his homemade ice-cream flavors in a space near **Sip Cafe** (p. 99) in East Nashville, where he also supplies a case of flavors. In the downtown location there's a coffee bar, too, for fueling up on caffeine with or without ice cream, like the warm cappuccinos and the frozen one. The shop has been featured in *Rachael Ray* magazine for its red velvet milk shake, a blend of milk and red velvet ice cream with cream cheese frosting swirl, and in *People* magazine for a sundae Gwyneth Paltrow created while filming in town; it's made with vanilla ice cream with dark chocolate sauce and dark chocolate–almond toffee.

The Peanut Shop, 19 Arcade, Nashville, TN 37219; (615) 256-3394; nashvillenut.com. This is the way snack shops should look in my opinion. Not modern, sleek, and neat, but cluttered like a great aunt's overstuffed purse. The Peanut Shop is pushing 90 years old and is a mainstay in The Arcade, an enclosed strip of businesses that stays busy with downtown office workers at lunch. The Peanut Shop has more than 100 varieties of candies, and it can be overwhelming as it's all crammed into a smallish space. But it's dripping in nostalgia. Many of the candies were created long ago, such as Necco Wafers and Goo Goo Clusters (p. 59), the 100-year-old Nashville based candy bar. You'll find the Chattanooga treat—moon pies—along with several types of taffy, triple-dipped malted-milk balls, gumdrops, and jelly beans. Then there's the aroma of freshly popped popcorn and roasted nuts like pecans, cashews, almonds, and Spanish peanuts perfuming The Arcade daily. The jumble of sights, smells, and sweets makes this place irresistible. While downtown workers often stop by on their way back to the office, many others make a special trip to this shop.

East Nashville

If a neighborhood makes its own bumper stickers, you can bet it's got pride. And no doubt, many who live on the east side of the Cumberland River love their 'hood. One of the stickers, for example, says "37206: We'll steal your heart and your lawn mower," which I thought was a joke until it happened to me. I had only lived in the neighborhood a couple of months before my initiation. But even with its reputation for crime and a gritty past that has seen tornado damage and fire, the neighborhood has come a long way in cleaning up and revitalizing itself, even catching the attention of the *New York Times* and *The Guardian* as a hip place to live.

Over the years it has attracted working musicians, artists, and creative bohemian types. But the pioneers in its latest renaissance might owe as much to the restaurateurs and food lovers. Chef Margot McCormack told me that when she opened Margot Cafe & Bar in the Five Points area in 2001, only Bob Bernstein was roasting coffee at Bongo Java, and John Dyke had taken a chance on opening The Turnip Truck Natural Market. Otherwise, "you could hear a pin drop," she said.

It's a much different scene today with pizza joints popping up next to packed bars, and new bistros and butchers opening their doors beside coffee shops that keep their houses packed. One visit to the annual East Nashville Tomato Art Fest, an event that started as a small art show and grew to a funky romp of tomato-themed contests, parades, and opportunities for live music and food, and you'll see the flavor and charm that has a diverse group of people calling home.

After several years, I moved out of East Nashville, but it remains my favorite place to turn when I feel like going out. So yes, I got another lawn mower, but the east side still has my heart.

 *Foodie Faves*

Batter'd & Fried/Wave Sushi Bar, 1008 Woodland St., Nashville, TN 37206; (615) 226-9283; batteredandfried.com; Seafood/Pub Food/Japanese; $$. Red Sox fans, this is your home base (so to speak). The TV will be tuned to your games, you'll find scads of Sox memorabilia on the walls, and Sam Adams flows from the tap. Owner Matt Charette hails from New England and borrowed a few recipes from his father, a chef in Massachusetts for more than 50 years. You'll find oysters, clams, and lots of fried options—as the name implies—such as the cod breaded with flour, egg, and panko and dusted with Lawry's. Fries come in paper sacks for tossing with malt vinegar should you wish. And, of course, there's clam chowder. (But a warning to thin chowder purists: This one comes thick.) Also inside the restaurant is Wave Sushi Bar for those who want their fish in a different way. There are traditional rolls on the menu but also options like the shrimp pad thai roll with shrimp, a cube of "sweet omelet," red bell pepper, cilantro, red cabbage, spicy Thai sauce, peanuts, and a lime to squeeze on top.

Beyond the Edge, 112 S. 11th St., Nashville, TN 37206; (615) 226-EDGE; beyondtheedge.net; Pub Food; $. Well it's definitely a bar with 2 pool tables, darts, enough flat screens to wallpaper a bachelor pad's basement, and a wall of taps including local **Yazoo** (p. 264) and **Jackalope** (p. 263). But the crowd is mixed, and a whole section of the menu is vegetarian options. It might not wow you in a haute cuisine sort of way, but items are creative and tasty, like the black-bean veggie-burger quesadilla, a spicy mixture of chopped-up veggie burgers held together with plenty of melty cheddar, diced jalapeños, and onion, warm between a grilled tortilla. Or you can order the hummus pizza, a Boboli crust layered with hummus, mozzarella, diced jalapeños, onion, banana pepper, tomato, and black olives. The carnivores have plenty of options, too—giant nachos with chicken chili, buffalo wings, wraps, burgers, and a signature Amaretto chicken salad with grapes, sunflower seeds, almonds, and Amaretto liqueur on a croissant or over greens.

Bolton's Spicy Chicken & Fish, 624 Main St., Nashville, TN 37206; (615) 254-8015; Hot Chicken; $. It might look just like a shabby block of concrete with barred windows and door from the outside, but this tiny hot chicken joint delivers big-time on the bird. It's one of a handful of major Nashville-style hot chicken joints. Bolton Polk worked at a hot chicken joint with employees who later went on to work at Prince's Hot Chicken Shack before Bolton opened a restaurant of his own, passing his hot chicken recipe on to his nephew and current owner Bolton Matthews. Inside, the walls are Pepto pink, and that's what you might need later if you're not down with spicy food. Hot chicken purists will tell you that Bolton's offers a milder version overall, though, compared to some others—which isn't necessarily a bad thing. Place your order by poking your head in the window at the back of the room, where you'll likely see someone standing over an iron skillet. Choose from fried breasts, leg quarters, wings, or fish with crispy cayenne added at a mild, medium, or hot level. Follow your heart on sides, but you can rest assured your chicken will arrive with at least two classic accoutrements—white bread and dill pickles.

Castrillo's Pizza, 1404 McGavock Pike, Nashville, TN 37216; (615) 226-2900; castrillos.com; Italian/Pizza; $. Once upon a time, not so many years ago, the people of this section of East Nashville were likely left to the pies of Domino's and Pizza Hut. But then along came development in the Riverside Village area with **Mitchell Deli** (p. 79), **Sip Cafe** (p. 99), **Village Pub** (p. 85), and Castrillo's Pizza blazing the trail. Castrillo's is carryout and delivery only, with just a counter for ordering and a kitchen where a team tosses dough and slides pizzas into ovens. The pies come

in either thin or hand-tossed crust. Some of the more interesting specialty pizza options include the Flamethrower with jalapeño, banana peppers, pepperoni, Italian sausage, crushed red pepper, and cayenne; and the chicken Alfredo with Alfredo sauce, chicken, onion, broccoli, and feta cheese. Of course the more typical options can be had, too, like the Greek, BBQ chicken, and Hawaiian, as well as build-your-own with standard toppings as well as artichokes, sun-dried tomatoes, and buffalo chicken. The menu keeps going beyond pizzas—wings, subs, or pasta dinners like beef lasagna, chicken Alfredo lasagna, and a few types of raviolis.

Drifters, 1008-B Woodland St., Nashville, TN 37206; (615) 262-2776; driftersnashville.com; Barbecue; $$. After East Nashville entrepreneur Matt Charette opened his homage to his native New England with **Batter'd & Fried** (p. 64), as well as other ventures, he decided to take a stab at barbecue with Drifters. The smoker out back keeps the parking lot perfumed, and it draws neighbors in for a bite or a drink. This building has good bones as a watering hole, too, having hosted many as Drifters and previous incarnations. For a bit of variety, choose the BBQ sliders—one pork, one chicken, and one brisket—with fries and 5 types of sauces on the table for sampling. While there are smoked sausages, brats, wings, and ribs on the menu, too, you'll also find plenty of vegetarian options, like barbecued tofu; a vegetarian burrito stuffed with avocado, rice, black beans, pico de gallo, and cheddar; and black bean nachos drizzled with smoky Texas barbecue sauce sweet with molasses. The patios—one out front and another that is covered in the back—often host bands.

Eastland Cafe, 97 Chapel Ave., Nashville, TN 37206; (615) 627-1088; eastlandcafe.com; Bistro; $$$. There are many reasons to love this neighborhood restaurant beginning, in my opinion, with happy hour. Every day from 5 to 6:30 p.m., you can order from the $5 happy hour menu of specialty martinis, premium beers, and dishes like fish tacos with slaw, chipotle ranch, and lime; stone-baked pizzas; pot stickers; and spring rolls, to name a few. The atmosphere is lively and open with a soaring ceiling, but it also stays warm with mahogany panels and candles on the table. It has a long welcoming bar and a kitchen you can peek into from nearly any seat in the house. And in warmer weather, don't miss the back patio dripping with white lights and wisteria. On the menu, the goat cheese brûlée with local honey is a favorite—a warm crock of the cheese with roasted tomatoes and peppers, chives, drizzled with balsamic syrup, and served with flatbread. And though menu items change to reflect the seasons, you can always find a steak, like the grilled flat-iron with smoked ketchup and pommes frites as well as fish dishes like pan-seared shrimp with a coconut-ginger crepe and Asian slaw. As for sides, the green-chile mac and cheese is a favorite

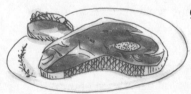

at this restaurant, as well as at the owner's restaurant in West Nashville, **Park Cafe** (p. 221).

Eastside Fish, 2617 Gallatin Pike, Nashville, TN 37216; (615) 227-8388; eastsidefish.com; Seafood; $. It's billed as the "crunkest fish in town," meaning so good it makes you feel half crazy and half drunk, I think, because that's what it does to me. I love the cornmeal batter for a crisp finish on the classic whiting fish, trout, or US farm-raised catfish for a sandwich or plate. I prefer the whiting sandwich, which comes on plain white bread with pickles, the crunch of white onions, a smear of mustard, and a peppering of hot sauce. Sides include country favorites like white beans, turnip greens, fried okra, and green beans. Slaw always goes well with a spicy fried-fish sandwich, as do fries or onion rings. And then there's spaghetti. It might not seem to fit at first, but a small portion of noodles and sauce in a takeaway container seems just right when the mood strikes. This place also offers wings and burgers. But don't expect much in the way of atmosphere. It's mostly a takeout place with a just a couple of chairs along busy Gallatin Pike.

The Family Wash, 2038 Greenwood Ave., Nashville, TN 37206; (615) 226-6070; familywash.com; Pub Food; $$. A true Nashville gem, this funky little turquoise building with yellow trim is both restaurant and listening room with some of the city's best musicians dropping in to serenade you with jazz, rock, country, and all manner of genres as you eat and drink. You might hear David Bowie's guitar player one night, for example, and the Black Crowes guitarist the next, or maybe just a quiet singer-songwriter session with the guy who wrote "Private Eyes" (Warren Pash). The cozy interior is lit with Christmas lights and paper Chinese lanterns and a folk art American flag canvases the wall behind the stage. As for food, the shepherd's pie is legendary. The traditional version layers ground beef and lamb with vegetables, and it's topped with a blanket of mashed potatoes and extra-sharp cheddar. The vegetarian option replaces the meat with lentils. Stop by on Tuesday for Pint and Pie Night when you'll pay just $10 for both. Beyond pies, the remainder of the menu is comfortable, too—meatloaf, chicken potpie, bangers and mash with buttered green peas, and macaroni and cheese served as an entree with either salad or the vegetable of the day.

Far East Nashville, 1008 Fatherland St., Nashville, TN 37206; (615) 228-0991; fareastnashville.com; Vietnamese; $. East Nashvillians rejoiced when this Vietnamese restaurant came along, because it added a fresh ethnic option to the neighborhood's restaurant repertoire. Hau and Hang Nguyen, a brother and sister team, created a bright, contemporary space in a renovated brick storefront with a small patio along the side of the building. I also appreciate that the menu here is well edited, which has taken some self-control given all the fabulous options the cuisine has to offer. But it's just one page, including appetizers of spring rolls; *banh mi* (sandwich of pork); *banh xeo* (pancake with shrimp, pork, bean sprouts, herbs, and fish sauce for dipping); a few options for bowls of steaming pho; and entrees grouped by type of protein including lemon salmon with asparagus, spicy tamarind tiger shrimp, coconut curry chicken with Yukon Gold potatoes, and a 12-ounce rib eye with asparagus, onion, and mushroom. There are also vegetarian options like grilled eggplant with mushroom, onion, bamboo, and fish sauce. Will Motley, owner of the neighborhood Woodland Wine Merchant, created a list of mostly French wines for the restaurant. You can also find jasmine teas, Vietnamese coffee, and soda *chan,* a house-made limeade with soda water, among beers and other beverage choices.

Five Points Pizza, 1012 Woodland St., Nashville, TN 37206; (615) 915-4174; fivepointspizza.com; Pizza; $$. A pizza joint in this particular block of bars and restaurants in Five Points seemed overdue. So it's no wonder that once this spot opened in 2011, it's been gangbusters ever since. Lucky for us, these guys also happen to turn out excellent pie. It's New York in style—big 14- or 18-inch pies with thin crust that you can buy by the slice or the entire pie. The dough is made fresh daily and topped with hand-crushed plum tomato sauce. Slices swallow a paper plate (and even hang over in places) in cheese, pepperoni, or the slice of the day, which often includes a gourmet flair like a drizzle of balsamic syrup. The full pie offerings such as vegetarian, bianca, Greek, and supreme come loaded with the freshest ingredients. Or build your own masterpiece with toppings like fresh basil, fresh jalapeños, artichoke hearts, Peppadew peppers, Gorgonzola, feta, Genoa salami, and anchovies among many more. To start, the garlic knots with soppy bits of fresh garlic, Parmesan, olive oil, and marinara for dipping are hard to resist. There are two types of salads and quality beers on tap, such as local **Yazoo** (p. 264) or Sweetwater and Lazy Magnolia Southern Pecan.

Germantown Cafe East, 501 Main St., Nashville, TN 37206; (615) 242-3522; germantowncafe.com; Bistro; $$$. Over in Germantown proper, **Germantown Cafe** (p. 146) put down roots in 2003. Then almost 10 years later, this East Nashville outpost opened, offering some of the dishes that make the original across the river so popular. At lunch, you'll see business meetings as well as social ones over crocks of french onion soup, or the black bean–quinoa burger with corn-avocado relish, or the indulgent BBQ shrimp and grits with a zesty-sweet sauce over a bowl of creamy Pepper Jack grits. Dinner favorites include mussels steamed with shallot-white wine; plum pork over mashed potatoes with green beans; coconut curry salmon with risotto, spinach, and asparagus; healthy farm-fresh oven-roasted chicken; and a vegetable "green plate" of the chef's seasonal choices. Brunch is a popular option, too, when you'll find egg dishes but also several favorites off the weekday menu. Touches of decor remain similar at both locations—eggplant walls or Gerbera daisies for a dot of color on white tablecloths, giving the room a warm, comfortable, and upbeat vibe. But despite the similarities, each of these restaurants has its own special touch, including views of downtown from two different vantage points.

Holland House Bar & Refuge, 935 W. Eastland Ave., Nashville, TN 37206; (615) 262-4190; hollandhousebarandrefuge.com; American; $$$. Walk in this room after dark and you're bathed in a soft golden and amber glow. Chandeliers drop from the exposed beams, and in places, brick walls peek through plaster at this refurbished former grocery. Take your pick from two bars in the room—a square centerpiece just as you enter or a smaller bar in the back. And it's at the bars where servers in suspenders create drinks made popular in another era such as the sidecar and old-fashioned as well as creative options like the Clover Club with egg white, gin, raspberry syrup, and bitters. The menu changes regularly but might include plates of charcuterie and cheeses, pickled vegetables, and main dishes of bistro steak, scallops, risotto, veal, and a burger dressed up with caramelized shallot, blue cheese, and oven-roasted tomato on a locally made bun from **Provence Breads & Cafe** (p. 196). Happy hour happens all night on Thursday.

I Dream of Weenie, 113 S. 11th St., Nashville, TN 37206; (615) 226-2622; Hot Dogs; $. This hot dog stand operates out of an old VW bus painted sunshine yellow. Parked up on a porch-like structure with roof and drooping lights, you order from a side window of the van, and then enjoy your dog on a street corner, picnic table, or from a blanket on the grassy patches in this happening block of Five Points. The people watching is good as the stand sits near a popular neighborhood bar, a coffee shop, and Franny's House of Music, a used and new music store in a refurbished home. As for

the food, I love the Rebel Yelp, a dog with Tennessee chowchow (sweet-tangy relish), mustard, onion, and jalapeño. Others to try include the Pimento Cheese Weenie with homemade pimento cheese; or even just the Frank and to the Point with mustard, ketchup, onions, and sweet relish. You won't find it on the menu, but order the Hot Southern Mess if you'd like to try pimento cheese and chowchow on your dog. Specials rotate regularly, so go with an open mind. Vegetarian dogs are available as well as turkey dogs and beef dogs. **Porter Road Butcher** (p. 99) brat braised in local Dos Perros beer also makes the menu when available.

Italia Pizza & Pasta, 1600 Woodland St., Nashville, TN 37206; (615) 262-5001; italiapizza37206.com; Italian/Middle Eastern/ Pizza; $. Don't let the empty seats in the dining room throw you. This place stays hopping with carryout and delivery of their hand-tossed pies. The restaurant also happily caters to those who want to do without gluten by offering a crust option that's gluten-free. In the "Drag It through the Garden" pie, Italia showcases the toppings that help set it apart from some other pizza joints—fresh broccoli, artichokes, and fresh basil along with the more standard mushrooms, green peppers, onion, and tomatoes. Chef-Owner Salem Elkhatib also offers Mediterranean options from his native Iran, like tabouli and baba ghanoush, falafel, and stuffed grape leaves. And bringing the two cuisines together even more completely is the "Peace in the Historic East Nashville Hummus Pizza" that layers hummus with tomatoes, olives, feta, onion, basil, and pepperoncinis with melted mozzarella.

Las Maracas, 2704 Gallatin Pike, Nashville, TN 37216; (615) 227-8000; Mexican; $. The thing I love most about this restaurant is the collection of people who frequent it. It brings together a diverse group of East Nashvillians for affordable Mexican food and strong margaritas. The front patio, which is heated during the winter, is my favorite place to sit when I'm meeting friends here. As for the menu, it seems they've hired a math whiz to figure the probability on every tortilla, sauce, bean, and cheese combo imaginable. Chips and salsa will hit your table within seconds of arrival, and you'll be on your way to a feast of enchiladas, fajitas, a fish bowl of Mexican-style shrimp cocktail, or a burrito stuffed to your liking alongside refried beans and rice. I often enjoy the regularly recurring special of fish tacos for a lighter bite or just shrimp tacos with fixings of queso fresco and pico de gallo. You'll occasionally find live music in the form of a roving fiddle and guitar serenading you tableside with a country-mariachi-bluegrass blend, and though the lighting isn't sexy, the walls are painted in a faux finish for a Mexican stucco theme. Finally while it's not on the menu, ask for the extra spicy salsa if you want to feel the heat.

Lockeland Table Community Kitchen & Bar, 1520 Woodland St., Nashville, TN 37206; lockelandtable.com; Bistro; $$. Hal Holden-Bache earned a following for his comfortable but refined bistro-style food after many years as chef at Eastland Cafe. But in

2011, he struck out on his own and opened the doors to his own restaurant in fall of 2012 with former Eastland manager and wine expert Cara Graham. Hal and Cara wisely tapped into the neighborhood love by keeping future patrons abreast of their every move on Facebook, such as installation of the restaurant's wood-fired oven for pizzas, the construction of the blackboard with antique frame for listing specials, and the hanging of the rustic wooden outdoor sign. Inside the restaurant, Hal and Cara put in antique church pews as banquettes and a communal farm-style table reclaimed from Cara's family near the bar. As for the menu, Hal has a knack for offering food that's rooted in classic preparation while also modern and locally sourced—from cheeses and affordable appetizers to local beers, fresh produce, fish, and meats. Take a seat at the short chef's bar to watch the pizza-making or choose the secluded and romantic booth with curtain at the back of the restaurant. See Hal's recipe for **Butternut Squash Soup** on p. 289.

Marche Artisan Foods, 1000 Main St., Nashville, TN 37206; (615) 262-1111; marcheartisanfoods.com; French/Bistro; $$. On Saturday and Sunday, lines of people waiting for a table at this European-style cafe spill out the doors. But there's hot Drew's Brews coffee, lattes served in bowls, and cocktails like the blood-orange mimosas from a small counter while you wait. You can also browse around the perimeter of this open space stocked with imported products, like special tubes of anchovy paste, marmalades, and

olive oils along with loaves of house-baked brioche and a refrigerated case of house-made ketchup, marinated olives, and stocks to take home. As the more casual sister restaurant to **Margot Cafe & Bar** (below) around the corner, this restaurant also has French influence. There's usually an omelet on the menu, an artisan cheese plate and toasted bread with fruit, mascarpone, and balsamic reduction. The restaurant is open for breakfast through the week, lunch, and dinner, too, with menu items ranging from house-made beet and ricotta ravioli with swiss chard, walnuts, and brown butter to pork osso bucco with cranberry bean and kale stew with preserved lemon gremolata.

Margot Cafe & Bar, 1017 Woodland St., Nashville, TN 37206; (615) 227-4668; margotcafe.com; French/Italian/Bistro; $$$. When Margot McCormack spotted a former service station in a sketchy neighborhood, she somehow recognized the fabulous bones of this restaurant, now more than 10 years old. And Margot Cafe has that savory stew of elusive elements that gives a place good vibe—a melding of food, service, atmosphere, and energy from diners hungry with anticipation. Inside it has exposed brick walls—some bedecked with copper pots—a triangular-shaped bar in the middle of the room under a soaring ceiling, and a staircase that leads to a loftlike second floor overlooking the first. The food takes its influence from France and Italy, and the menu changes daily on the whims of what local farmers bring. You might find, for example, marinated Provençal olives with fennel and orange or curried carrot and rutabaga soup for a first course, then a grilled tuna with chickpeas, escarole, garlic, and chiles, or maybe a linguine with lamb sausage, roasted red pepper, olives, and tomatoes. At Sunday brunch, the votives on clothed tables give way to a flood of natural light; the menu might offer lemon-curd crepes with strawberries and cream, steak and eggs with hand-cut fries and house steak sauce, or frittata with peas, feta, and mint. There's really not a bad seat in the house, though many prefer the side sunroom with brick floor and windows that fling open during warmer months. See Chef-Owner Margot McCormack's recipe for **Grilled Trout with Bacon, Red Onion & Tomato Butter** on p. 300.

Mas Tacos Por Favor, 732 McFerrin Ave., Nashville, TN 37206; (615) 543-6271; Mexican; $. This teeny restaurant in a nondescript cinder-block building first started as a food truck in a 1970s Winnebago. You'd often see owner Teresa Mason behind the wheel and perhaps holding her breath as she rolled through East Nashville hoping the truck would make it to the next destination. Though the truck still makes occasional cameos around town, now it's the brick-and-mortar operation that does the bulk of the business. Patrons spill outside the door to line up at the counter and chalkboard wall where daily menu items are scrawled. Order the superb chicken tortilla soup, fresh with hunks of queso fresco, grape tomato halves, bright sprigs of cilantro, and strips of crispy tortilla. I also love the *elote* and Veracruz-style tamales, and of course, the tacos, such as fried avocado, cast-iron chicken, sweet potato with quinoa, and chorizo with pickled cactus, red cabbage, and queso fresco. Bring your own if you'd like alcohol, or cool off with a bottle of Mexican Coca-Cola or refreshing house-made agua fresca with flavors like cilantro pineapple or cantaloupe. See Owner Teresa Mason's recipe for **Chicken Tortilla Soup** on p. 301.

Mitchell Deli, 1402 McGavock Pike, Nashville, TN 37216; (615) 262-9862; mitchelldeli.com; Deli; $. It's one of those important life questions as far as I'm concerned: Where were you the first time you tasted Benton's bacon? I was at Mitchell Deli. I'm really not bacon obsessive, but the deli had just opened in 2008 when one of the cooks at the restaurant insisted—insisted!—that I try a piece, and I loved it so much that I carried a bite of it wrapped in a napkin back to the office for my editor. Mitchell Deli still sells the bacon, made by the Prince of Pork, Allan Benton, whose "hillbilly" (as he calls it) operation in Madisonville, Tennessee, has captured the attention of chefs from New York to Los Angeles. The deli also serves it on sandwiches like the turkey sandwich on wheat with cheddar, spouts, avocado, tomato, mayo, and Benton's bacon. Owner David Mitchell offers many excellent sandwiches with the freshest ingredients—local when possible— that have included a BBQ Asian tofu, a Reuben with locally raised corned beef, the grilled veggie sandwich, and a turkey apple brie. But another draw at this spot is the hot bar for breakfast (another chance for Benton's bacon) with scrambled eggs and cheesy grits, and lunch with braised beef, green beans, and other savory vegetables with homemade soups such as tomato dill and chicken andouille. The deli also serves as a small market for some locally made products such as Silke's Old World Breads.

Pepperfire Hot Chicken, 2821 Gallatin Pike, Nashville, TN 37216; (615) 582-4824, pepperfirechicken.com; Hot Chicken; $. This is one of the newer hot chicken joints on the scene, but since it opened in 2011 it has been earning a steady following. It's a take-out place mostly, with a window at the front for walk-up orders and a drive-through in the back, though there are a few tables out front along busy, eclectic Gallatin Pike. In addition to breast or leg quarters—and a half chicken or whole chicken for bigger appetites or groups—the menu includes its popular hot version of chicken tenders as well as a chicken tender sandwich with tomato, lettuce, and blue cheese. Sides include the usual—crinkle fries, baked beans, fried okra, and the palate-cooling potato salad and coleslaw. Perhaps the most progressive aspect of this joint is that you can place your order online, an important point of differentiation as some hot chicken joints come with a wait for the fried-to-order chicken. The owners also will let you sample the various levels of heat, so you know what you're getting into before you begin.

The Pharmacy Burger Parlor & Beer Garden, 731 McFerrin Ave., Nashville, TN 37206; (615) 712-9517; Burgers/German; $. The debate over who makes the best burger in this town—or any town—is fierce. And it's not one I'm going to touch. But if you want to sink your teeth into a contender, head to this spot. More than burgers, though, this space has good mojo—not necessarily because of its past (it was a day care)—but because of its comfortable design. It has various levels to find a spot for eating or drinking, such as the fenced-in beer garden out back on a gently sloped hill—with small playground, too—or the 2-level back patio and bar, or interior space warm with dark reclaimed wood. The menu gives a nod to Terrell Raley's Texas Hill Country roots with German food inspired by settlers of that area: house-made sausages like bratwurst and kielbasa served with house-made kraut, horseradish, beer mustards, and sides including German-style potato salad. And obviously there are burgers.  Based on Raley's favorite at Chris Madrid's, an icehouse in San Antonio, these burgers have a flatter, more irregular patty on a freshly made bun. There's a farm burger loaded with ham, bacon, and oozing egg, as well as a stroganoff burger and chili burger. More health conscious patrons can go turkey burger or black bean. Choose from a variety of craft beers to drink, or try the old-school phosphate sodas, malts, and shakes made from local **Pied Piper** (p. 98) ice creams.

Pomodoro East, 701 Porter Rd., Nashville, TN 37216; (615) 873-4978; Italian; $$. Guillermo "Willy" Thomas came to Nashville from New England and worked at the **Capitol Grille** (p. 28) and **Bound'ry** (p. 123). But where he has really made his mark in town is at the independent neighborhood restaurants he opened such as **Park Cafe** (p. 221) in the Sylvan Park neighborhood of West Nashville and **Eastland Cafe** (p. 68) in East Nashville. His latest venture, open in spring of 2012, is Pomodoro East, a farm-to-table Italian restaurant with Chef Joe Shaw, a veteran of several Music City restaurants. Pomodoro East has a warm but modern feel with

open kitchen and bar before a brick, wood-burning pizza oven, and a large patio connected to the main dining room by a garage door that goes up on warmer days. In addition to pizzas such as lamb sausage or roasted chicken with garlic, provolone, and wild mushrooms, the menu includes antipasti, a selection of pastas, and main entrees such as fish of the day and beef with pancetta braised in red wine.

Rumours East, 1112 Woodland St., Nashville, TN 37206; (615) 262-5346; rumourseast.com; Wine Bar; $$$. This funky little 1900s Victorian home is painted the color of an eggplant. During cooler temperatures, you'll find the best seat in the house among the local artwork at the curved bar handcrafted of hardwood, a piece of artwork in itself. But during warmer months, don't miss the patio under the pergola, dripping white lights, and the stars in a spacious fenced-in backyard. Argentinean chef Hernan Borda brings a touch of South America and Spain to the restaurant with his daily black-board specials that might include duck breast, steak or scallops; a house pizza with mozzarella, cherry tomatoes, prosciutto, and arugula; the popular steamed mussels; or Borda's version of shrimp and grits, a sophisticated take with arugula and balsamic drizzle. On Wednesday nights during the summer, the restaurant often showcases local songwriters and offers wine specials. On Sunday, bottles purchased from the well-edited wine list are half off with purchase of an entree.

Silly Goose, 1888 Eastland Ave., Nashville, TN 37206; (615) 915-0757, sillygoosenashville.com; Cafe; $$. Chef-Owner Roderick Bailey opened this shop with just a few tables and hardly more than a George Foreman grill. It was an instant success, though, as patrons swooned over his innovative sandwiches and couscous platters with fresh ingredients. Bailey eventually expanded just enough to give him room to move, but not enough to disturb the cozy vibe. He added some stylish touches like silverware wrapped in red hand-kerchiefs and simple, refreshing artwork such as a giant SG with marquee-style lights. But even among the changes, the favorites on the menu remain, such as the Mexico City: red chile couscous with grilled chicken, poblano pepper, cilantro, goat cheese, mango, and lime juice. As for sandwiches, I love the Zipper: smoked salmon, honey black-pepper goat cheese, caramelized onion, and baby aru-gula on toasted rye. Bailey has a knack for combining ingredients with punch in ways that work together, too. And for dessert, you should probably have Sex, the dark chocolate mousse in a milk chocolate vessel with blackberry cream, white chocolate rum sauce, and hazelnut crunch.

Sky Blue Cafe, 700 Fatherland St., Nashville, TN 37206; (615) 770-7097; skybluecoffee.com; Cafe; $. None of the coffee mugs match in this cozy little restaurant. Add to that the worn decks of Trivial Pursuit cards on each table and local art on the walls, and you'll almost feel like you're dining in your cousin's house. Begin the day here with hot coffee and classics like plates of eggs, bacon or sausage, home fries and toast, omelets, breakfast burrito, eggs Benedict, french toast, and pancakes. But there are more innovative options, too, like the popular french toast pancakes stuffed with banana and Nutella. For lunch it's mostly sandwiches and the fresh homemade chili that happens to be vegan—not that you'd miss the meat with all the full flavor. Another good choice is the homemade black-bean burger with spinach, hummus, tomato, and onion, stacked on french bread. Brunch can be busy on weekends with diners waiting it out on a grassy area across the street, while others sip mimosas and Bloody Marys at a few iron tables on the sidewalk. At the time of publication, restaurant owners were also testing a dinner menu.

Thai Phooket, 207 Woodland St., Nashville, TN 37213; (615) 248-7933; thaiphooket.com; Thai; $. I've heard it called the Thai trailer, and, well, it is just a plain white double-wide near the Titans football stadium with a simple red sign painted in block letters. But this is one of the most popular Thai restaurants in town. The inside is cozy, with red walls and tables often full with lively conversation. Thai music videos play on the televisions. I love that the first couple pages of the menu commit to teaching about the properties

of Thai ingredients in the cuisine including paragraphs on kaffir lime leaves, Thai lemon basil, and galangal. As for dishes, there are many to choose from, including steaming bowls of soups like *tom yum* (hot and sour) and *tom kha* (coconut soup) as well as noodle dishes like the trusty pad thai and *pad kee mao* (drunken noodles) and red, green, and panang curries chock-full of vegetables and spice. One of my favorite dishes is the spicy mango, a blend of the sweet fruit with chicken, basil, and vegetables such as bell peppers, carrots, onion, mushrooms, and bamboo shoots.

The Village Pub & Beer Garden, 1308 McGavock Pike, Nashville, TN 37216; (615) 942-5880; riversidevillagepub.com; Pub Food; $. This place is more of a pub than a beer garden, but a fabulous pub it is. Located in a former 1940s home in the Riverside Village neighborhood of East Nashville, it has a wraparound porch where those seated are sometimes treated to live acoustic music. The inside is dimly lit, with dark wood and mustard walls for a warmer vibe. The bar menu includes a hearty selection of craft brews and imports on tap, but also don't miss the Moscow mule served in a cold pewter mug. As for the food menu, it's pub fare (not necessarily "bar" fare, thankfully) with giant soft pretzels for dipping in cheddar dip made with local Yazoo (p. 264) beer or with stone-ground mustard. Pretzels come "stuffed," too, as sandwiches with beer-cooked brats, kraut, and other fixings. The "local platters," with local artisan cheese, Silke's bread, Benton's country ham, and accoutrement such as marinated olives and pepperoncini, are great for sharing.

Watanabe, 1400 McGavock Pike, Nashville, TN 37216; (615) 226-1112; watanabesushibar.com; Japanese; $$. This place is named for its cofounder and former sushi chef Hide Watanabe, who came to Nashville from Kobe, Japan, to play banjo. Yes, banjo. Hide heard bluegrass on the radio as a kid, which brought him to Nashville at age 18 and put him in the company of Earl Scruggs and the like. But it was sushi that kept Hide in America when he trained at **Ichiban** (p. 50) restaurant downtown. He later worked for Matt Charette at Wave Sushi Bar inside **Batter'd & Fried** (p. 64). And then in 2008, he and Charette opened Watanabe together. From the outside, you might not expect much of this black cinder-block square of a building in the Riverside Village neighborhood. But inside it's

decorated with punches of red accent and a long turquoise bar that looks like a sliver of the ocean. The bar is a good spot for meeting a friend or dining alone, but larger parties should snag one of the round booths along the wall for optimal conversation. Though Hide no longer works at the restaurant, his legacy lives on in the traditional sushi as well as inventive rolls like the Riverside with fried asparagus, cucumber, radish sprouts, spicy tuna topped with avocado and pistachios, and spicy mayo. Beyond sushi, Watanabe has entrees that incorporate other elements of Asian cuisine including a bibimbap with local beef, and poached egg over sticky rice with vegetables.

The Wild Cow, 1896 Eastland Ave., Nashville, TN 37206; (615) 262-2717; thewildcow.com; Vegetarian; $. One of the few vegetarian-only restaurants in town, The Wild Cow opened in this bustling mixed-use space of condos and shops like **Ugly Mugs** coffee (p. 102), **Silly Goose** restaurant (p. 83), and a **Jeni's Splendid Ice Creams** (p. 96). It's a casual spot with options for vegans and those with gluten intolerances as well. Specials are posted daily and might include balsamic-roasted mushrooms with pearl couscous, spinach, grilled tempeh, and romesco sauce. And the restaurant sometimes donates to charitable causes such as Blood Water Mission, a local organization helping to bring clean drinking water to Africa. Regular menu items include the simple but fresh and filling veggie bowls of quinoa with grilled vegetables and a drizzle of the sauce of your choice (garlic aioli, peanut, ginger miso, or green goddess dressing) as well as sandwiches with tempeh, tofu, and seitan transformed into veggie versions of buffalo grinders, Reubens, and french dips. Visit on Tuesday for the Be Hive, a themed vegetarian buffet that changes each month and has featured Jamaica themes or breakfast for dinner with mini banana pancakes, cashew jalapeño grits and blueberry quinoa, and Bloody Mary soup. The $12 buffet benefits a different charity each week, such as Urban Green Lab.

Landmarks

Bongo Java East, 107 S. 11th St., Nashville, TN 37206; (615) 777-3278; bongojava.com; Cafe; $. When the wind blows the right

way in the Five Points area of East Nashville, you might catch the aroma of roasting coffee beans coming from Bongo Java. In addition to the roaster and burlap sacks behind the counter, though, this gathering space with bohemian tendencies shows local artwork on its mocha-colored concrete walls and a menu of coffee drinks and sandwiches on bagels (called "bombs"), salads, or panini like the tuna melt with tomato and Jack cheese, and snack plates such as hummus with pita, cucumbers, and olives. Options can be sweet, too, like toasted PBG wrap: Technically a breakfast dish, but served all day, it's a whole wheat tortilla swaddling peanut butter, banana, and granola with vanilla yogurt for dipping. Owner Bob Bernstein opened the shop when the neighborhood was still up-and-coming in 2000. He owns several other spots across town now including **Grins** (p. 191) vegetarian restaurant near Vanderbilt, **Fido** (p. 189) coffee shop, and **Hot & Cold** (p. 208) in Hillsboro Village. An additional Bongo Java location, the original in Bernstein's empire, is at 2007 Belmont Blvd., Nashville, TN 37212; (615) 385-JAVA.

The Gerst Haus, 301 Woodland St., Nashville, TN 37213; (615) 244-8886; gersthaus.com; German; $$. The Gerst name has a long history in Nashville beginning first as a brewery in the late 1800s. Though the brewery closed in 1954, a grandson of the original William Gerst opened the Gerst Haus Restaurant in 1955 as Gerst Amber beer continued to be brewed for the restaurant from Evansville Brewing Company in Evansville, Indiana. The restaurant sat just a couple of doors down 2nd Avenue from Courthouse Square, drawing politicos and newsmen. Yes, mostly men at least until the about the mid-1960s, when the Civil Rights Act began loosening things up. Nowadays the Gerst Haus welcomes all, of course, from a stone structure on the edge of East Nashville near the Titans football stadium. The menu still has wiener schnitzel, bratwurst, pig knuckles, and corned beef with cabbage. And last year, local **Yazoo Brewing Company** (p. 264) even took over the brewing of Gerst Amber, bringing it home for the first time in many years. But even if the Amber doesn't suit you, there are more than 20 additional drafts and bottled imports for choosing. For the full experience, drop by on a Friday or Saturday night to hear live polka music in a setting that feels appropriately old-school.

Prince's Hot Chicken Shack, 123 Ewing Dr., Nashville, TN 37207; (615) 226-9442; Hot Chicken; $. This place is downright legendary with a past that goes back the 1940s when a scorned lover made blazing hot chicken to torture her cheating man. He loved it. And Nashville-style hot chicken was born. At its current location (it's not really in a shack) just a few white booths sit among the turquoise walls. Order at the window, where you can peek in to see chicken getting happy in cast-iron skillets. You'll have a choice of mild, medium, or hot, which comes in breast and leg quarters. Though an extra-hot option also exists on the menu, it's typically not suggested for newbies: This chicken in a cayenne paste brings

NASHVILLE-STYLE HOT CHICKEN

When I spotted "Nashville-Style Hot Chicken" on a menu in Brooklyn, I figured Music City's culinary contribution had finally arrived. Fast forward a few hours, and I stood in LaGuardia Airport waiting for a flight home while eating a leg of that chicken without a single drop to drink. Turns out the New York version wasn't so hot.

Still, I couldn't have been happier about the homage to it, and that Nashville had something to export besides country music.

Indeed, expertly fried spicy chicken is hot in Nashville, and it has been for a while now. It all started back in the 1940s when a scorned lover tried to take revenge out on her man with cayenne. But he said bring it on, baby. He couldn't get enough of it. And so **Prince's Hot Chicken Shack** (p. 89) was born. Since then, a few former Prince's fans have opened up shops with their own renditions including **400 Degrees** (p. 31) and **Bolton's** (p. 65), each of them offering unique touches. But almost all of them serve the bird over a couple of slices of plain white bread for soaking up rusty-red grease like the sweat of the Devil. Dill pickles almost always arrive on top.

the thunder. Sides like baked beans, fries, coleslaw, and desserts are offered as well, but the chicken is king on grease-and-spice soaked white bread and pickles on top.

Rosepepper Cantina, 1907 Eastland Ave., Nashville, TN 37206; (615) 227-4777; rosepepper.com; Mexican; $$. The mural of a pepper and a rose on the outside wall of this reddish-pink

In 2007, former mayor and hot chicken fanatic Bill Purcell helped begin the Music City Hot Chicken Festival, which draws thousands each year for an amateur cook-off and tasting of several different varieties of bird. Meanwhile the hot chicken joints continue to draw their regulars, visitors, musicians, and celebrities. Even the famed chef Thomas Keller stopped by Prince's in 2010. His publicist called a few days later to say he was still talking about it on his book tour in Denver.

Beyond its ability to bring tasters to tears and other physiological reactions spurring shenanigans in, say, the backseat of a sedan, hot chicken has helped bring us all together. In Prince's earliest days, it had a mostly black clientele. When the mostly white Opry musicians caught wind of the tasty chicken, they wanted to try it too but were kindly asked to sit in the back. Race relations improved over the years, and now we all, thankfully, commiserate together when we cry and pant and reach back in for another addictive bite. After all, cayenne doesn't discriminate, so why should we?

cinder-block building kind of looks like the building's tattoo, which couldn't be more appropriate for this funky little Mexican restaurant. Inside it's eclectic with Christmas lights, and outside there's a spacious covered patio with lazy ceiling fans to keep you cool. First you'll be treated to a basket of warm chips and three varieties of salsa. Then it's margarita time for many as Rosepepper eschews sour mix for tequila and Rose's Lime Juice. Highlights for eating include the tamales, little pillows stuffed with vegetables or shredded chicken and then wrapped in banana leaves for cooking. They aren't made with lard like a lot of traditional tamales, but you'll only miss it in fat content, not in taste. I also like the fish tacos—either fried Baja style or grilled—with a crunch of slaw, as well as the *borrachos,* shrimp sautéed in tequila and lime served with flour tortillas. There's plenty more to choose from on the menu including standards like chiles rellenos, fajitas, enchiladas—both with tomatillo sauce or chile rojo sauces and a variety of fillings such as pork, chicken, and fish.

Meat-and-Threes

Bailey & Cato Family Restaurant, 1307 McGavock Pike, Nashville, TN 37216; (615) 227-4694; baileyandcatorestaurant.com; $. Long before Riverside Village was a hip hang in East Nashville, the folks at Bailey & Cato were slowly smoking barbecue ribs and pork shoulder and frying chicken, and thankfully, they're still at it today. The space is a bit cramped in this old home with its name scrawled right onto the siding, but that's part of the charm. Regulars know the daily specials by heart, which include baked neck bones and meatloaf on Tuesday, for example, and fried catfish and oxtails in gravy on Friday, along with sides like turnip greens, white beans, candied yams, and mac and cheese. Barbecue ribs are offered daily, and keep on the lookout for the smoked chicken and pork shoulder. Also don't miss the hot water cornbread as it's perfect in its simplicity and for scooping and sopping any gravies, sauces, or the like. Finally, it's best to complete any meal here with a glass of sweet tea.

Specialty Stores, Markets & Producers

Bagel Face Bakery, 700 Main St., Nashville, TN 37206; (615) 730-8840; bagelfacebakery.com. Owner and baker Kristen Skruber was only in her 20s when she opened Bagel Face Bakery. But the Nashville native, who majored in chemistry in college and later spent some time in New York City, noticed a need for good bagels upon her return to town. So she put her chemistry degree to good use in the matters of yeast and fermentation. She hand rolls her bagels and uses only five ingredients—flour, water, salt, yeast, and malt. No preservatives, chemicals, dough conditioners, or even honey, which the vegans appreciate at her shop as well as the many places she supplies around town such as **The Hermitage Hotel** (p. 34), and the fine coffeehouses of **Crema** (p. 58), **Dose** (p. 240), **Ugly Mugs** (p. 102), **Frothy Monkey** (p. 191), and **Sky Blue** (p. 84), among others. She has a roster of regular flavors available daily— plain, salt, sesame, poppy seed, whole wheat, everything, onion, garlic, blueberry, and cinnamon raisin. Specialty bagels rotated daily include options like chocolate espresso, basil mozzarella, rosemary garlic, and pumpernickel. Skruber does have a few spreads and sandwich-type offerings—cream cheese, peanut butter, honey, and Shuckman's smoked salmon with cream cheese, red onions, tomatoes, and capers. But she mostly keeps her concentration where it should be—on the bread.

Barista Parlor, 519B Gallatin Ave., Nashville, TN 37206; (615) 712-9766. Four large garage doors painted the color of a traffic cone roll up to welcome guests at Barista Parlor, one of the newest and hippest coffee shops in Nashville located in a former transmission shop. Take a seat near the center station of spiraling cold-brew towers and Seattle-made Slayer espresso machine or pick a spot around the edges of the room for more hand-offs service. The knowledgeable staff grind and brew the finest in beans to order by the cup and serve it to you in a mug with your own glass carafe for topping off. Proprietor Andy Mumma installed a filtration system to adjust minerals left in water for various espressos. And while Mumma keeps a collection of fine coffees and chocolates on hand—such as Mast Brothers and **Olive & Sinclair** (p. 97)—he also partners with nearby **Porter Road Butcher** (p. 99) to provide his guests snacks like sausage on house-made biscuits with local Kenny's Farmhouse Cheese and locally made jams. The coffee and the room are works of art. You can't miss, for example, the mural artwork along the back wall that brings together 4,000 letterpress squares from Nashville-based Isle of Printing.

East Nashville Farmers' Market, 210 S. 10th St., Nashville, TN 37206; eastnashvillemarket.com. This little farmers' market outgrew its first grassy patch across from the **Turnip Truck** (p. 101), and moved to a bigger lot on 10th Street about a block away, where it has added many more vendors, cooking demos, more live music, and the SNAP program to help promote healthier, fresher eating for lower income visitors. Every farmer here is local and most grow organically, like Delvin Farms, the largest organic farm and CSA in the area. In addition to produce, you can browse the tented booths for grass-fed meats, fresh eggs, artisan cheese, and prepared foods like fruit pies by **Foxy Baking Co.** (below), bottles of *kombucha,* samples or full loaves of **Provence Breads** (p. 196). Stop for a minute to take in the music, as it will no doubt be good and the crowd will be characteristically funky in that East Nashville way, and then maybe cool off with a scoop of Italian ice from Izzie's Ice, a small cart often pulled to the center area of the market.

Foxy Baking Co., 707 Porter Rd., Nashville, TN 37206; (615) 260-6457; foxybakingco.com. Self-taught baker Katy Branson says her business was born from a mid-life crisis when she started selling her pies and baked goods—that were already popular among her friends—at local farmers' markets. But that was just a couple years ago, and now she has a brick-and-mortar location along a quiet section of East Nashville to help support the business. Patrons can visit the small shop to smell and peek behind the counter for treats she makes from fresh, local, and seasonal ingredients. Options might include pies like Shaker Lemon, Buttermilk, Nutella Custard, and Chocolate Chip Pecan. Branson also makes quiche in various sizes in flavors such as Bacon and Onion as well as cakes like Rosewater Pound Cake and Cinnamon-Sour Cream Coffee Cake, and squares of fudge brownies and Strawberry Jam bars. Look for her baked goods—such as her popular zucchini muffins—at local coffee shops, too, such as **Ugly Mugs Coffee & Tea** (p. 102).

Jeni's Splendid Ice Creams, 1892 Eastland Ave., Nashville, TN 37206; (615) 262-8611; jenis.com. Though I've focused on local, independent restaurants in this book with a few home-grown chains, the Ohio-based Jeni's Splendid Ice Creams offered enough flavors, I mean reasons, to make an exception. First off, the James Beard award–winner Jeni Britton Bauer chose Nashville as the first (and only, so far) location to expand outside of Ohio just because she likes our town. Second, Jeni also likes her operations to remain as locally run as pos-sible, and she makes a commitment to using local ingredients when she can, such as the Tennessee strawberries in the Roasted Strawberry Buttermilk ice cream. And finally, Jeni's Splendid Ice Creams is just an exceptional product. Since the store opened in 2011, it seems to have had a line filing up to the ice cream cases ever since for scoops with cream-cheese in the base and inventive flavors such as Bangkok Peanut, Reisling Poached Pear, Pistachio and Honey, Goat Cheese and Red Cherry, Whiskey and Pecans, and many more. Plus they'll let you sample everything in the case before you make your final decision. Seriously. A smaller selection of Jeni's Splendid Ice Creams also can be tasted at **Hot & Cold** (p. 208) in Hillsboro Village, 1804 21st Ave. South, Nashville, TN 37212; (615) 767-5468.

✓**Olive & Sinclair Chocolate Company,** 1404 McGavock Pike, Nashville, TN 37216; (615) 262-3007; oliveandsinclair.com. Scott Witherow, a local boy with a highfalutin culinary background overseas, opened his bean-to-bar chocolate factory in Riverside Village in 2009. Since then business has exploded, and it has been voted "America's Best Chocolate" by *Southern Living* magazine, among many other accolades. Still, though, Witherow and his small staff make their Southern artisan chocolate in a single room—roasting cacao beans from stacked burlap bags, then grinding the roasted beans in a Mexican corn grinder that was once use to make tortillas. After adding pure brown sugar, it's poured into molds to form bars. Witherow now makes about 10 varieties of the chocolate including a 67 percent cacao that he sprinkles with salt and pepper; a Mexican-style cinnamon-chile chocolate; buttermilk white chocolate; and a couple varieties including a brittle that he makes using cacao nibs smoked in Allan Benton's famous woodstove smokehouse for his hams in Madisonville, Tennessee, as well as a bourbon brittle made with nibs aged in barrels. Witherow's shop used to be just for chocolate making, as his products are sold in retail locations like Whole

Foods Markets, but these days he has opened up the operation for tours on certain Fridays. Call the shop or check the shop's Twitter handle (@oliveandsinclair) for availability.

Pied Piper Creamery, 114 S. 11th St., Nashville, TN 37206; (615) 227-4114; thepiedpipercreamery.com. The Trailer Trash ice cream might have made them famous, but this ice-cream shop is actually located in a purple- and turquoise-trimmed bungalow in East Nashville's Five Points. When owner Jenny Piper moved to East Nashville, she bemoaned the absence of an ice-cream shop in her neighborhood until she finally took matters in her own hands and opened one in 2007 following a stint at Frozen Dessert University in Winston-Salem, North Carolina. These days you'll find about 24 flavors at the shop at any given time, with about 12 of them permanent, including Trailer Trash (vanilla ice cream with Oreo, Twix, Butterfinger, Nestle Crunch, Snickers, M&Ms, and Reese's Pieces), Oatmeal Raisin in the Sun (cinnamon ice cream with oatmeal raisin cookies), Movie Star (a lemon-ginger custard), and of course chocolate, strawberry, and vanilla, among others. But Jenny's always thinking up something interesting and has produced more than 225 flavors and counting, including Red Velvet Elvis (red velvet cake ice cream with a swirl of cream-cheese icing); and Little Debbie Does Ice Cream, named for the Little Debbie store-bought cakes called Swiss Rolls that she combines with vanilla ice cream and a fudge swirl. There is an additional location at 2815 Bransford Ave., Berry Hill, Nashville, TN 37204; (615) 516-9219.

Porter Road Butcher/The Bloomy Rind, 501 Gallatin Ave., Nashville, TN 37206; (615) 650-4440; prbutcher.com; thebloomy rind.blogspot.com. This butcher shop in Nashville is owned by two friends, James Peisker and Chris Carter, with impressive resumes in the culinary arts and butchery despite their young age. It's best to get on their e-mail list or visit their social media sites or website to stay up on what's fresh and available and to hear about specials such as the Tennessee Pâté, a blend of local pork, coriander, nutmeg, cloves, white pepper, garlic, and other spices, with Jack Daniel's whiskey, finely ground and pressed into a mold. The butchers stock the shop with grass-fed beef and offer cuts like rib eye, flank, tenderloin, and porterhouse, as well as tongue and marrowbone. As for hogs there's chops, loin, shoulder, trotter, and even skin. Also look for sausages and chicken as well as stocks and fats. The building also shares space with Kathleen Cotter, the cheesemonger behind The Bloomy Rind, a cheese distribution business that she started from a cart at various farmers' markets. Cotter set up shop with the butchers and offers handcrafted cheeses from around the country, with special love for southeastern Cheese. In fact, Cotter spearheaded the first Southern Artisan Cheese Festival Nashville in 2011.

Sip Cafe, 1402 McGavock Pike, Nashville, TN 37216; (615) 227-1035; mikesicecream.com. This Riverside Village nook brings together two of my favorite vices: coffee and ice cream. The frozen case holds 23 flavors that pack a big punch, like oatmeal cookie dough and Nutter Butter. They're handmade at Mike Duguay's factory, located underneath the Sip Cafe building, both for the case at Sip as well as his Mike's Ice Cream Shop location downtown. As for the coffee drinks, they're written on the blackboard wall behind the counter and make use of locally roasted Drew's Brews coffees. For the best of both worlds, Sip has frozen espresso drinks like the mint mocha, raspberry mocha, or caramel latte. You'll find local art on the walls and a deck out back near a community garden for the businesses in this block, including **Mitchell Deli** (p. 79).

Sweet Betweens, East Nashville Farmers' Market, 210 S. 10th St., Nashville, TN 37206; sweetbetweens.com Alexandra Payne's Sweet Betweens falls into the category of a "nonstaurant": Not quite a restaurant and not a storefront, she brings her food and talents to the people in an alternative way. Look for her at the **East Nashville Farmers' Market** (p. 95) on Wednesday, for example. You'll want to seek her out for her creative takes on whoopee pies and sandwich cookies that she calls cookiewiches. For example, she has made bacon chocolate-chip cookiewiches with brown sugar–chile candied Benton's bacon, as well as vanilla bean, honey, and lavender or chai whoopee pies. Though you can find more classic cookie and buttercream fillings, too, like dark chocolate buttercream filling or salted chocolate chip cookies for the 'wich part, it's the interesting combinations and fresh, local ingredients—including honeys, eggs, milk, and herbs—that will have you saving room for dessert.

Sweet 16th Bakery, 311 16th St. North, Nashville, TN 37206; (615) 226-8367; sweet16th.com. Dan Einstein, a 22-year veteran of the music business and cofounder of Oh Boy Records, left the music biz to open a bakery with his wife Ellen in 2004, and East Nashvillians who drop by their shop in the mornings couldn't be happier. The couple greets patrons with a smile and hot local Drew's Brews coffee in the mornings, and in the pastry case, you'll find trays of scones, coffee cakes, breakfast casseroles, cookies, cupcakes, and savory salads like the couscous version. The couple's breakfast sandwich also has been named one of the "Best Breakfast Sandwiches in America" by *Food & Wine* magazine. Known by locals as "one to go," it's an egg and cheese casserole with green chiles on a cheddar scone. Though there's bar seating along the front window and a couple of high-top tables in this comfortable, fresh-looking space, a large part of the business is grab and go.

The Turnip Truck, 970 Woodland St., Nashville, TN 37206; (615) 650-3600; theturniptruck.com. Long before this neighborhood enjoyed write-ups in national newspapers and magazines for its hipness, John Dyke took a chance by opening a natural and organic market in a transitioning neighborhood. That was 2001, and the Turnip Trunk still thrives today with a second location, too, in the Gulch that opened in 2010. Stroll down the aisles and you'll find bins of local heirloom tomatoes and green leafy heads of local lettuces, colorful bottles of *kombucha,* blocks of local cheeses and eggs, and a freezer case of vegetarian products, Amy's Organic frozen meals, and loaves of Ezekiel bread. It's also great for picking up organic or low-sodium canned goods and good-for-you snacks like rice chips, hummus, locally made salsas, or bars of raw chocolate. There's a natural health section, knowledgeably staffed for help on supplements, vitamins, and herbs for what ails you. But yet another draw to this spot is its prepared food. Soups made fresh daily might include potato leek or Indian lentil as well as sandwiches such as curried chicken salad, and tubs of black bean and corn salsa, vegan pad thai, or barbecued tofu.

Ugly Mugs Coffee & Tea, 1886 Eastland Ave., Nashville, TN 37206; (615) 915-0675; uglymugsnashville.com. In the interest of full disclosure you should probably know that the book you're holding was mostly written in this coffee shop. It is my favorite. But that's not to say that it's the best coffee shop in Nashville, because people choose their coffee shops for myriad reasons. For me, Ugly Mugs has good working energy, I feel comfortable there, and I appreciate that the caffeine comes in the form of Drew's Brews locally roasted beans. Other popular coffee drinks include the blend of espresso, vanilla, cinnamon, honey, and milk called In Da Hood, or a the Bingster, a three-shot espresso drink with sweetened condensed milk. As for the food, indulge in the chocolate chip cookies from **Dozen** bakery (p. 156) for just the right amount of salt and organic butter with sugar and chocolate chips. The menu also includes sandwiches at breakfast (with eggs for example) or for lunch with the El Pico, a tasty toasted number with turkey, roasted red pepper, spinach, and spicy mayo on ciabatta. As for the room, this coffee shop has clean lines in black and gray, a rotating lineup of local art on the walls, brushed concrete floors and garage windows that roll up during warmer days. Often on Saturday evenings, you'll be treated to live music by quality singer-songwriters.

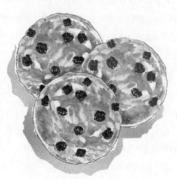

Green Hills

There's a reason four lanes of traffic back up along Hillsboro Road heading through Green Hills every day. And no, I'm not talking about matters of city planning and roadways and such. That would fall outside my area of expertise. But as a food lover I suspect that many of these cars inch toward the neighborhood—especially on weekends—toward Nashville's first Whole Foods Market, which came along in 2008, and the Trader Joe's, which followed in 2009. They're also probably coming for posh boutiques and chain restaurants like the Cheesecake Factory, Carrabba's Italian Grill, and California Pizza Kitchen. And they're coming for the mall.

The Mall at Green Hills is Nashville's largest and finest, with shops like Tiffany, Louis Vuitton, BCBG, Nordstrom, and standards like J. Crew, Williams-Sonoma, and Gap. Among all that glitzy retail, finding the local mom-and-pop restaurants can feel like rooting around in the sale rack hunting down the perfect dress. But tasty local joints have roots in this neighborhood, too. For finding them, here's help.

Foodie Faves

August Moon, 4004 Hillsboro Pike, Nashville, TN 37215; (615) 298-9999; Chinese; $. Though the ambience is nothing special, the menu at this Chinese restaurant folds out like a giant placemat with rows and rows of inexpensive options. Watch for the AUGUST MOON sign in faux bamboo lettering at the Green Hills Court strip mall. Tucked toward the back, parking here is easy, which can often be a rarity in Green Hills. Inside it's dark and plain with just the food and daily buffet keeping it bright. The lunch buffet is just $5.99 through the week, and an only slightly more expensive version is offered Thursday through Sunday nights. The menu is divided into type of protein—chicken, beef, seafood, duck, pork—and it also includes sections for fried rice, chow mein, and lo mein. In addition to the buffet, the Family Dinner, which can serve 2 or more, is a steal at $9.95. It includes egg roll, choice of soup (wonton, egg flower, or hot and sour), choice of entree like cashew chicken, Mongolian beef, or *tsao san shien*. The meal also includes hot tea and fortune cookie, of course. There's also a daily happy hour of 2-for-1 draft beers from 4 to 7 p.m.

Bread & Company Bakery & Cafe, 4105 Hillsboro Rd., Nashville, TN 37215; (615) 29BREAD; breadandcompany.com; Deli; $. The simple, clean color scheme of silver, white, and a touch of blue keeps the focus on the fresh food at this popular local chain. Though it's open for breakfast and dinner hours, it seems most fitting at lunch when favorite sandwiches and salads shine. Try the Iroquois sandwich, for example, with almond-tarragon chicken salad, lettuce, and tomato on freshly baked bread dense with pecans and cranberries. A favorite salad includes the Strawberry Fields: mesclun greens tossed with strawberries, blue cheese, and pecans, and drizzled with a sesame vinaigrette that is so popular diners buy it by the jug from refrigerated cases. But if you're feeling more creative, you can build your own salads and sandwiches choosing toppings and breads like the fiesta jalapeño, New York rye, and sourdough along with soups like tomato basil (in a bread bowl if you'd like) or prepared dishes from behind a glass case including edamame succotash with corn, red pepper, and basil in a white vinaigrette. And I haven't even gotten to the pastries, cookies, or breakfast options that include omelets, breakfast sandwiches, waffles, and french toast. Additional locations at 6051 Highway TN 100, Nashville, TN 37205; Cool Springs Blvd., Franklin, TN 37067; 2525 West End Ave, Nashville, TN 37203.

Chinatown, 3900 Hillsboro Pike, Nashville, TN 37215; (615) 269-3275; Chinese; $. It's oddly ornate with a tiny strip of bamboo-colored light emanating in a line along the top of the room, and glass panes rimmed in brass around the tops of each booth. But coming from the kitchen in the back, you can hear chicken, steak, and vegetables sizzling in woks, and it smells like sweet soy sauce for a long list of familiar dishes such as sesame chicken, orange beef, moo shoo pork, kung pao chicken. The menu goes on and on; it is categorized by protein type and offers plenty of opportunity for branching out, too. Then for a value and a bit of variety choose the combination dinner—a soup, appetizer, main course, and dessert of a chocolate-covered cinnamon-and-cheese wonton. This restaurant also sits next to **Ginza Japanese Restaurant** (p. 110) in a strip mall tucked quietly off the main thoroughfare through Green Hills, which helps lend it a more comfortable and tranquil vibe.

Crow's Nest Restaurant, 2221 Bandywood Dr., Nashville, TN 37215; (615) 783-0720; crowsnestnashville.com; Pub Food; $$. If there's a sporting event you need to watch, this is your 2-story palace of TVs and taps. But it also happens to have food that goes beyond the typical bar bites. Yes, you'll find smoked wings (with sauce options like barbecue and spicy honey), fried pickle chips with horseradish cream sauce, burgers, po' boys, and oysters on the half shell that also can be served grilled and stuffed with spinach and Parmesan. But this sprawling bar also offers options like a sesame-seared ahi tuna salad with wasabi peas, wonton strips, and miso vinaigrette, and a selection of tacos stuffed with pork, wrapped in banana leaves, and marinated overnight. Entrees have a heavy Southern theme—steak or chicken on silver-dollar biscuits, shrimp and grits, and jambalaya. During warmer days, the windows are thrown open, and there's a brunch menu, too, on Saturday and Sunday from 11 a.m. to 3 p.m. Options on that menu include eggs Benedict, Belgian waffles, and omelets as well as more inventive dishes like the Green Eggs and Ham—pesto egg omelet with ham, tomato, green onions, and provolone.

El Palenque, 2210 Crestmoor Rd., Nashville, TN 37215; (615) 383-6142; Mexican; $. With its location in a strip mall next to the beloved **F. Scott's Restaurant & Jazz Bar** (below), this little Mexican restaurant can often be overshadowed. But it shouldn't be, as it offered Nashville one of its first tastes of house-made tortilla chips, salsa, and authentic Mexican dishes from its original location off Nolensville Road. These days, it's situated near The Mall at Green Hills, and it offers a welcome respite from the larger chains in the area. It also fills the void that La Paz restaurant left, when the Green Hills landmark closed to make way for  **Tokyo Japanese Steakhouse** (p. 116). Though you won't find any major surprises on the menu— burritos, enchiladas, taco, fajitas, margaritas—it's still a delight. And for those who like to dine al fresco, there are a few tables on the back balcony dressed up with brightly colored tablecloths and potted plants.

F. Scott's Restaurant & Jazz Bar, 2210 Crestmoor Rd., Nashville, TN 37215; (615) 269-5861; fscotts.com; Contemporary; $$$$. The restaurant has been a launching pad for some of the best chefs in town who have gone on to open their own spots—and it's still great in its own right after 25 years in Green Hills. You'll often find low light and live jazz in the bar area as you enter, and then cozy rooms with low ceilings and beige walls throughout. The menu has a seasonal and local focus, changing often and thankfully fitting comfortably on a single page. Options to begin might include rabbit confit with wild mushroom and caramelized onion cakes or a salad of spinach and mâche with malted sorghum vinaigrette and local **Yazoo** (p. 264) brew–poached apple, spiced walnuts, and house-cured beef sausage. Main courses could include braised Berkshire pork osso bucco served with black-eyed-pea cake and sautéed kale or maybe the butter-poached lobster with Tennessee buttermilk white-cheddar potato gratin and grilled broccoli rabe. Wines by the glass also reflect the seasons by changing monthly, and the cellar also holds about 2,500 bottles. For a value, make a reservation after 9 p.m. in the dining room for Nine Dine when entrees are half off.

Firefly Grille, 2201 Bandywood Dr., Nashville, TN 37215; (615) 383-0042; fireflygrillenashville.com; Bistro; $$. The red door and awning grab your attention first at this inviting little gray building that could nearly pass for a home. It's a welcome smidge of quaint among all the brick, chains, and retail in this area near The Mall at Green Hills. Inside is warm, too, but casual, with whimsical decor like Mardi Gras beads stapled to the ceiling, colored Christmas lights around the windows, and tabletops painted in colorful designs. The menu is seasonal, small but eclectic, and packed with flavor. To begin, you might find rock shrimp dumplings with a Thai chile coconut broth, red and orange *tobiko*, and an herb salad. As an entree, there's often a pasta and catch of the day as well as steak, poultry, and a vegetarian dish—much of which is tricked out with sides and sauces such as the duck leg confit or flaky puff-pastry strudel stuffed with spinach, walnuts, golden raisins, and a blood orange *gastrique*. The burger is a popular item, too—10 ounces, grilled and topped with bacon and white cheddar on a Kaiser roll.

Ginza Japanese Restaurant, 3900 Hillsboro Pike, Nashville, TN 37215; (615) 292-1168; Japanese; $$. This restaurant is just off the main drag through busy Green Hills, but it's tucked away in a more serene stretch of the strip mall behind a nail salon and **Fox's Donut Den** (p. 117). Inside it's bright with white walls and pale wood. Softly glowing paper lanterns hang along the edges of a sushi bar in the back of the room. The menu includes lots of sushi options, of course, along with hibachi dinners, rice bowls, and warm, comforting dishes of noodles. If you've got the appetite, choose a Dream Box, which includes miso soup, house salad, rice, gyoza, edamame, a California roll, and your choice of main dishes such as chicken teriyaki, beef *yakiniku,* or *yasai* tempura. And, of course, the Dream Box ends with a scoop of ice cream. But even if you don't go the gamut from appetizers to desserts, they'll bring you a sweet orange at the end of the meal, peeled and perched artfully with toothpicks for plucking out perfect sliced wedges.

Kalamatas, 3764 Hillsboro Rd., Nashville, TN 37215; (615) 383-8700; eatatkalamatas.com; Mediterranean; $. The owners of this Mediterranean restaurant in a brick strip mall keep the focus on health. Chef Beth Collins met co-owner and registered dietician Kitty Fawaz while teaching at the St. Thomas Hospital heart-healthy cooking school. Meanwhile, Kitty's husband, Maher, brings his

Lebanese roots. The result is a casual spot with counter service and a menu that includes the great Greek salad with romaine, tomatoes, cucumbers, red onion, and Lebanese dressing, which can be topped with kebabs of your choice such as grilled marinated chicken, vegetables, Persian lamb, beef tenderloin, or a falafel, and then finished with a bright bit of tabouli and cooling tzatzaki sauce. Various combinations of salad and meat can be stuffed into freshly baked pita as well. For sides and appetizers there's freshly made hummus; Lebanese pies stuffed with spinach, cheese, or meat; baba ghanoush; and grape leaves stuffed with rice and vegetables. Of course if you'd like to indulge, there's pistachio baklava, too. Additional location at 330 Franklin Rd., Brentwood, TN 37027; (615) 221-4002.

Macke's, 4009 Hillsboro Pike, Nashville, TN 37215; (615) 292-3838; mackesgreenhills.com; Southern/Bistro; $$. It might seem like an odd spot for a lovely restaurant on the second floor of a posh strip mall near The Mall at Green Hills, but the ladies who lunch have worn a beelined path to it for years. The menu appeals to the clientele with sophisticated Southern and sophisticated salads at lunch. For instance, starters include dishes like fried green tomatoes and shrimp and grits, and there's a daily blue plate special that might include home-made meatloaf with gravy, roasted red

HOMEGROWN CHAINS:
CHRISTIE COOKIES & BRAVO GELATO

You know the warm gooey cookies you receive at Doubletree Hotels upon check-in? They come from **Christie Cookies** (christiecookies .com) in Nashville. Christie Hauck quit his corporate job to pursue a quest for the perfect cookie in his apartment kitchen, and in 1984 he opened his first shop. Nowadays he has four locations. But Hauck's business really took off when he tapped back into the corporate and wholesale world with his cookies. Each year he ships hundreds of thousands of cookies—frozen in boxes or wrapped and packed in tins and printed with various company logos. The recipe has stayed the same with quality butter, vanilla, brown sugar, and additional ingredients still measured by hand. Hauck has thankfully stayed with just a few core products—chocolate chip, oatmeal raisin, chocolate macadamia nut, and brownies.

potatoes, and glazed carrots on Tuesday, or crispy fried chicken and comforting mashed potatoes with steamed broccoli on Wednesday. But then there are light salads such as crab and avocado tossed with greens, grapefruit, mango, and Champagne-Dijon vinaigrette as well as entrees such as shrimp stir-fry and a chef's special pasta. Staples on the menu include tearoom classics such as chicken salad, tuna salad, or pimiento cheese with a cup of soup, or even a quiche of the day.

Several years later, Hauck started a second company at the urging of his stepson who traveled and trained in Italy—**Bravo Gelato** (bravogelato .com). Creating unique flavors like **Yazoo** (p. 264) Hefeweizen, bacon maple, and double chocolate with local

Olive & Sinclair (p. 97) chocolate bars, the company tapped into the restaurant industry by working directly with chefs and at retail locations including the local Whole Foods Markets. Locations at The Mall at Green Hills, 2126 Abbott Martin Rd., Nashville, TN 37215, (615) 386-6730; Village Green Shopping Center, 4117 Hillsboro Rd., Nashville, TN 37215, (615) 297-0274; Creekside Crossing Shopping Center, 101 Creekside Crossing, Brentwood, TN 37027, (615) 678-7658; Gaylord Opryland Hotel, 2800 Opryland Dr., Nashville, TN 37214, (615) 458-2637.

Nero's Grill, 2122 Hillsboro Dr., Nashville, TN 37215; (615) 297-7777; nerosgrill.com; Steak House; $$. The original restaurant in this space called Nero's Cactus Canyon opened in 1962 and closed in 1976. But the property stayed in the family. So in 2007, John Griswold, son of Nelson "Nero" Griswold Jr. opened Nero's Grill, and you'll often see him bustling around the place. On the menu you'll find the white-bean soup recipe that has been there since the '60s, and soon after you take a seat, a basket of corn cakes—just like the ones that John helped roll as a young boy in the kitchen—will hit your table with crispy outsides and warm moist insides. The valet parking, warm lighting, and stone fireplaces make for a cozy, convenient meeting place both day and night for a varied crowd. On one lunch visit, I sat between a table of young businessmen and a group of white-haired, retiree-age men. At lunch you'll find sandwiches and salads and lighter dishes like grilled tilapia with strawberry salsa and steamed seasonal vegetables. At dinner, you'll see much more steak—filet mignon (bacon wrapped and blue-cheese stuffed if you like), rib eye, and even elk with a peppercorn crust. All steaks come with house or Caesar salad and baked, mashed, or stuffed potato.

Shalimar, 3711 Hillsboro Pike, Nashville, TN 37215; (615) 269-8577; shalimarfinedining.com; Indian; $. It's next to a Krystal fast food restaurant and near the mall on busy Hillsboro Pike, but this place has been offering an exotic little retreat from all that since 1990. Look for the small building with the green-and-white awning, and then once inside you'll find tables covered in linens and a vibe that's romantic and intimate. I appreciate the layout of the menu—appetizers like samosas and pappadams start off the meal. Then there are beverages including lassis, juice, and tea (it's BYOB for alcohol, with no corkage fee). Breads follow, including several types of naan, poori, and chapatti; entrees are grouped by protein such as lamb, chicken, and vegetarian. The favorites are familiar, such as the chicken tikka masala and lamb vindaloo. The dessert menu is short but worth checking out with just *gulab jama,* dough in rosewater with pistachios, or rice pudding jazzed up with saffron and pistachios. If you'd like a sample of more items in an environment that's a bit more hurried, go for the lunch buffet.

Table 3, 3821 Green Hills Village Dr., Nashville, TN 37215; (615) 739-6900; table3nashville.com; French; $$$. It's a welcome bit of sophistication in the area around the Mall at Green Hills with decor that puts you in France from the minute your step onto the octagon tile floor. The lights are low, and the color scheme is a subdued gray with mirrored walls like that of a brasserie. The menu is mainly French comfort food served on fine china, such as steak frites (filet or rib eye), cassoulet, and blue plate specials like bouillabaisse on Friday; a rich, fall-from-bone coq au vin on Saturday; duck confit shepherd's pie on Sunday; and Alsatian pork schnitzel on Monday. There are lighter dishes, too, like the niçoise tuna salad, herb- and Dijon-roasted chicken, grilled trout and salmon, and the omelet of the day. Also worth digging into at lunch or dinner at the bar, maybe before catching a movie at the nearby cinema, are the comforting croque madame of grilled ham and gruyère with Mornay sauce and sunny-side-up, farm-fresh egg on top; the duck burger with thyme aioli and Boursin cheese; and the Table 3 Burger of house-ground beef, local Kenny's aged cheddar, caramelized onions, and mayo, with an optional fried egg on top. Don't miss the desserts, which change with the seasons and might include vanilla bean crème brûlée, profiteroles, Olive & Sinclair salted chocolate mousse, and apple galette with caramel sauce and vanilla whipped cream, or you might choose a sweet treat to go at the restaurant's market next door.

Tokyo Japanese Steakhouse, 3808 Cleghorn Ave., Nashville, TN 37215; (615) 297-6698, Japanese, $$. It's slightly bizarre in an endearing way, with live piano playing, laser lights in the bar, and a broad collection of patrons—from large parties rowdy at a birthday celebration, to families with kids in tow, and couples on dates. But the main draw at this restaurant near The Mall at 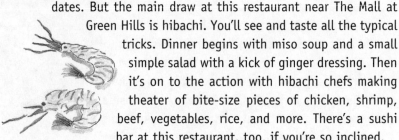 Green Hills is hibachi. You'll see and taste all the typical tricks. Dinner begins with miso soup and a small simple salad with a kick of ginger dressing. Then it's on to the action with hibachi chefs making theater of bite-size pieces of chicken, shrimp, beef, vegetables, rice, and more. There's a sushi bar at this restaurant, too, if you're so inclined.

YOLOS Restaurant & Bar, 3805 Green Hills Village Dr., Nashville, TN 37215; (615) 292-5535; yolosnashville.com; American Contemporary; $$$. The decor in this place is so polished and sleek you might suspect it's a chain. Not so. And even though the locally owned restaurant has a lounge groove coming from the sound system, gigantic glowing lampshades hanging from the ceiling, and wisps of white tree sprigs in rows as decor, it manages to be comfortable, too, with lunch, dinner, and brunch service, and a covered, open-air front deck area. It's a place where guests drop by for happy hour after work, before catching a movie at the nearby cinema, or after shopping at The Mall at Green Hills next door. The menu is comfortable, too, with familiar starters like spinach artichoke dip, though some are dressed up a bit like the red pepper hummus with fresh herbs, Asiago, pico de gallo, and drizzles of sweet balsamic glaze. One of the most popular dishes on the menu is the lobster mac and cheese, a main entree with lobster and shrimp sautéed with bell pepper and scallions and tossed with smoked Gouda cream and penne pasta. You'll find filet, pork chops, goat cheese–stuffed chicken, salads, flatbreads, mahimahi tacos, and a burger of the week.

Landmarks

Fox's Donut Den, 3900 Hillsboro Rd., Nashville, TN 37215; (615) 385-1021; foxsdonutden.com; Bakery; $. When owners tried to swank up this strip mall where Fox's Donut Den sits, they took down its 30-plus-year-old neon sign and replaced it with a plain black-and-white one while they weighed options on changing the building's facade. Public uprising ensued. The sign is back now, all aglow, just as the glazed doughnuts have been the treat to shine at this landmark near Hillsboro High School. The shop is otherwise no-frills with checkered floor and old-school pastry cases piled with cake doughnuts as well as glazed, frosted yeast versions and trays of piled-up doughnut holes in flavors like chocolate, maple, or cinnamon. Other pastries include apple fritters, chocolate éclairs, cinnamon rolls, and muffins in familiar poppy seed, bran, blueberry, and cranberry-walnut. Owner Norman Fox can also fix you up with oversize shaped and decorated doughnuts for celebrations or savory items such as sausage rolls, *kolaches,* and bagels in spinach-Parmesan, poppy seed, cranberry, or just plain, spread with cream cheese.

Specialty Stores, Markets & Producers

The Food Company, 2211 Bandywood Dr., Nashville, TN 37211; (615) 385-4311; thefoodcompanynashville.com. It's connected to the funky Greenhouse Bar (yes, drinking happens inside a domed, plastic-walled greenhouse, and it's awesome). So after 5 p.m., you can take your food inside and sit for a bite. But The Food Company is really more of a take-out place and catering operation. The sandwiches are pretty straightforward but super fresh. There are 3 variations of herb-roasted turkey sandwiches, for example—on farm bread with sharp cheddar; a version on sourdough with artichoke spread, roasted red peppers, and baby spinach; and on a tortilla with Jarlsberg, bacon, and basil mayo. Also consider their alternative version of pimento cheese (sans pimientos) with bacon and almonds. But setting this place apart is its brilliant casserole menu priced for the number of folks you need to feed. Options might include black bean enchiladas, classic lasagna, wild mushroom lasagna, chicken enchiladas, spinach and artichoke lasagna, and turkey tetrazzini. Other catering options go from more casual boxed lunches to layered three-pesto terrine, grilled beef tenderloin with horseradish, biscuits and lollipop lamb chops with fig-mint jelly, and much more. Finally there's brunch to-go, too, feeding a 12-person minimum; it includes a package of muffins, fruit with honey-lime mint sauce, homemade ham biscuits and herbed butter, and a casserole.

The Painted Cupcake, 2014 Glen Echo Road, Nashville, TN 37215; (615) 279-8055; thepaintedcupcake.com. This cupcake shop began downtown in 2009 but moved to Green Hills in 2011, taking with it a style of fancy black chandeliers, striped walls, and scratch-made, artfully designed cupcakes. Look for its famous flavor the Rockin Turtle, chocolate cake with caramel filling, roasted marshmallows, caramel drizzle, and toasted pecans. Others include the Black Velvet, chocolate cake with cream  cheese icing; The Bugsy, carrot cake with cream cheese icing; and Peanut Butter Surprise, chocolate cake with peanut butter morsels and peanut butter frosting. You'll find more straightforward flavors, too, such as Coconut or The Conventional, vanilla bean cake topped with chocolate butter cream frosting. Make-your-own cupcake parties also can be booked the shop. For orders of a dozen or more, the shop also will deliver.

Table 3 Market, 3821 Green Hills Village Dr., Nashville, TN 37215; (615) 739-6900; table3nashville.com. This open, airy little space is the more casual and carryout counterpart to **Table 3 Restaurant** (p. 115) next door. Shelves stay stacked with tins of bourbon smoked sea salt, jars of Amish jellies, and crocks of herbs de Provence, and the counter is lined with cake plates holding up bacon-cheddar scones, plum-filled sablé cookies, French apple turn-overs, and almond cupcakes topped with caramel but-tercream icing. If you arrive early, try a warm breakfast panini layering Nutella, banana, and drizzle of honey, or a panini with Benton's country ham, caramelized onion, Amish pepper jam, and Kenny's aged cheddar. At lunch, check out the blue plate sandwiches piled on breads baked in-house—from a simple grilled cheese with roasted tomato on homemade Texas toast to spicy fried chicken with red pepper jam, pickle chips, and Gorgonzola aioli on challah. The folks at Table 3 can also hook you up with platters of cheese; charcuterie with baguette, mustards, chutney, and pickles (among many other combinations both savory and sweet); or boxed lunches including sandwich, chips or apple, and chocolate chunk cookie.

The Gulch & Midtown

Like the ugly duckling of neighborhoods, The Gulch has traded its empty warehouses and industrialization in recent years for hip condominiums, restaurants, and trendy shops. But even with the new additions, The Gulch has come into its beauty in a gritty kind of way. Situated under the Broadway bridge that runs into downtown, The Gulch gets its named for being topographically depressed from the city above it, and it also still holds a web of train tracks that have hauled goods into the city since the 1880s.

As development took hold in the early 2000s, it became what real estate agents call a mixed-use neighborhood where residents can work, live, and play. But as food lovers, the important question is, where can we eat?

While The Gulch does make it easy to fall into its collection of higher-end chains, the local culinary centerpiece worth checking out instead is Chris Hyndman's M Street project. Just off its namesake McGavock Street, Hyndman opened Whiskey Kitchen in 2009. He relocated his popular sushi den and cocktail lounge to a renovated newspaper warehouse across the street in 2010, and in April 2011 added a modern steak house called Kayne Prime, named for the historic Kayne railroad switchyard across the street.

Just next to The Gulch, heading away from downtown, you'll find Midtown and Music Row. Though the famed Music Row sounds glamorous, it's not much more than office buildings and rows of bungalows converted to studios. However, this area's Division Street and section of Broadway hold some of the city's most talked-about restaurants and bars—from the New York–style deli Noshville to the gussied-up pub fare of Tavern.

Along Division Street you'll find the speakeasy-style cocktail lounge The Patterson House operated by brothers Benjamin and Max Goldberg. Above it sits the brothers' crowning jewel, The Catbird Seat. Then farther up Division, it's Midtown's older guard—the crab shack called South Street and the more upscale Bound'ry. Between the two lies a hot spot for nightlife, drawing a mix of Vanderbilt students and young professionals. If the country music and pine walls of a bar named Losers doesn't appeal, there's a watering hole beside it by a different name: Winners, of course.

Bound'ry, 911 20th Ave. S., Midtown, Nashville, TN 37212; (615) 321-3043; pansouth.net; American Contemporary; $$$$. Oh, if these walls could talk. Located in the former digs of the Rock and Roll Hotel, a rollicking music scene joint in the '70s and '80s, the Bound'ry still has a kicking bar of its own (both the main bar downstairs and a smaller lounge upstairs). Yet it also offers a dining room with soaring ceiling as well as several nooks and crannies for tucking away for a quieter night. Its wilder days shouldn't over-shadow the menu either. While you can still grab a bar bite of pizza (which comes from the brick oven in the former hot tub room) in options like lobster BLT or the Ring of Fire with four-chile barbecue chicken, the entrees include steaks, pancetta-wrapped halibut, braised veal cheeks, and magret duck with baby turnips, pomme frites, and a red wine, chocolate, and orange emulsion.

The Catbird Seat, 1711 Division St., Midtown, Nashville, TN 37203; thecatbirdseatrestaurant.com; Eclectic; $$$$. Everybody's talking about it. And by everybody, I mean every food lover in Music City plus the *New York Times, W* magazine, and *GQ* (which named it one of the hottest 10 new restaurants of 2011). This tiny space perched above **The Patterson House** (p. 128) cocktail lounge (with the same owners, brothers Benjamin and Max Goldberg) looks unassuming from the street. But once led inside, it's a culinary jewel box with just 30 seats around an open kitchen where chefs Josh

Habiger (formerly of CRAFT and Alinea) and Erik Anderson (stints at The French Laundry and Noma) prepare plates and serve them directly to diners. You won't find a menu, just inventive seasonal dishes on the chefs' whim. Tastings have included sous-vide Wagyu rib eye, dusted in kale ash, resting on warm potato-horseradish puree, and garnished with nasturtium petals. Also look for a swish take on Nashville-style hot chicken—a square bite of crispy chicken skin, sweetened with sorghum, dusted with cayenne, and topped with a twirl of Wonder Bread puree and a fleck of dill-pickle salt. Reservations required, and dinner is a 9-course tasting beginning at $100 per person. Special dietary menus upon request.

Corner Pub Midtown, 2000 Broadway, Midtown, Nashville, TN 37203; (615) 327-9250; cornerpubtn.com; Southern/Barbecue; $. Don't even think about getting a seat at this place during, say, March Madness (or any other major sporting event). But the early bird does get the chicken nachos in this case. Or perhaps just visit during less-busy hours. Though it does stay popular as a watering hole for students and young professionals, it offers a menu with plenty more than nachos, such as burgers and sandwiches (they hang their hat on the club) as well as Southern touches like the fried bologna sandwich, marinated steak on biscuits, fried pickles, and the Corner Pub's take on Nashville hot chicken—hot chicken tenders in "magic hot dust." But for a treat, visit on Smoking Monday when Corner Pub owners load the house smoker with hickory in the parking lot—filling Midtown with the smell of barbecue ribs, chicken, and wings.

Giovanni, 909 20th Ave. S., Midtown, Nashville, TN 37203; (615) 760-5932; giovanninashville.com; Italian; $$$. A server at Giovanni once spotted Reba, Lionel Richie, and Ryan Seacrest at separate tables in a single sitting at this Midtown restaurant. So yeah, it can be that kind of place with its dimly lit, warm design of terra cotta and wood, with white tablecloths and Northern Italian fare. But owner Giovanni Francescotti, who had a New York City restaurant by the same name for more than a decade before he relocated to Music City, keeps the vibe friendly by stopping to check on tables or across the bar laid with imported Italian marble. On the menu you'll find anti- pasti of imported *salumi* as well as carpaccio, and mussels in garlic tomato sauce. There's pastas, too, including house- made beef ravioli with tomato sauce and homemade tagliatelle with Bolognese sauce. Traditional entrees like veal scaloppine make the menu, but so does salmon over broccolini with celery-root puree and toasted almonds. Also look for special treats like the *patate al tartufo e parmigiano*—truffle Parmesan fries.

Kayne Prime, 1103 McGavock St., The Gulch, Nashville, TN 37203; (615) 259-0050; mstreetnashville.com/kayne-prime; Steak House; $$$$. Steak houses are often more men's club than hip haven, but Kayne Prime is a modern yet warm respite from the older school version. Part of owner Chris Hyndman's M Street Project (it's off

McGavock in The Gulch and across from the historic Kayne switch-yard), this restaurant wraps its chic clientele with a mix of natural and rustic elements. Servers stay attentive but keep the vibe lower-key, wearing denim, crisp white shirts, and aprons cinched and folded at the waist. On the menu, you'll find classics like filet (both 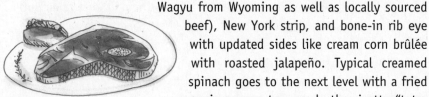 Wagyu from Wyoming as well as locally sourced beef), New York strip, and bone-in rib eye with updated sides like cream corn brûlée with roasted jalapeño. Typical creamed spinach goes to the next level with a fried organic egg on top, as do the risotto "tater tots" and sake-steamed baby brussels sprouts with grana cheese and truffle oil. As for salads, check out the black kale with currants, marcona almonds, and lemon. But if you want a traditional iceberg wedge, they've got that, too.

Ken's Sushi & Japanese Restaurant, 2007 Division St., Midtown, Nashville, TN 37203; (615) 321-2444; kenssushi.com; Japanese; $. Located in a stand-alone building, Ken's Sushi sits like a lone red-and-yellow box in the midst of Midtown. It's no-frills, but it has been a long-time favorite of students and professors at Vanderbilt, who work and study just across the street. Owner Kenji Ohno puts together a fine roster of sushi—standards like yellowtail, eel, crunchy shrimp, and spicy tuna. But if you're not feeling that type of fish, choose appetizers like the popular gyoza and seaweed salad or entrees such as teriyaki chicken or beef; traditional noodle dishes; or *tonkatsu*, pork loin in panko. I enjoy the variety of a

HOMEGROWN CHAINS: GIGI'S CUPCAKES

The first part of Gina "Gigi" Butler's story is a Nashville classic: Aspiring singer/songwriter moves to town with just $500—no job, no apartment, no plan. She eventually worked her way into gigs singing for tips at honky-tonks by night, cleaning houses, and waiting tables at Red Lobster by day. But as performing until 3 a.m. started to grow old, she took a tip from her brother. He called her after waiting in line 2 hours at a New York City cupcake shop, but he said they weren't nearly as good as the cupcakes Gina and her mother had made. She planned to open her own cupcake shop in Nashville, borrowing money along the way. When the doors opened in 2007, she had $33 in her checking account with more than $4,000 in rent, payroll, and other bills to pay in less than a week. She made it happen with $300 to spare, and she now has more than 50 Gigi's Cupcakes locations in three states. And the cupcakes? They have the size and weight of a softball, but they're moist on the inside and with icing twirled on top in tufts of pink, white, and various shades of chocolate brown The creative flavors change regularly, but keep an eye out for banana cream pie, yellow cake with a vanilla filling topped with banana buttercream frosting and crushed vanilla wafers on top; or Midnight Magic, a devil's food cake with dark chocolate chips topped with a chocolate buttercream frosting and more chocolate chips as garnish. Main location at 1816 Broadway, Midtown, Nashville, TN, 37203; (615) 342-0140; gigiscupcakesusa.com. Additional location at 1000 Meridian Blvd., Ste. 112, Franklin, TN, 37067; (615) 472-1508.

bento box as well, which comes with miso soup, salad, steamed veggies, rice, and an entree such as ginger pork (plus the addition of sushi at dinner). If you're thirsty, too, go during happy hour, which happens daily between 5 and 8 p.m., for 2-for-1 hot sake or Kirin Ichiban draft.

The Patterson House, 1711 Division St., Midtown, Nashville, TN 37203; (615) 636-7724; thepattersonhousenashville.com; American; $$. It's the spa treatment of cocktail lounges with the scent of house-made bitters filling a space that feels sepia-toned between its back wall of books and thick velvet curtain at the front. With a speakeasy style, the vibe is more tranquil and sophisticated than many of Nashville's watering holes, but don't let that throw you. It's certainly a bar, and these expertly crafted artisanal cocktails are the real deal. Guests are seated by a hostess, which keeps parties together in cozy booths surrounding the outskirts of the room or around the 30-seat square bar that takes center stage both in location and as focal point of the action. While the cocktails keep the attention of most patrons, the menu stays fresh, too. I like the playful snacks like black-eyed-pea hummus, truffled deviled eggs, rosemary pork rinds, and creative panini concoctions like the Elvis, with peanut butter and banana. Be sure to finish with the warm doughnuts—soft pillows dusted with sugar and cinnamon. For more on the cocktails, see The Patterson House entry in this guide's Craft Cocktails section on p. 266.

Tavern, 1904 Broadway, Midtown, Nashville, TN 37203; (615) 320-8580; mstreetnashville.com/tavern; American; $$. The TV count in this restaurant could qualify it as a sports bar, but the food, vibe, and attractive clientele make it much more. Located in the heart of Midtown, it's a project by Chris Hyndman, who classed-up The Gulch with his M Street development. Tavern feels more modern and sleek than its name implies, with diners ensconced in rich layers of expensive-looking wood. Though there's open patio seating by busy Broadway, the covered side patio dripping with rows of hanging white bulbs on string makes for a great perch. The menu is funky and fun with nods to Southern roots in the Brown Bag Special—grilled Kutztown bologna, hot-pepper mayo, yellow cheese, white bread, and Yukon Gold truffle chips—and more worldly in other offerings of Vietnamese lemongrass-chicken tacos and Maine lobster sliders on Parker House rolls.

Tin Roof, 1516 Demonbreun St., Midtown, Nashville, TN 37203; (615) 313-7103; tinroofbars.com; Pub Food; $. It's a music venue and bar first and foremost, so don't expect a quiet dinner at this rowdy spot off Demonbreun, but the Tin Roof does offer a bite to eat among the tunes. Located among a stretch of eateries along this street that connects The Gulch and Midtown, it draws a mix of students and young professionals as well. Between catching a live band or just grabbing a beer, you'll find fresh salads and classics like wings, jalapeño poppers, and a host of quesadilla choices including spicy corn, vegetable, classic chicken, and barbecue chicken. The sandwich list also reaches from Cuban to Reuben and peanut butter and banana on Texas toast. You can find another location called Tin Roof 2 at 9135 Carothers Pkwy., Ste. 100, Franklin, TN 37067; (615) 435-8100.

Virago Robata Grill & Sushi Bar, 1126 McGavock St., Midtown, Nashville, TN 37203; (615) 254-1902; mstreetnashville.com/virago; Sushi/Japanese; $$. On a warm day, this restaurant should be on your list for the patio alone. It overlooks the twinkling lights of downtown as well as the rooftops of the gritty Gulch, where you'd almost expect to see a *Mary Poppins* chimney sweeper clicking his heels. Choose a booth with a dining surface that converts to cocktail table or a seat at the long bar beside the outdoor fireplace that looks straight out of the pages of *Dwell*. Venturing inside this restaurant, which is part of the M Street development, it's a labyrinth of rooms and bars laid with exotic-looking timbers and stones and dripping in swank lights. It's a world away from The Gulch (and there are no windows for reminders). In addition to sashimi, nigiri, and inventive maki like the Phantom roll (tempura calamari, poblano peppers, cucumber, and avocado wrapped in black rice with soy *tobiko,* balsamic soy, and Sriracha), consider entrees like the Colorado lamb lo mein, Wagyu brisket udon, or the Japanese-style grilling technique, *robatayaki.*

Watermark, 507 12th Ave. South, The Gulch, Nashville, TN 37203; (615) 254-2000; watermark-restaurant.com; Contemporary Southern; $$$. Before the high-rise condominiums took root in The Gulch, Nashvillians in the know ventured to this neighborhood almost solely for an unassuming cinder-block building—and legendary live-music venue—The Station Inn. But then in 2005, came Watermark. This fine dining establishment, located on the second floor of a brick building with industrial bones, offers a sleek, urban, and subdued space of concrete, brick, and glass as well as a rooftop patio overlooking The Gulch and downtown. It boasts the largest wine list in town, and the menu brings together sophisticated Southern sensibilities and seasonal ingredients. You might find sautéed Islamorada yellowtail snapper over poached fingerling potatoes, or a Duo of Duck—roasted breast over a Granny Smith compote in a cider-sorghum glaze along with sweet potato–cat head biscuit stuffed with duck-neck confit and *foie gras* scented with bourbon maple syrup.

Whiskey Kitchen, 118 12th Ave. South, The Gulch, Nashville, TN 37203; (615) 254-3029; mstreetnashville.com/whiskey-kitchen; American; $$. Watch the game, split a pizza, and sink into a burger at this . . . oh wait, is that a King of Leon? This M Street property might be the most casual of the bunch—**Virago Robata Grill & Sushi Bar** (opposite) and **Kayne Prime** (p. 125) are the others—but its stylish sophistication still draws a trendy crowd to its crocodile-print walls studded with bold finishes and low lights. During warmer months, a wall of windows in the front fly up, airing out the room, and a small patio along the side of the building stays busy despite the weather with its mod fireplace (and inventive cocktails with names like Fate) keeping guests toasty. The menu of upscale pub grub is for every man—and woman—including popular Tennessee Whiskey Yam Fries seasoned with sea salt and brown sugar with jalapeño ketchup for dipping. You'll also find 4 types of gourmet wings (including the Aristocrat with butter, garlic, Parmesan, pepper, and parsley), pizzas, fish-and-chips, entrees like grilled chicken tacos, and the restaurant's take on Nashville hot chicken—skillet fried with market vegetables and chipotle mac and cheese.

Landmarks

Broadway Brewhouse & Mojo Grill, 1900 Broadway, Midtown, Nashville, TN 37203; (615) 340-0089; broadwaybrewhouse.net; Cajun / Pub Food; $. Yes, it's a great place to drink, with its long bar and plethora of no-frills places to perch under a shedlike space that opens up during warmer months. And yes, you'll find a vast variety of beers on tap and frosty bushwackers (an alcohol-laden milk shake kept cold in Styrofoam), but locals in-the-know will tell you Broadway Brewhouse has some of the best bar food in town. The wings in particular are a favorite with choices of Panama, the spicy-sweet option; Mojo, blazing habanero hot; and Gringo, which taste perfectly smoky with just minimal seasoning. But beyond the wings, burgers, sandwiches, and nachos, there are simple, hearty plates of beans and rice with andouille sausage, which make it worth coming for the drinks—or maybe the day after for the hangover cure. Additional locations downtown at 317 Broadway, Nashville, TN 37201, (615) 271-2838; Brewhouse West at 7108 Charlotte Pike, Nashville, TN 37209, (615) 356-5005; Brewhouse 100 at 8098 Tennessee 100, Nashville, TN 37221, (615) 673-2981; and Brewhouse South at 1855 Galleria Blvd., Franklin, TN 37067; (615) 778-1860.

Noshville, 1918 Broadway, Midtown, Nashville, TN 37203; (615) 329-6674; noshville.com; Deli; $. The faux Statue of Liberty atop this restaurant helps tip visitors off that's it's a New York–style deli. If not, the menu will surely seal the deal with bagels from H&H and cheesecake from Carnegie Deli along with standards like matzo ball soup, homemade blintzes, and Reuben sandwiches piled high with corned beef and kraut. The restaurant has a mustard-and-ketchup color scheme with chrome stools and booths over black-and-white tile floors. It sits near Music Row and draws a music business crowd as well as lines of locals for breakfast on the weekends. Celebrity designer Manuel, who dressed Elvis in jumpsuits and made Johnny Cash the Man in Black, might also be spotted at the counter for breakfast. Try the corned beef and cabbage, homemade meatloaf, or sandwiches of pastrami, brisket, and rare roast beef. Or for breakfast, there's french toast made with challah with a host of omelets and sides like silver dollar pancakes. Additional locations: 4014 Hillsboro Circle, Green Hills, Nashville, TN 37215, (615) 269-3535; 1000 Meridian Blvd., Franklin, TN 37067, (615) 771-6674; Nashville International Airport, 1 Terminal Dr., Nashville, TN 37214, (615) 275-6674.

South Street Original Smokehouse, Crab Shack & Authentic Dive Bar, 907 20th Ave. South, Midtown, Nashville, TN 37212; (615) 320-5555; pansouth.net; Barbecue/Seafood/Southern; $$. It's the closest you'll get to a beach bar in Nashville at this laid-back restaurant with walls of convertible windows that make it breezy in the open air. Though it sits amid Midtown's concrete, it's a place where you can order trays of oysters, and the Steam Pot Bucket, a pail of mussels, shrimp, smoked sausages, corn on the cob, and new potatoes in a Cajun boil along with Red Stripe and Coronas with lime. Take the stairs up to the "tree house" to where you'll find yet more windows that roll up for an open vibe on summer nights, or visit during the popular big ol' smoke house brunch from 11 a.m. to 3 p.m. on Saturday and Sunday. I visited once when the windows stayed open even during a refreshing summer thunderstorm. The bartender just turned up the music and doled out a round of shots for us all until the dark clouds parted. In addition to seafood, there's barbecue on the menu, too—ribs, pulled pork, smoked sausage, and smoked rotisserie chicken.

Sub Stop, 1701 Broadway, Midtown, Nashville, TN 37203; (615) 255-2782; substopbroadway.com; Deli; $. No chance missing this shop with its bright pink and blue color scheme painted boldly on brick. The Sub Stop's building could fit right in at a Florida beach town, but it's near Music Row instead and has been pulling crowds for more than 30 years. The decor and menu are simple, but the food is fresh—ham, turkey, tuna mixed just with mayo. The bigger daddies include Italian meatball, corned beef and swiss, or the Super— ham, turkey, cooked salami, genoa salami, and mozzarella. Choose your freshly baked 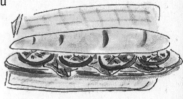 bread and know that "all the way" includes tomatoes, lettuce, pickles, onion, oil and vinegar, and dash of oregano (mustard and mayo on request). There's a rotating roster of soups such as Whamo Chili or chicken noodle, and the red velvet cake is made in-house too. While you wait, read the jokes printed from someone's personal e-mail and taped to the wall, as well as newspaper articles—not about the restaurant but about the music-industry types who frequent the place. The Sub Stop acknowledges who keeps them busy with a sign painted on the front glass: THANK YOU, MUSIC CITY.

Meat-and-Threes

Lucy's Country Cafe, 1911 Broadway, Midtown, Nashville, TN 37203; (615) 410-1311 for catering; (615) 354-8900 for delivery; lucyscountrycafe.com; $. As if five number-one hits weren't enough, professional songwriter and musician Bobby Pinson wanted to open a meat-and-three, too. Along with his wife, Lucy, he now serves dishes like pot roast, country fried steak, chicken and dumplings, cornmeal-crusted okra, mashed potatoes, corn muffins, and banana pudding for lunch each day during the week and at a "Sing for Your Supper" dinner on Wednesday featuring live music from his song-writing friends. He said he wanted to offer a low-cost, home-cooked (and delivered if you want it) option to the musicians and suits that work in the area. After all, he writes songs in the space above the restaurant at the Blue Bar. Pinson's personality comes through in his writings as well as his menu, so with the real-deal menu items he offers tongue-in-cheek dishes, too, like fried Spam.

The Pie Wagon, 1302 Division St., Midtown, Nashville, TN 37203; (615) 256-5893; thepiewagon.com; $. Located near the offices and studios along Music Row, this meat-and-three has been called the Music Row Commissary because it draws executives and musicians craving a home-cooked meal at lunch. But even before it's "commissary" days, this meat-and-three's roots run deep in Nashville. It began as a trolley car that served hot meals—known in the 1920s as "pie wagons"—and parked near downtown. In 1965, the wagon found a home in a brick-and-mortar building in The Gulch under its original name, The Majestic Cafe. But its more general moniker of "pie wagon" had longer sticking power. The restaurant moved again toward Midtown in 2002 where these days the regulars line up to take a tray at the steam tables holding favorites like hot 'n' spicy fried chicken or fried catfish. You also will find a host of sides such as mashed potatoes, turnip greens, green beans, white beans, and squash casserole.

Specialty Stores, Markets & Producers

Casablanca Coffee, 602 12th Ave. South, The Gulch, Nashville, TN 37203; (615) 942-7666; casablancacoffee.com. This coffee shop opened its doors just outside the lobby of the trendy ICON condominium complex in The Gulch in 2009. But situated between a Cantina Laredo and Music City Flats restaurant, Casablanca Coffee serves locally roasted coffee from Drew's Brews and Nashville Coffee Company. It also offers **Yazoo** (p. 264) beer brewed just around the corner. The menu begins with bagels and breakfast sandwiches through the morning, salads and snacks like a half avocado for a $1 at lunch to sandwiches such as the grown-up grilled cheese panini with caramelized onion, cheese, and tomato on grilled local sourdough from Silke's Old World Breads. And for dessert, you'll find

Nashville Cake Pops and locally made Mexican-style popsicles from Chilly Pops. While Casablanca Coffee keeps regulars caffeinated by day, this coffee shop also hosts poets and musicians on a regular basis in the evenings and features art and photography from locals on its walls.

J&J's Market, 1912 Broadway, Midtown, Nashville, TN 37203; (615) 327-9055. The neon sign has a peeling backdrop of turquoise and white, but once inside you'll find J&J's Market to be a gem. It began as a grocery in 1974, and the front of the shop continues to operate as one. There's a newsstand and magazine rack as well as a cabinet of cigars beside tins of Cafe du Monde coffee, Toblerone chocolate, bars of Scharffen Berger, and other European treats such as Belgium *stroopwafel,* which is a thin syrup-filled sandwich cookie for warming over a cup of coffee (also sold in singles from a jar at the counter). The coffee shop in the back has a soaring

ceiling, exposed brick, and crumbling concrete walls painted a mustard color. The dark wood tables, wingbacks, and sofas are all mismatched but neatly arranged. Coupled with the classical and opera music, it has a feel that's more hip, studious library than rambunctious coffee shop. And if your coffee window has closed? Choose from beers on tap such as Lazy Magnolia's Southern Pecan or locally made **Yazoo** (p. 264) and **Jackalope** (p. 263) brews. You can walk out with a mixed sixer (or keg), too, from the fine selection in the market's cooler.

The Turnip Truck Urban Fare, 321 12th Ave. South, The Gulch, Nashville, TN 37203; (615) 248-2000; theturniptruck.com. This mom-and-pop natural and organic market based in East Nashville (see p. 101) makes a healthy second home in The Gulch, where it draws nearby residents and businesspeople to its rows of organic produce. It also offers an organic meats counter, bins of dried beans and granola, yogurts, *kombuchas* and coconut waters, and aisles filled with healthy snacks, nutrition bars, organic frozen meals, and supplements. Or join those who visit for the fresh lunch at this spot. They come for its brightly colored salad bar, a shot of wheatgrass or ginger at the juice bar, prepared sandwiches like curried chicken salad or organic turkey breast. The hot bar offers vegetarian, vegan, and carnivorous options such as lasagna, Indian-spiced chicken, or simply roasted brussels sprouts and pans of healthy, lightly seasoned broccoli. Additional location: 970 Woodland St., East Nashville, Nashville, TN 37206; (615) 650-3600.

Germantown & North Nashville

German immigrants who worked in the meatpacking industry in the area north of downtown built many of the 19th-century homes that set apart the concentrated area known as Germantown. North Nashville as a whole was the heart of the black bourgeoisie with Jefferson Street as its main street, and later a hangout for the likes of Jimi Hendrix. The northern area of town had one of the most interesting ethnic and racial mixes in the city, says Nashville author John Egerton, who has written books about the civil rights movement as well as food. Fisk University, which began in the mid-1800s before Vanderbilt University, Meharry College, also founded in the 19th century, and Tennessee State University helped bring together black professionals. It remains diverse today in people and in architecture as the 19th-century gems sit alongside new developments.

For the food lover, the area north of downtown holds one of Nashville's most talked-about restaurants, City House, as well as the independent restaurant pioneer Mad Platter, the popular Germantown Cafe, and the famed soul food of The Sands. For handmade pasta and sauces visit Lazzaroli Pasta, then to The Cupcake Collection for sweets. The Nashville Farmers' Market, a local mecca for seasonal fruits and vegetables, also provides a one-stop shop for authentic Jamaican food that has been featured on the Food Network's *Diners, Drive-Ins, and Dives* to Southern barbecue and grits, mom-and-pop Indian cuisine, homemade pies and pastries, and an eclectic lunch from a former *Top Chef* contestant. Also look for the market's special events, including cooking demonstrations by local chefs and roundups of artisan food producers and food trucks that make for an appetizing night out.

Foodie Faves

AM@FM, Nashville Farmers' Market, 900 Rosa L. Parks Blvd., North Nashville, Nashville, TN 37208; (615) 291-4585; amfmnashville.com; Eclectic/Bistro; $ This outpost of local chef and *Top Chef* contestant Arnold Myint brings a touch of upscale service to the **Nashville Farmers' Market** (p. 145). Guests can order at the counter or take a seat in Myint's modern space in the open Market House. A server will deliver a bowl of house-made potato chips, mint-infused water, and a glass of wine if you'd like, while on the menu, Myint incorporates seasonal ingredients from the market with a worldly flair in dishes such as Moroccan chile stew with couscous and saffron, and smoked tomato soup with *crema,* dill, and shallots. The deli case holds sandwiches for both grab-and-go and table service, including roasted vegetable hummus naan and the excellent moo shu chicken salad wrap. Myint's salads also shine: kale with nuggets of sweet raisins and walnuts, smoked fennel and carrot slaw, curried roasted vegetable quinoa, and just simple roasted beets with herbs or roasted brussels sprouts. On the weekends, patrons can take a shopping break with mimosas and a crostini bar, which has toppings like farm egg salad available. For dessert try the toasted-coconut brownies. Arnold Myint also owns restaurants **Cha Chah** (p. 186), **PM** (p. 195), and **Suzy Wong's House of Yum** (p. 226).

B&C Market BBQ, Nashville Farmers' Market, 900 Rosa L. Parks, North Nashville, Nashville, TN 37208; (615) 770-0032; baconand caviar.com; Barbecue/Southern; $. This barbecue shop inside the Market House at the **Nashville Farmers' Market** (p. 145) is known nearly as much for its grits as its pork. Garlic and cheese grits are served daily, with each day of the week also offering a special such as jalapeño grits on Thursday and tomato gravy grits on Friday, for example. But the barbecue here edges out as star of this show. The hickory-smoked pulled pork can be ordered on a sandwich or as a plate with house-made sides, or you can order the pork over grits. Other barbecued meats include pulled chicken, beef brisket, smoked salmon, baby back pork ribs, and smoked bologna (on Saturday only). The sides are fresh and include baked beans, corn pudding, mac and cheese, green beans, and homemade cornbread. Look for the pulled-pork egg rolls as an appetizer and the occasional special of Nashville-style hot chicken egg rolls. For dessert, try to save room for the Chocolate Gravy Cake, peach cobbler, or chess pie. Additional location at 2617 Franklin Pike, Nashville, TN 37024; (615) 457-3473.

Bella Nashville, at the Nashville Farmers' Market, 900 Rosa L. Parks Blvd., Nashville, TN 37208; (615) 457-3863; facebook.com/ BellaNashville; Italian/Pizza; $. Like a lot of newcomers to the area, Dave Cuomo came to Nashville for music with his wife, Emma, and their duo called Chicken Little. But when he learned that the **Nashville Farmers' Market** (p. 145) wanted a pizza place inside its Market House, Dave knew it was a nook he could fill. He had been a student of pizza while working at a shop in Brooklyn, and he had worked as chef at **The Patterson House** (p. 128), so he fell right in place at the market, with Emma foraging for their fresh ingredients among the farmers' stalls. The couple keeps things simple on the menu with just about 5 choices of pizzas daily, all of which are 9-inches and New York style. Offerings usually include a Margherita, a meat pizza, a hummus pizza, and then a weekly special featuring the freshest ingredients from the market such as a chicken pizza with organic zucchini, South American *mojo* sauce, and sheep's milk cheese from local cheese shop **The Bloomy Rind** (p. 99).

City House, 1222 4th Ave. North, Germantown, Nashville, TN 37208; (615) 736-5838; cityhousenashville.com; Italian/Pizza/Southern; $$. It's a place where you could bump into musicians like Michael Stipe or Dan Auerbach from The Black Keys, but a conversation with Chef-Owner Tandy Wilson reveals that it's regulars—no matter what occupation—who matter to him the most. Though Wilson has an impressive resume that includes a stint in Italy, the Nashville native is just as likely to call his mom for a family recipe or consult a Junior League cookbook. The result is a blend of regional Italian with Southern American that's expertly executed with a commitment to sustainability and whole-animal cooking. Located in the former studio of sculptor Alan LeQuire, the res-

taurant's warm, open vibe brings together a soaring ceiling and long chef's bar for watching Wilson and team before a wood-burning oven, which turns out pizza like the popular house-made belly ham with oozing egg on top. Also look for fresh pasta dishes, bread gnocchi, and entrees often including trout with bread crumbs, peanuts, raisins, lemon, and parsley. At Wilson's Sunday suppers, many of his chef friends come in for "snacks" of tenderloin on biscuit with sorghum bacon butter, house-made sausage, offal, and entrees for sharing like pork meatballs and garlic toasts. See Chef-Owner Tandy Wilson's recipe for **Orange & Fennel Roasted Pork Butt** on p. 302.

Nashville Farmers' Market

During the devastating Tennessee Floods of May 2010, marketing manager Jolie Yockey evacuated the Nashville Farmers' Market as she watched a car float down Rosa L. Parks Boulevard. Floodwaters soon rose to 18 inches inside the Market House at the farmers' market. But even after waters subsided, drywall had to be ripped out, equipment had to be removed and cleaned, and walls had to be swabbed for disease-causing bacteria. The market did not celebrate its grand reopening until 3 months later.

Thankfully, though, as Metro picked up the bill for the city-owned building, the community also came together during those post-flood days. Not even a week after the flood, when farmers had returned to the outdoor sheds (and the Market House remained closed), I watched a farmer offer a customer a discount on a plant that had suffered a bit of flood damage. But rather than the $12 he suggested, she handed him back $25 instead.

These days, the market is back in full swing and better than ever. While the market is open daily, its special events and Night Markets bring enough food-filled fun to qualify for date night. The Market House's new Grow Local Kitchen hosts cooking demonstrations and classes from local chefs, and the farmers' market also accepts applications for its community kitchen, a place for locals with ideas and recipes who want to take their products to market. (See Grow Local Kitchen's Laura Wilson's recipe for **Roasted Cauliflower with Turmeric, Peanuts & Raisins** on p. 293.) And of course you'll find the farmers and vendors who give us inspiration in the kitchen and in life with their hard work and creativity. 900 Rosa L. Parks Blvd., North Nashville, Nashville, TN 37208; (615) 880-2001; nashvillefarmersmarket.org.

The Garden Brunch Cafe, 924 Jefferson St., North Nashville, Nashville, TN 37208; (615) 891-1217; gardenbrunchcafe.com; Brunch; $$. Once home to William Strickland, the architect who designed the Tennessee State Capitol in the 1800s, this gray brick bungalow with red door now welcomes guests as The Garden Brunch Cafe. Chef Jennifer Carpenter renovated and opened the spot with her husband, Karl, and she opens just on Fri, Sat, and Sun from 9 a.m. to 2 p.m. Though Carpenter was a Realtor for 20 years, she has good cooking roots and repertoire. Her father came from New Orleans and her mother from Baton Rouge, and from them, she learned a lot, including the influence for her bananas Foster pancakes and fish and grits. She also made a point of cooking often for her five children, so she's committed to health as well: She doesn't use artificial ingredients, processed food, or pork products; she prefers turkey and organic beef instead. Look for the Germantown Benny, her version of eggs Benedict with smoked salmon, sautéed spinach, caramelized onions, cherry tomatoes, capers, and house-made hollandaise sauce, as well as garden omelets and steak and eggs.

Germantown Cafe, 1200 5th Ave. North, Germantown, Nashville, TN 37208; (615) 242-3226; germantowncafe.com; Bistro; $$. Talk of Germantown Cafe usually comes with a mention of the downtown view. Perched on a hill at the edge of Germantown, it offers a clear line of sight to Nashville's twinkling skyline. While the best spot is from the tables near the front window, the room here has good energy throughout, thanks to its aubergine walls and gerbera daisies giving a spot of bright color to each table. At lunch you'll see celebratory birthday meals as well as business ones over crocks of french onion soup and fresh salads or maybe the black bean–quinoa burger with corn-avocado relish. At dinner, signature dishes include the plum pork, mustard-marinated tenderloin medallions with plum sauce, mashed potatoes, and green beans, or coconut curry salmon over risotto with asparagus. The cafe also offers a popular brunch with crab cakes Benedict and shrimp and grits as well as omelets and frittatas of the day.

Jamaicaway Restaurant & Catering, Nashville Farmers' Market, 900 Rosa L. Parks Blvd., North Nashville, Nashville, TN 37208; (615) 255-5920; jamaicawaycatering.com; Jamaican; $. Native Jamaican Ouida Kalokoh-Bradshaw runs this restaurant inside the Market House at the **Nashville Farmers' Market** (p. 145), with her son Kamal Kalokoh as chef. Customers take a tray and head through the line at the steam table for jerk chicken, fried plantains, sweet potatoes with hunks of pineapple, callaloo greens, fried johnny-cakes, and rice and peas. Ouida and Kamal keep close to their roots, offering many authentic Jamaican dishes as well, such as braised oxtail and curried goat with thyme and pimento. To drink, try the ginger beer, Irish moss (a sweet blend of boiled seaweed, flaxseed, and soy milk), as well as sorrel juice brewed from a blossom native to the island along with ginger. Jamaicaway is a favorite among vegetarians as the menu includes curried tofu, jerked meat substitute, and barbecued portobello mushrooms. The tables at the restaurant are lacquered with photos from Jamaica, and the walls are decorated with a map of the island and photos of that famous Jamaican who reminds us that every thing's gonna be alright. As Seventh-Day Adventists, Ouida and family observe the Sabbath on Saturday, so you'll find the restaurant closed on that day.

The Mad Platter, 1239 6th Ave. North, Germantown, Nashville, TN 37208; (615) 242-2563; themadplatterrestaurant.com; Contemporary; $$. Craig and Marcia Jervis, owners of the Mad Platter, blazed a trail as pioneers of Germantown's revitalization and to the local farm-to-table movement from the quaint brick Victorian restaurant and home. They've long had a garden out back for plucking seasonal vegetables and herbs, and after an impressive 23 years in business, the restaurant completed the rigorous Green Restaurant certification at the end of 2011, becoming only the second restaurant to do so in the city. Signature dishes include the rack of lamb with seasonal accoutrement that might include chickpeas, roasted garlic, kalamata olives, grape confit, eggplant, and pomegranate reduction, and the duck breast with Falls Mills grits, pearl onions, roasted beets, turnips, fennel, cranberry compote, and orange *gastrique*. For dessert you can't go wrong with many of the options—classic crème brûlée, bananas Foster, or the Chocolate Elvis, a tart of bittersweet, white, and milk chocolate ganache. Simply add $20 to the price of your entree for the 5-course dinner, which adds choice of appetizer, soup, salad, and dessert. The restaurant serves lunch, too—fresh salads, homemade soups, a Reuben the menu claims as Nashville's best, and entrees like crab cakes, pan-seared trout, and petite filet.

Savannah Tea Company, 707 Monroe St., North Nashville, Nashville, TN 37208; (615) 248-2288; savannahteacompany.com; Tearoom; $$. Taking proper tea is a treat, and there aren't a lot of places in the area to do it. But this Victorian with high ceilings and hardwood floors serves as both tearoom and tea shop with light tea or full tea options. You can begin by choosing an elaborate hat to wear from the restaurant's collection while dining— totally optional, of course. Then it's on to a quiet table with just the lilt of classical music playing in the background. The tea menu is fairly large— over 100 to choose from, divided into tea type like black tea, oolong, rooibos, Earl Grey, many flavored ones from pome- granate and rosehips to pumpkin spice and chocolate mint, or lavender and hibiscus herbal teas. As for the menu, you might as well pay the extra $3 for full tea, which includes cup of soup and quiche in addition to scones, muffins, jam, clotted cream, assorted finger sandwiches, fruit, and dainty desserts and pastries. There's a regular menu, too, with classic ladies-who-lunch fare such as strawberry-spinach salad, tuna salad on tomato, and chicken salad on croissant. The tearoom also caterers, hosts events, and offers a custom wedding- cake service.

Siam Cafe, 316 McCall St., Nashville, TN 37211; (615) 834-3181; sites.google.com/site/siamcafenashville; Thai; $. The Silpacharn family brings us the Thai cuisine at this restaurant located along the cultural smorgasbord of Nolensville Road. Open for nearly 30 years, it's a beloved spot for Thai food in town. And while there's a steam table buffet for a variety of Asian items, it's best to take a seat in the dining room and order specialties off the menu. For groups, the soups arrive in raised silver serving bowls heated underneath, holding options like Tom Yum Koong (hot and sour shrimp with lemongrass, kaffir lime leaves, mushrooms, lime juice, and chile paste) or Tom Ka Kai (chicken coconut with lemongrass, galangal, mushrooms, lime juice, and chile paste). I could make a meal on the rich soups alone. But the menu goes on with lots more options including Pla Jian, deep-fried whole red snapper topped with ground pork, vegetables, and ginger sauce to a host of curries such as standards like green and red as well as Hunag Ray, red curry with ginger and cashews.

Silo, 1121 5th Ave. North, Nashville, TN 37208; (615) 750-2912; silotn.com; American/Southern; $$. After his time as chef at Virago and Lime, a trendy Midtown spot by restaurateur Chris Hyndman, chef Clay Greenberg took a hiatus to hone his next project, Silo, which food lovers find well worth the wait. He opened the doors in 2012 to the Southern bistro with a farm-to-table focus in the heart of Germantown among the Vista Germantown apartments. Collaborating with Greenberg is Paul Cercone, previously of Normandy Farm Artisan Bakery in Charleston, South Carolina.

Choose from seats at the community table, patios, bar area, or private dining rooms for dishes from an open kitchen. First courses include house charcuterie of root beer pork belly to deviled eggs and hot chicken with pickled peach puree on Sunbeam bread to second courses of smoked pork pot pie with biscuit topping and grilled summer vegetables or steelhead trout with fairytale eggplant, zephyr squash, and tomato nage. Sides might include field pea salad with lemon vinaigrette, heirloom tomatoes, and cracklin' cornbread with jalapeño-honey butter.

Swagruha Indian Restaurant, 900 Rosa L. Parks Blvd., North Nashville, Nashville, TN 37208; (615) 736-7001; swagruhaindian restaurant.com; Indian; $. Though it looks like an even smaller version of a mall food court shop—just a short steam table with a small lit menu on the wall behind it—this Southern Indian restaurant sits in the midst of the Market House at the **Nashville Farmers' Market** (p. 145), and its name translates to "home." Indeed it's a full-on family affair. The woman in charge is Siva Pabuluri, and on weekends you might find her children and husband all helping put food on trays. "He's a doctor during the week and dishwasher on the weekends," I once heard Siva's daughter say of her father, who came to the states from India in 1972. He helped his wife open the business as she cooked so well at home and had even been approached about catering, a service that she offers from the restaurant today. But at the market restaurant, just $6.49 will fill your tray with rice, naan, and two curries, including chicken biryani, butter chicken, chicken tikka masala, chicken curry, chile chicken, goat curry, vegetable korma, channa masala, dal, and *mutter panir*. The menu also includes samosas, *dosas,* and mango smoothies as well as other beverages.

Zackie's Original Hot Dog, 1201 5th Ave. North, #103, Germantown, Nashville, TN 37208; (615) 291-8311; zackies.net; Hot Dogs; $. This hot dog shop isn't owned by a man named Zackie, but it's named after one. Zackie Wakin was a family friend and "colorful character" in the life of owner Mike Trigiani, who manned his first hot dog stand when he was just a 10-year-old boy in Big Stone Gap, Virginia. Trigiani later moved to Nashville from New York City and decided to go back into the hot dog business in 2006 when he noticed a need for more hot dogs in Nashville. His tiny shop is clean and no-frills; the best spot to park with lunch is at the patio tables out front. When ordering at the counter, begin by choosing dog type—Nathan's beef, turkey, veggie, Johnsonville beer brat, Polish sausage, TJ's Italian sausage and peppers, or spicy Cajun sausage. Toppings include the standards like yellow mustard, ketchup, coleslaw, chili, cheese, and onions. But you'll also find

Chicago relish, sautéed onions, sauerkraut, jalapeños, celery salt, banana peppers, and more. Sides include french fries, onion rings, and pierogies. Buns are baked fresh locally at Charpier's Bakery, and Trigiani practices

what he calls "Italian hospitality"—he'll remember your name and your order.

Meat-and-Threes

Monell's Restaurant, 1235 6th Ave. North, Germantown, Nashville, TN 37208; (615) 248-4747; monellstn.com; $$. Diners who come to Monell's, located in a historic redbrick building in the heart of Germantown, sit at communal tables where the food is served family style as if this were a boarding house. Once seated, out come heaping bowls of skillet-fried chicken as well as the famous corn pudding, which *Garden & Gun* magazine called one of the 50 best foods in the South. Otherwise dishes vary by day such as chicken and dumplings and meatloaf on Monday; spinach lasagna and pot roast on Tuesday; pork chops on Wednesday; fried catfish on Friday, and so forth. On the weekends, you can have a full country breakfast with sausage, bacon, country ham, scrambled eggs, hash browns, fried apples, pancakes, cheese grits, biscuits and gravy, hot coffee, and, of course, more fried chicken and corn pudding. Though it's busy at breakfast and lunch, dinner is served Tues through Sat as well from 5 to 8:30 p.m. An additional location called Café Monell's is located at 2826 Bransford Ave., Nashville,TN 37204; (615) 298-2254; and Monell's at the Manor also serves as a wedding venue. It is located at 1400 Murfreesboro Pike, Nashville, TN 37217; (615) 365-1414.

The Sands Soul Food, 937 Locklayer St., North Nashville, Nashville, TN 37203; (615) 742-1652; $. I wonder if people who don't like soul food also don't like butterflies and chocolate chip cookies. I mean, it's soul food. And this restaurant represents that genre at its finest. From a simple cinder-block building on a side street near the **Nashville Farmers' Market** (p. 145), you'll find regulars lining up for breakfast and lunch. In fact, the day starts at the Sands with customers loading their trays at the short cafeteria line with bacon, sausage, country ham, grits, biscuits, pancakes, and eggs to order. Not to be missed: the hash browns. As the pans behind the line morph into lunch options, the choices turn

to fried pork chops and chicken wings in gravy with sides like white beans, turnip greens, and macaroni and cheese. *Southern Belly*, the app that complements the book by the same name by John T. Edge, will direct you to the pork neck bones in gravy over rice. And while I trust the recommendation, I had my mind blown at the Sands by a bowl of chicken and dumplings. There are a few tables in this plain butter-colored room, but the Sands does a busy takeout, too, sending guests walking with bulging containers that will perfume their cars.

Swett's Restaurant, 2725 Clifton Ave., North Nashville, Nashville TN 37209; (615) 329-4418; swettsrestaurant.com; $. David Swett Jr. is the grandson to Swett's founder, Walter Swett, who opened the restaurant in 1954, and he once told me that the humble meat-and-three is one of the most diverse places in Nashville: "You can sit here with every walk of life," he said. And true, it draws politicians and celebrities as well as neighborhood folk who just want some country cooking. The restaurant has endured flood and fire. In fact, David Swett said he had no interest in running the business until he helped his family rebuild it after it was burned to the ground. Then in May 2010, the Swett's location at the **Nashville Farmers' Market** (p. 145) flooded along with many other businesses in town, and the family decided not to reopen there. Regulars have never failed the Swett family, though, lining up at the steam table for a cornucopia—fried chicken, meatloaf, barbecue chicken, turnip greens, fried apples, pinto beans, candied yams, okra, squash casserole, and creamed corn. Sop it up with cornbread and finish with fruit cobblers like peach and blackberry or a slice of sweet potato pie. The only additional location is in the Nashville International Airport at Concourse C.

Specialty Stores, Markets &Producers

The Cupcake Collection, 1213 6th Ave. North, Germantown, Nashville, TN 37208; (615) 244-2900; thecupcakecollection.com. Mignon Francois had almost hit financial rock bottom when she began selling her cupcakes at $1.50 apiece. And through one sweet bite at a time, and lots of family teamwork, she has built a business that now regularly sees lines of guests out the front door of the bungalow she also calls home. The business, which opened in 2008, remains a family affair, and the price of the cupcakes thankfully h a s n ' t changed. In the age of massive over-the-top

treats, I love the size of these cupcakes that feel genuinely old-school— enough to feel like a treat, but not an overindulgence. Mignon uses no artificial ingredients and keeps the flavors fresh with   specials like Key lime coconut, pineapple upside down, banana nut cake, and cookies 'n' cream, as well as flavors that you can find daily such as red velvet, strawberry, and sweet potato, which was inspired by a family dessert. Keep on the lookout, too, for The Cupcake Collection's bus, which parks at special events around town.

Dozen—A Nashville Sweet Shop, 900 Rosa L. Parks Blvd., North Nashville, Nashville, TN 37208; (615) 509-9680; dozen-nashville .com. Owner/baker Claire Meneely's "shop" consists of a table with banner sign at the **Nashville Farmers' Market** (p. 145). But it's the products she sells that matter most, and Claire's expertly handcrafted cookies and sweets are at once professional and just like you'd find at home. Claire baked in San Francisco and Paris before coming to Nashville, and she has a deep commitment to using local products that you might find at the market, such as milk from Hatcher Family Dairy, fresh butter from JD Country Milk,

GAYLORD OPRYLAND RESORT & CONVENTION CENTER

As a Nashvillian, this sprawling 9-acre complex with its well-groomed gardens, fountains, waterfalls, shops, restaurants, elaborate decorations at Christmastime, and live music—not to mention the **Grand Ole Opry** (p. 275) nearby—offers one of the best spots possible for being a tourist in your own town. Though it's built for visitors, even locals like making a visit.

You'll find at least 10 bars and restaurants inside the property offering vast varieties for dining from Mexican to Italian and Irish to Tennessee barbecue. But the **Old Hickory Steakhouse Restaurant** is my top choice. Located in an antebellum-style mansion, the restaurant's terrace overlooks the indoor river in the Delta Atrium. Or book a spot in the Library Lounge for classic cocktails or wine and desserts like bananas Foster Napoleon or crème brûlée. On the main menu, you'll find escargot, Reisling-poached *foie gras,* grass-fed steaks such as the dry-aged Kansas City strip with blue-cheese butter, filet, porterhouse, and bone-in rib eye with sides like asparagus in hollandaise sauce, blue cheese and thyme potatoes au gratin, mascarpone creamed spinach, and garlic truffle mac and cheese. And speaking of cheese, don't miss the cheese cart experience when the *maître fromager* brings cheese choices to your table and helps you select artisanal varieties in groups of 3 or 6. It's worth a trip to the hotel alone. 2800 Opryland Dr., North Nashville, Nashville, TN 37214; (615) 889-1000; gaylordhotels.com/gaylord-opryland.

farm-fresh eggs from Wedge Oak Farms, as well as organic sugars and flours. Her chocolate chip cookies bring together just enough sweet, salt, and butter for a rich and chewy version. Other popular cookies include the oatmeal cranberry with walnuts, peanut butter and ginger made with molasses and crystallized ginger pieces. Claire also specializes in *dulce de leche* brownies, almond cherry bars, linzer cookies, traditional madeleines with lemon glaze, and her mother's recipe for gingerbread, a dark-molasses baked version. You can also find her products at coffee shops around town and at a booth on Saturday at the **Franklin Farmers' Market** (p. 259) in Franklin, Tennessee.

Drinkhaus Espresso & Tea, 500 Madison St., Germantown, Nashville, TN 37208; (615) 255-5200; drinkhaus.com. This bright spot of a coffee shop gives a nod to its Germantown roots with its name. Clean white walls bedecked only with local art and just a few tables fill the small space. But up by the counter you'll find lots of options such as locally made Tutto Bene biscotti, hiply packaged Halo nutrition bars, and a refrigerated case with juices and spring water called Fred filling up cool bottles. You'll find the lattes and mochas you'd expect from a coffee shop, and if you ask for just a coffee, they'll serve you an Americano with cream that comes from local Hatcher Family Dairy, should you choose to add it, and a sleeve made of cork and stamped with the shop's logo to wrap around hot cups. Items of note on the menu include the peanut butter mocha and fruit crèmes in various flavors, such as the strawberry made with blended fresh fruit and iced milk. During warmer months the elderflower lemonade brings a taste of refreshment.

Geraldine's Pies, 900 Rosa L. Parks Blvd., North Nashville, Nashville, TN 37208; (615) 310-8908; geraldinespies.com. It's a pleasure to spot Geraldine Bell's table at the farmers' market both for her collection of pies and her wide smile. Bell spent many years perfecting her grandmother's chess pie recipe, and in 2003 she began selling them door-to-door at beauty shops and nail salons and markets and any place she could get the word out. These days, you'll often find her at the farmers' markets around town, and her offerings have expanded beyond classic chess—though she always has that one on hand. She often has chocolate chess, pecan chess, and lemon chess as well as other traditional pies like pumpkin and chocolate. Almost all of the pies she bakes are also available "diabetic," or without sugar. Geraldine is happy to bake pies for special events with some advance notice, and she sells pies in two sizes—regular pies for $11 and miniature pies for $2.

Lazzaroli Pasta, 1314 5th Ave. North, Germantown, Nashville, TN 37208; (615) 291-9922; lazzaroli.com. Tom Lazzaro grew up in the 1970s on the fresh pasta of his Grandmom Amoroso, an immigrant from Sicily who combined flour and whole eggs on the countertop in South Philadelphia. About 30 years later in 2002, he began taking the family tradition of homemade pasta to market in small batches from a commercial kitchen out of his Hendersonville garage. In 2007 he opened his shop, a nook of paradise for food lovers, where he keeps making pasta and ravioli stuffed with kale, pancetta, duck, or Chianti beef short ribs. You'll also find tubs of house-made ricotta and tomato sauces like Bolognese, lemon mascarpone, arrabbiata, and puttanesca. Cases hold hard-to-find *salumi*, sopressata, prosciutto, boudin, and andouille. Cheeses include Parmigiano Reggiano, caciocavallo, Romano, pecorino, and locals like Kenny's Farmhouse cheddar. The shelves are lined with olive oils and vinegars as well as Sicilian anchovies, breads from local Silke's Old World Breads Bakery, dried pastas, crackers, amaretti cookies, and *pizzelles*.

Shreeji's International Market, 900 Rosa L. Parks Blvd., North Nashville, Nashville, TN 37208; (615) 254-1697. This is the type of place where food lovers could get lost browsing for hours among the rows of beans, nuts, teas, and sauces. Sitting in the heart of the Market House at the **Nashville Farmers' Market** (p. 145), Shreeji's International Market brings together interesting treats from throughout Asia and the Middle East. Though there are a couple rows allocated for produce such as onions, cilantro, limes, and long green beans used in Thai and Szechuan dishes, I find the inner aisles to be of most interest, even if they do seem a little stuffed and chaotic—bags of yellow-orange turmeric, coriander seeds, and all sorts of spices and rice flours in bulk as well as burlap sacks of basmati rice, jars of ginger paste, tins of tea, bags of naan, chutneys, oils, nuts of all sorts, and a vast selection of hot sauces. The refrigerated cases hold imported beverages like Jamaican root or sweet Champagne colas and tubs of exotic ice creams with rosewater.

The Sweet Stash, 900 Rosa Parks Blvd., North Nashville, Nashville, TN 37208; thesweetstash.com. Whitney and Vaughn May started The Sweet Stash out their home—transforming their kitchen into a commercial workspace—in 2008. You can find them inside the Market House at the **Nashville Farmers' Market** (p. 145) where they sell their cupcakes, cookies, truffles, and breads. If you can only try just one thing, I recommend the oatmeal sandwich cookie—two oatmeal cookies held together by a lightly spiced cinnamon cream-cheese filling. But you also can't go wrong with the gingersnap with its lemon zest filling or the peanut butter cookies with milk chocolate and peanut butter filling and the edges rolled in salted, crushed peanuts. Whitney bakes whoopie pies as well and loaves of bread such as banana walnut and blueberry lemon. I've heard these cupcakes in flavors such as red velvet or banana cream and mocha called the best in town. The Mays also prepare special orders for weddings, showers, and other parties.

8th Avenue South, Melrose, Berry Hill & South Nashville

There's a strip mall along Nolensville Road in South Nashville where you can visit six countries from the same parking lot. You'll find an Indian market sitting next to a Vietnamese nail salon, which sits near a Hispanic law office beside a Kurdish market with a bakery in the back for picking up freshly prepared lavash bread. Though the Hispanic community makes up Nashville's largest immigrant population, Music City also has the second-largest Kurdish population in the country.

The variety in cultures shines through most in this part of town where I also once took a Nolensville Road cross-culture tour offered by *Alimentum* literary journal. Along one stretch of South Nashville we hopped from Thai curries to Ethiopian stews scooped up with *injera* to *barbacoa* tacos to Turkish coffees and Persian rosewater ice cream, golden with saffron and flecked with crushed pistachios.

Leading down to this southern section of town, though, is 8th Avenue South. It was rough and tumble just a couples decades ago—even causing Jack Arnold of the famed Arnold's Country Kitchen to carry a gun in a hip holster during lunch service—but it has since become an area of focus for new businesses. On 8th Avenue, you will find the black tablecloths of Flyte World Dining & Wine, and as the road turns into Franklin Pike and the area called Melrose, you'll find the bar stools and burgers of the popular M. L. Rose.

But also in this section of town sits the quirky and charming Berry Hill neighborhood. Home to recording studios, musicians, and artists, it brings an independent spirit to the shops and, of course, an eclectic mix to the food.

Foodie Faves

Abay Ethiopian Restaurant, 3792 Nolensville Pike, South Nashville, Nashville, TN 37211; (615) 834-8885; Ethiopian; $$. I first visited this restaurant on a tour of Nolensville Road's ethnic spots led by Paulette Licitra and Annakate Tefft of the literary journal *Alimentum*'s food tours. If it weren't for the tour, I might not have realized the place existed, because it's easy to miss, tucked into a strip mall off the main road. But it's certainly worth seeking out. The room is relatively plain and spacious, and the service is friendly with owners offering descriptions and education on the dishes. We received bowl after bowl of Ethiopian stews, both vegetarian and meat-based with baskets of rolled up *injera,* the spongy, flat sourdough bread for scooping it up. I find it's best to go here with an open mind and just ask what's on the menu that day. Some of these dishes are complex and take time to make, and if you ask, you'll get what's most fresh.

Athens Family Restaurant, 2526 Franklin Pike, Melrose, Nashville, TN 37204; (615) 383-2848; athensfamilyrestaurant.com; Greek/Breakfast; $$. The Food Network's Guy Fieri made a stop here for an episode of *Diners, Drive-Ins, and Dives,* and indeed, it's a popular spot for many locals along 8th Avenue for both a traditional breakfast of eggs with all the fixings, pancakes, omelets, and eggs Benedicts, as well as fresh Greek food on blue-and-white checked tablecloths. Dishes include homemade spanako-pita (phyllo dough with spinach and feta), moussaka (layers of eggplant, ground beef, cheese, and béchamel sauce), *suzukakia* (beef meatballs with tomato sauce), pastitsio (ziti pasta casserole with beef and cheese and topped with béchamel sauce), and appetizers such as hummus, dolmades (stuffed grape leaves), and snacks of feta and olives. You'll find plenty of dishes that fall between Greek and American such as the bacon lamb burger. For dessert, try the scratch-made baklava and crème caramel. And Thurs through Sat, this restaurant keeps its doors open 24 hours, bringing in a hungry crowd of all sorts through the night.

Back to Cuba Cafe, 4683 Trousdale Ln., South Nashville, Nashville, TN 37204; (615) 837-6711; Cuban; $. It's a restaurant located inside a small strip mall attached to a service station at a busy intersection near the I-65 on-ramp. So the outside atmosphere is hardly a view of the Caribbean Sea. But it's the food that really matters, and Back to Cuba has the best Cuban sandwich you'll find in Nashville. It's layered, as one would expect, on Cuban-style bread with ham, pork, pickles, and mustard, and then pressed flat. Owner Alex Martinez, who is of Cuban descent, also serves arroz con pollo (chicken and rice), empanadas of chicken or beef (the latter studded with green olive a la picadillo), *lechon asado* (roast pork) and *pechuga a la plancha* (grilled chicken). Many of the dishes are accompanied by sweet plantains or yuca. While they don't serve alcohol, you can bring your own, or maybe just order a Cuban coffee. Martinez and his wife, Rebecca, who is from Central America, have long owned nearby **Mama Mia's** (p. 172) Italian restaurant as well.

Baja Burrito, 722 Thompson Ln., Berry Hill, Nashville, TN 37204; (615) 383-BAJA; bajaburrito.com; Mexican; $. Burrito and taco shop chains seem to be a dime a dozen, so it might be shocking to find that Baja Burrito is a locally owned, one-shop burrito restaurant in Berry Hill. But it fits right into the neighborhood with its artists and free-thinking style. Just a little beige box, you enter under a

turquoise awning with sunshine-dotted *j* (in the word *Baja*) to see a well-edited menu (especially when it comes to burrito and taco shops) on a blackboard. Menu items are prepared in front of you the way you want them in either small or large flour tortillas. Choose from stuffings that include chicken, steak, veggie (a mix of peppers and onions sautéed with garlic), or "maximum r&b" (Mexican rice and choice of beans). Fixings include what you'd probably expect—rice, beans, salsas, sour creams. The taco menu offers similar choices, except with the addition of fish. Dressings for salads are homemade and include a tomatillo vinaigrette and chipotle honey-mustard. I also enjoy the frugality of the smartly named Peasant Plate: beans, rice, guacamole, salad, and corn tortillas for $5.25.

Calypso Cafe, 700 Thompson Ln., South Nashville, Nashville, TN 37204; (615) 297-3888; calypsocafe.com; Caribbean; $. One of several locations around town, this Caribbean-themed and locally owned restaurant was one of my favorite discoveries for an inexpensive and healthy meal when I moved to Nashville. The vibe is laid-back, but the service is speedy for both takeout and dine-in (the tables are covered in brightly printed patterns). The rotisserie chicken is a highlight ordered in quarters or halves with sauces such as a thin, tangy barbecue, a Jamaican curry, or spicy jerk. Sides include packed-with-flavor Cuban black beans, Martinique callaloo (mustard greens with tomato and onion), or spiced mashed sweet potatoes, sprinkled with coconut if you'd like. The black bean salad also keeps customers returning for a plate of green leaf lettuce and tortilla chips topped with a generous helpings of black beans, cheddar cheese, tomatoes, sour cream, red onions, and your choice of chicken, beef, or rice. The house barbecue sauce comes warm on the side as dressing—an unconventional combo that works well. The Lucayan salad is another favorite with chicken, mandarin oranges, toasted almonds, and vinaigrette served with *boija* muffins, Caribbean cornbread topped with coconut, that are sweet enough to serve as dessert. Additional locations at 2424 Elliston Place, Nashville, TN 37203, (615) 321-3878; 5101 Harding Pike, Belle Meade, Nashville, TN 37205, (615) 356-1678; 600 Frazier Dr., Franklin, TN 37067, (615) 771-5665; 1101 Gartland Ave., East Nashville, Nashville, TN 37206, (615) 227-6133.

Ellendale's, 2739 Old Elm Hill Pike, South Nashville, Nashville, TN 37214; (615) 884-0171; ellendales.com; American Contemporary; $$$. There's something for everyone on the menu and buffet at this restaurant in a farmhouse with a sprawling organic garden. Owner Julie Buhler has been personal chef to Dolly Parton, and she named the restaurant after her grandmother, a woman who devoted her life to helping those in need. Though the menu changes often, it always offers fresh, scratch-made cooking like pork shoulder with mango salsa, beef stroganoff, creamed spinach, mashed potatoes, sautéed green beans, and asparagus. On the dinner menu, you'll find steaks, seafood, chicken, pasta, and even game like local rabbit in white wine sauce with rosemary, thyme, and portobellos and served with ginger mashed sweet potatoes and grilled vegetables. The Saturday and Sunday brunch features stations for customizing omelets, pasta with Alfredo or marinara sauce, and a bar of staples like sausage, bacon, cheddar grits, waffles, and biscuits and gravy, as well as homemade soups, salads, and chocolate fondue dessert. Ellendale's also features live music every night of the week.

Flyte World Dining & Wine, 718 Division St., 8th Avenue, Nashville, TN 37203; (615) 255-6200; flytenashville.com; Eclectic; $$$. This sophisticated and modern restaurant with spicy red walls and exposed ductwork opened in SoBro (South of Broadway) before the area's cool moniker had fully taken root and when the vibe of the neighborhood was a bit grittier. But Flyte has kept its

footing with a creative menu that supports local farmers and producers who provide free-range meats and line-caught fish. You can sample wines by the glass, bottle, or "flyte," (a riff on the term "flight" often used by wine tasters to describe a group of three or more) and you can do the same with some menu items. The salads and soups can come in smaller-portioned trios, for example. And though the menu changes often, soup options might include a trio of turnip, carrot-ginger, and anasazi beans. For main dishes you'll likely find fish, beef, lamb, local vegetable dishes, and poultry like confit Sonoma duck leg with brussels sprouts, braised cabbage, and mustard jus.

The desserts also offer creativity such as the Heirloom "Carrot Cake," a walnut cake with cream cheese, carrot sorbet, and raisin *gastrique*. A prix fixe is offered every night (except some holidays): starter like soft-poached egg with chorizo-pistachio cake and bacon sorghum, a choice of entree, and choice of dessert for $35.

Gabby's Burgers & Fries, 493 Humphreys St., 8th Avenue, Nashville, TN 37203; (615) 733-3119; gabbysburgersandfries.com; Burgers; $. Owner Doug Havron knew his burger joint had good bones being located in the old Hap Townes building, a beloved meat-and-three. And even though Doug serves a different sort of fare, the vibe is convivial and the food comforting. Just around the corner from the Nashville Sounds baseball stadium, this cottage of a restaurant serves grass-fed beef burgers to all types of folks who take a seat at one of the few tables or sit at the bar around the grill where the action happens. Though Gabby's, named for Doug's daughter Gabrielle, serves several types of burgers including a bacon-swiss or a chili burger as well as a house-made veggie burger, I say you can't beat the Seamus, a single 5-ounce patty of grass-fed beef (order the Gabby for two patties) topped with cheese and loaded with traditional fixings such as lettuce, pickle, tomato, mustard, onion, mayo, and ketchup. Both the regular fries and sweet potato fries are perfect. But for those who want a little something out of the ordinary, Gabby's has that, too, with toppings that include kickin' ketchup, a fried egg, grilled onions and peppers, jalapeños, and banana peppers.

Gojo Ethopian Restaurant, 415 Thompson Ln., South Nashville, Nashville, TN 37211; (615) 332-0710; gojoethio.com; Ethiopian; $. This orange box of a building along Nolensville is one of the few Ethiopian restaurants in town. If you want to experience many of the flavors and dishes, there's a lunch buffet Monday through Sunday. But one of my favorite things about the Ethiopian dining experience is how communal it can be when dishes are shared at the table. I prefer to go for dinner, and usually just skip the appetizers and salads and order a combination of meat and vegetable stews (you can select 2 vegetable dishes and 2 meat dishes for $13.95 here). The options come served over *injera,* the spongy, flat sourdough bread for scooping. Favorites include the *kitfo,* a spiced and buttered version of a steak tartare; *qey-w'et,* beef stew with onion, garlic, ginger, berbere spice, hot pepper, and butter; and *doro w'et,* marinated chicken legs served with a hard-boiled egg. Vegetarian dishes might include *miser w'et,* lentils cooked in spices; *ye'atkilt w'et,* green beans, carrots, and onions in a flavorful sauce; and *shiro w'et,* ground chickpeas seasoned with onion and garlic. Don't forget to sample the Ethiopian coffee served in a traditional *jebana,* or Ethiopian coffee pot.

La Hacienda Taqueria, 2615 Nolensville Rd., South Nashville, Nashville, TN 37211; (615) 256-6142; lahaciendainc.com/restaurant .html; Mexican; $. This popular Mexican restaurant along the stretch of world-cuisines restaurants on Nolensville Pike welcomes a variety of diners through its doors at both lunch and dinner. The decor is cheery and bright, and almost every table has curved-back, rattan chairs. While you'll find every bean-cheese-rice combination imaginable in enchiladas, burritos, chimichangas, and fajitas, La Hacienda has more authentic dishes like tripe soups and *molcajete* bowls loaded with ingredients rather than wrapped in tortilla. The Yepez family opened the restaurant when they were starting their tortilla-manufacturing facility. They now ship to seven states and, of course, to La Hacienda. The Yepezes, who moved to Nashville from San Ana, California, also own the market next door, **La Hacienda SuperMercado** (p. 180), so if you don't order the flan at the restaurant (and, well, even if you do), you can stop there for freshly baked Mexican breads like a round loaf of *concha* with its sugar-crusted top.

M. L. Rose Craft Beer & Burgers, 2535 Franklin Pike, Melrose, Nashville, TN 37204; (615) 712-8160; ml-rose.com; Burger/American; $. It might seem more like a neighborhood bar at first with its lived-in vibe, back patio, and pool table, and indeed it excels as such with about 15 beers on draft like local **Yazoo** (p. 264), Calfkiller from Sparta, Tennessee, and Thunder Ann APA by **Jackalope** (p. 263), which is brewed just up the street, as well as a long list of bottled craft beers. But the menu at M. L. Rose is not to be overlooked. The beef for the burgers is raised without hormones or antibiotics, hand-formed into patties, and served on locally made buns. Just a few of the choices include a blue-cheeseburger with bacon, grilled onion, and creamed blue

cheese; the Texas chili burger with sharp cheddar, chipotle barbecue sauce, red onion, and, of course, the chili; and the five-alarm burger with a spicy but creamy sauce, jalapeños, cheddar, lettuce, and tomato. Burgers are served in paper-lined red plastic baskets, and waffle fries can—and probably should—be ordered a la carte either plain or loaded with various combinations of cheddar, Jack, or blue cheese as fixings. Or choose the ranchero fries with a thick homemade dressing and diced tomato. There are salads, wraps, and sandwiches on the menu as well, but the burgers are M. L. Rose's best choice.

Mama Mia's, 4671 Trousdale Dr., South Nashville, Nashville, TN 37204; (615) 331-7207; Italian; $$. This small neighborhood Italian restaurant is nothing fancy location-wise, but it's been a favorite for decades for basics like tomato sauce and pasta (and dishes from Bolognese to manicotti) as well as cheese and cream over pasta (like carbonara) as well as chicken and 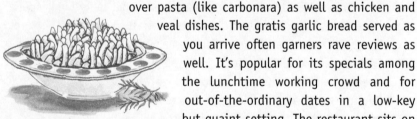 veal dishes. The gratis garlic bread served as you arrive often garners rave reviews as well. It's popular for its specials among the lunchtime working crowd and for out-of-the-ordinary dates in a low-key but quaint setting. The restaurant sits on the corner of Harding and Trousdale behind a service station, and it has a BYOB policy with a small corkage fee. But lucky for those who arrive unprepared, there's a liquor store (with wine, too, of course) just a couple doors down. Owner

Rebecca Martinez hails from Central America, and her husband Alex is from Cuba; they own **Back to Cuba Cafe** (p. 165) in the same area as well.

Phat Bites Deli & Coffee Shop, 940 Allen Rd., South Nashville, Nashville, TN 37214; (615) 871-4055; phatbites.com; Deli; $. With mostly fast food restaurants along Donelson Pike, Phat Bites offers a fresh break from all that with its gourmet sandwiches and salads. The 3-salad plate is a popular choice and lets you build your own plate from the choices behind the deli case: honey nut chicken, tuna salad, pesto pasta, tomato-mozzarella, sesame noodles, loaded potato salad, and more. You'll also find quiche and soup on the menu, as well as a long list of sandwiches from the basic grilled cheese, BLT, and Reuben  to a buffalo chicken sandwich, muffuletta, the Big Jerk with spicy chicken, and wraps like the standard veggie wrap, turkey wrap, and the Ninja Bomb wrap. But even beyond the menu, this place has a cool vibe since they turned the abandoned car wash next to it into a canvas for colorful graffiti. The restaurant also hosts art shows and live music on occasion.

Pfunky Griddle, 2800 Bransford Ave., Berry Hill, Nashville, TN 37204; (615) 298-2088; thepfunkygriddle.com; Breakfast; $. The Berry Hill area has an eclectic mix of businesses, many of them in structures that look more like homes (even though they might be recording studios). But perhaps the funkiest of the bunch is the Pfunky Griddle, a place where every table has an inlaid griddle for cooking your own breakfast. Pancakes are the main draw, and servers will bring you pitchers of either organic five-grain batter or unbleached white batter along with ramekins filled with the toppings of your choice. One topping comes with the all-you-can-eat price of $5.99 for adults, but additional toppings include seasonal fresh fruit, pecans, coconut flakes, applesauce, M&Ms, Reese's Pieces, and more. You can also cook your own french toast, eggs with add-ins like a variety of cheeses, roasted red peppers, salsa, sour cream, spinach, and shredded steak, and side items like sausage and bacon. When you're not interested in breakfast, there's a lunch menu, too, of homemade soups, salads, and sandwiches like tofu vegan egg salad to the Island Breeze, chicken salad with pineapple, cranberries, and walnuts. You don't have to make those items on your griddle (phew).

Sam & Zoe's Coffee House and Cafe, 525 Heather Place, Berry Hill, Nashville, TN 37204; (615) 385-2676; samandzoes.com; Coffee/Sandwiches; $. This coffee shop in the eclectic Berry Hill neighborhood has just a few tables inside, rotating local art on the walls, and a porch out front where you'll often find students sitting, studying, and sipping coffee. The coffee is locally roasted Drew's Brews as well as a few other local roasts. But the food is good, too. I especially like picking up a breakfast sandwich, which comes wrapped neatly in waxed paper and will be perfectly steamed by the time I arrive at work. The Early Bird is a favorite with egg, cheddar, tomato, and swiss (I like to order it on cracked wheat rather than a bagel). Breakfast is served all day, but there's a lunch menu as well of wraps, sandwiches, and salads. Standouts include the Zoe's Hummus & Roasted Red Pepper sandwich with pesto, swiss, lettuce, tomato, cucumbers, and onions, as well as the TLT Deluxe, a spicy tofu sandwich with lettuce, tomato, soy mayo, avocado, cucumbers, and pesto.

Shish Kabob, 4651 Nolensville Pike, South Nashville, Nashville, TN 37211; (615) 833-1113; theshishkabob.com; Persian/Middle Eastern; $$. The name shouldn't peg this place into meat-on-a-stick only. Though, yes, you can find an entire section of kebabs (including lamb, chicken, *kubideh,* shrimp, and salmon), you'll find much more on this menu. You can make a Middle Eastern meal on appetizers alone, for example, with *dolmeh,* grape leaves stuffed with beef, rice, cracked wheat, and spices; *maast-o-khair,* refreshing yogurt with cucumber, dill, and mint; *kashke bademjam,* spicy sautéed eggplant topped with whey; *ash paz,* a feta and sour cream blend with walnuts and herbs; as well as favorites like falafel and hummus. Most dishes come with jasmine rice, there's sumac on the tables for sprinkling, and all dishes are served with fresh lavash flatbread made at the bakery a few doors down that is also run by the restaurant's Kurdish owner Hikmat Gazi. Shish Kabob is located in a strip mall that doesn't have a lot of character, but the interior of the restaurant is decorated with Persian artifacts between the burnt sienna-colored walls, and a section toward the front of the restaurant allows diners the opportunity to sit on cushions at low tables. Don't miss the Persian ice cream with saffron and rosewater for dessert.

Smiling Elephant, 2213 8th Ave. South, Melrose, Nashville, TN 37204; (615) 891-4488; Thai; $$. Owner Sam Kopsombut worked in car repair until he decided to open a Thai restaurant. And I know lots of fans of his cuisine are thankful he made the career switch. Sam also is the brother of Patty Myint, the woman who brought the first Asian restaurant to Nashville in the 1970s and uncle to *Top Chef* contestant and Nashville restaurateur Arnold Myint,

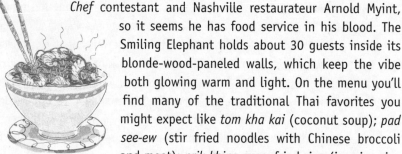

so it seems he has food service in his blood. The Smiling Elephant holds about 30 guests inside its blonde-wood-paneled walls, which keep the vibe both glowing warm and light. On the menu you'll find many of the traditional Thai favorites you might expect like *tom kha kai* (coconut soup); *pad see-ew* (stir fried noodles with Chinese broccoli and meet); *prik khing* curry fried rice (jasmine rice with curry, vegetables, egg, and your choice of meat), and a daily curry with rice. For dessert, check out the sticky rice in banana leaf, and if you like what you've had to eat, Sam will let you sound the gong by the front door.

The Yellow Porch, 734 Thompson Ln., Berry Hill, Nashville, TN 37204; (615) 386-0260; theyellowporch.com; Eclectic; $$. It sits just off a busy intersection along Thompson Lane, but the garden at The Yellow Porch helps keep this restaurant feel tucked away and intimate. This mainstay also serves as a gate to charming, whimsical Berry Hill with its independent spirit. So of course you'll find an independent spirit at The Yellow Porch, too, with a cozy environment both for lunch diners as well as a darker, candlelit space for dinner clientele. The menu is eclectic with a few Southern touches along with crowd pleasers that keep regulars coming back. The paella is a favorite, for example, with its hunks of fresh fish and shellfish in a spicy broth and saffron-rice base among onion, peppers, and tomatoes. And while the soups change daily, the blue cheese–celery is legendary with its sip and savor, a creamy blend of blue cheese brightened up by the celery. Among the steaks, lamb, and Sweet Tea Cured Smoked Pork Chop, you'll also find a favorite entree salad of port-poached sun-dried cherries with greens, spiced walnuts, goat cheese, and balsamic vinaigrette. See Executive Chef Guerry McComas Jr.'s recipe for **Celery & Blue Cheese Soup** on p. 288.

Meat-and-Threes

Arnold's Country Kitchen, 605 8th Ave. South, 8th Avenue, Nashville, TN 37203; (615) 256-4455; $. When the owner of this beloved meat-and-three got a call from the prestigious James Beard Foundation, Rose Arnold initially thought they were trying to sell her something. But then she realized that the Oscars of the food world wanted to give the restaurant, in a little red building, an American Classics award. Now the Beard medal is displayed on the wall along with photos of the famous musicians who visit this place for the reliable, perfectly cooked turnip greens, pork chops, fried chicken, roast beef, meatloaf, mashed potatoes, cornbread, macaroni and cheese, homemade slices of pie, and banana pudding. Just take a tray and stand in line at the great equalizer—the steam table—where Porter Wagoner had to wait for his mashed potatoes just like the rest of us. Though Jack Arnold used to be the man behind the carving station of roast beef, his son Kahlil is now in charge. Rose pours the tea and works the cash register. Though it stays busy, you'll somehow find a seat among the mix of policemen, truck drivers, professionals, and musician types for one of the best meals in town.

Luna, 2309A Franklin Pike, Melrose, Nashville, TN 37204; (615) 229-7000; lunanashville.com; $. From the outside, it's practically irresistible. Or to me, anyway, and that's even with its view of a Captain D's along 8th Avenue. But with its bright red brick LUNA sign in yellow letters, and a tagline of EAT, LIVE, LOVE, it draws me in the door or at least to the picket-fenced-in patio with umbrella-covered tables. The inside is just as charming with yellow walls, funky art, and framed album covers. The menu features fresh seasonal vegetables that change weekly or even daily. Billed as a gourmet meat-and-three, it tends to lean more toward comfort food than traditional Southern food. You might find chicken parmigiana, pot roast, meatloaf, corn pudding, peas, and carrots. While those who lunch at this bright spot might choose the popular scratch-made Caesar salad and sandwiches, the room turns to candlelight at dinner on Saturday nights (call for reservations) with dishes of baked grouper with crawfish Creole hollandaise, asparagus, and wild rice.

Specialty Stores, Markets & Producers

Azadi International Market, 391 Elysian Fields Ct., South Nashville, Nashville, TN 37211; (615) 315-0940. My favorite part of this market is the bakery in the back. A team of women in burkas works quickly, forming dough into mounds and then throwing it onto the sides of a round stone oven to make lavash, flat but spongy bread that sometimes gets spruced up with onion or spices. They'll stuff the large pieces into plastic bags that fog up with steam and pass the bags through the open window to waiting customers. But on the way to the bakery window, you'll also pass boxes of dates and bins of lentils, tins of teas, and burlap sacks of rice. There are rows of spices in bulk, and there's a Halal butcher as well for fresh meats. The shop is owned by Hikmat Gazi, the Kurdish immigrant who also owns the **Shish Kabob** (p. 175) restaurant nearby, where you'll also find fresh lavash on the tables each day and fresh lamb on the menu.

K&S International Market, 4225 Nolensville Pike, South Nashville, Nashville, TN 37211; (615) 832-8881. This is the international superstore of Nashville—a sprawling space of fascinating goodies from all over the world with a mixture of aromas to prove it. You'll find live fish in tanks in the seafood section as well as inexpensive produce just through the front door, including plenty of fruits and vegetables that a typical American grocery-store-shopper would consider exotic. Spices available in bulk also can be had for much less than your average American box store, as can staples of all cuisines like rice, noodles, and beans. Then there are rows upon rows of goods arranged by region—bottles of hot sauces, bags of noodles, jars of curries, packages of dried peppers or sheets of nori, cans of coconut milk, frozen goods, and boxed meals as well as all sorts of interesting candies and snacks. There is another location at 5861 Charlotte Pike, Nashville, TN 37209; (615) 356-8771.

La Hacienda SuperMercado, 2617 Nolensville Rd., South Nashville, Nashville, TN 37211; (615) 256-5066; lahanashville.com. This Mexican market opened in 1992, one year before the restaurant, **La Hacienda** (p. 170), next door. It was the first market in the area catering specifically to the Hispanic community; now there are many, especially in this stretch of Nashville. Owners Carlos and Lillian Yepez had moved to town from California, and at first they drove a trailer to Chicago weekly to shop for goods that they'd haul back down south for their market. These days, though, the selection has improved, adding a bakery with a large glass case along one wall with yellow- and pink-dusted rounds of *conchas* as well as *pan dulce* and *teleras*. There's a butcher offering chorizo and *adoboda puerco* as well as a case of a variety of chiles, rows of canned and bottled goods such as Jarritos sodas, and stacks of tortillas made on the premises and now shipped to more than 500 restaurants and shops in a seven-state area.

Vanderbilt, Hillsboro Village, Edgehill Village, Belmont & 12th South

Vanderbilt and Belmont Universities both fall into this area, which means the clientele keeps the neighborhoods vibrant and energized.

The 12th South neighborhood runs parallel to Belmont Boulevard through Belmont University's campus. Though it has had a grittier past with just a few restaurants and music shops, it's seen significant gentrification in recent years, bringing new condos and restaurants such as Urban Grub, Sloco, Edley's Bar-B-Que, and Burger

Up. A night out in this area might include a backyard party with music and the Mas Tacos food truck at Imogene + Willie, the hip purveyors of custom jeans, followed by drinks on the patio and more live music across the street at 12th South Taproom or a dessert of Las Paletas's Mexican-style ice pops, down the street.

Hillsboro Village lies at the heart of Vanderbilt University's social scene with old standbys like the Pancake Pantry with its line of students and visiting parents out the door, the Villager for beers and darts, the patio at Jackson's for people watching, Cabana for the night life, and the gourmet food mixed with a coffee-shop vibe at Fido.

And though Edgehill Village sits on the edge of Music Row and draws professionals from that area to its shops and restaurants like Bella Napoli and Dulce Desserts, it's still close enough to Vanderbilt to pull a strong college contingent.

Foodie Faves

Bella Napoli Pizzeria, 1200 Villa Place, Edgehill Village, Nashville, TN 37212; (615) 891-1387; bellanapolipizzeria.com; Italian/Pizza; $$. Hidden inside the open courtyard of Edgehill Village, a collection of eight 1920s industrial buildings that once housed a steam laundry, Bella Napoli has romantic but super-casual al fresco seating as well as a laid-back but bustling space inside. Outdoors there are picnic tables with Pellegrino umbrellas, for example, and

live music on occasion. Inside, the walls are exposed brick, and there's an open pizza kitchen where dough flies and a domed brick oven stays fired with Tennessee oak. Chef Paolo Tramontano, of the fancier Italian mainstay **Valentino's** (p. 237), brings influence from his hometown of Naples with San Marzano tomatoes on the pizza, fresh mozzarella, and finely milled "00" Caputo flour for soft dough. Paolo keeps the menu fairly simple in a refreshing and truly Italian sort of way, with a Margherita or a *bianche* pizza (no tomato sauce) such as the *salsiccia* with homemade sausage, mozzarella, broccoli rabe, and fresh garlic. The pastas include a hand-rolled gnocchi as well as lasagna, penne with vodka sauce, fettuccine with cream sauce, and spaghetti pomodoro with just diced cherry tomatoes, olive oil, basil, and roasted garlic. The panini selection is served between pizza dough, and just a few entrees include staples like pork saltimbocca.

Burger Up, 2901 12th Ave. South, 12th South, Nashville, TN 37204; (615) 279-3767; burger-up.com; Burgers; $$. The hip people who work at this restaurant can bring you a gourmet burger or maybe write you a song. But all are welcome as this stylish restaurant sits in the heart of the 12th South neighborhood and draws a mix of friends, families, and couples on dates. From the beginning, owner Miranda Whitcomb Pontes focused on the food. Burgers are made with local beef that's humanely raised at Triple L Ranch, and ingredients are sourced from nearby. As for decor, many of the rough-cut wood planks used to make the tables and barstools came from Miranda's grandfather or from Woodstock Vintage Lumber in Nashville, the namesake for the popular Woodstock burger made with Benton's bacon, Tennessee Sweetwater cheddar, and Jack Daniel's maple ketchup. Highlights include a quinoa black-bean burger; a lamb burger with Boursin, arugula, and honey-mint Dijon aioli; and the Ramsey Pimento Cheese Burger. Beyond burgers there's a host of salads and appetizers, and you shouldn't miss the cocktails like the seasonal Hayride with Bulleit bourbon, Rothman & Winter Orchard Apricot liqueur, lemon, homemade five-spice simple syrup, and apple cider.

Cabana, 1910 Belcourt Ave., Hillsboro Village, Nashville, TN 37212; (615) 577-2262; cabananashville.com; Eclectic/Southern; $$. Maybe it's the proximity to Vanderbilt or maybe it's the sexy cabana booths that guests can rent for the night, but this is where you'll likely find the pretty people on a Saturday night. Cabanas seat from 2 to 12 people and come with privacy curtain—for those who choose to use it—and a TV and iPod hookup for personalizing entertainment. Meanwhile, many other guests choose to dine or drink on the front patio or large open room in the back with rolling garage doors. The menu includes lots of small plates for sharing: Tennessee "sliders" served on mini sweet-potato biscuits with house-made peach preserves and choice of buttermilk fried chicken tenders or Benton's country ham. There are lots of entrees though that stay on the sophisticated Southern side including sweet tea smoked half chicken with country-style green beans, white cheddar scalloped potatoes, and apple butter; cornmeal-crusted bay scallops with local vegetables. A late-night menu served until 2 a.m. includes pizzas and several of the small plates and sweets like banana pudding and peanut butter pie with chocolate sauce.

Cha Chah, 2013 Belmont Blvd., Belmont, Nashville, TN 37212; (615) 298-1430; chachahnashville.com; Eclectic; $$. Chef-Owner Arnold Myint is restaurant royalty in Nashville; his mother opened the first Asian restaurant in the 1970s, and Arnold has earned fame himself on season 7 of *Top Chef*. The former professional ice skater has channeled his competitive streak into creativity for his restaurants with Cha Chah as his flagship; others include **PM** (p. 195) next door, **Suzy Wong's House of Yum** (p. 226), and **AM@FM** (p. 141) at the **Nashville Farmers' Market** (p. 145). At Cha Chah, near Belmont campus, the decor is hardwood floors and sophisticated clean lines, leaving most of the vibrant color and playfulness in the tapas-style menu. A favorite includes the warm brussels sprouts with marcona almonds, Thai chile, red onion, and smoked vinegar on the starters menu, or the lamb meatballs with herbed quinoa tabouli, cilantro yogurt, and lemongrass. Examples of entrees, which change seasonally: spice-rubbed venison with sage dumplings and candied garlic, or Duck Two Ways—the leg "au vin" and the breast seared with parsnip mash, ginger carrots, and kumquats. Dessert options might include a Banana Cream Pie of blondie panna cotta, graham wafer, salted caramel, and banana mousse. He also offers a chef's 5-course tasting menu for $65 or a 3-course tasting for $35.

Chago's Cantina, 2015 Belmont Blvd., Belmont, Nashville, TN 37212; (615) 386-0106; chagoscantina.com; Latin; $$. From the outside, this place looks like a party. The letters of the CHAGO'S sign are even in a rainbow of colors, and it's not uncommon to find a young adult crowd on the patio or just inside the lifted garage doors with Chago-Ronas, margaritas with an upside-down Corona coming out the top. But the menu brings some Latin surprises to this little fiesta. While you'll certainly find Mexican standards like fajitas, burritos, tacos, and enchiladas of various types, you'll also find El Salvadorian *pupusas con curtido,* handmade tortillas stuffed with beans and cheese, as well as *mofongo,* a Puerto Rican dish of mashed plantains topped with shrimp *criolla* (spicy tomato sauce). Chef-Owner Chad Head, who lived in San Diego and traveled in South and Central America, uses local ingredients when possible and makes everything from scratch. But lest things get too serious, you'll also find the largest margarita in Nashville on this menu—60 ounces for $30—as well as a menu item called the Tacos Borrachos: two tacos, a shot of tequila, and a can of Tecate for $10 served with beans and rice.

The Dog of Nashville, 2127 Belcourt Ave., Belmont, Nashville, TN 37212; (615) 292-2204; thedogofnashville.com; Hot Dogs; $.

Owner Adam Deal hails from the hot dog mecca of Chicago, so in 2007 he opened this spot in a bungalow near the heart of Hillsboro Village. While he serves up classics like the Chi Town with mustard, Kryponite-colored pickle relish, tomato, pickle spear, and celery salt on a poppy-seed roll, he also has a house-made chili dog and a hand-dipped corndog, as well as the Rise & Shine with bacon, cheese sauce, and fried egg, and the Barnyard with pulled pork, barbecue sauce, and topped with slaw. As for the dogs themselves, you can choose Angus beef, turkey, veggie, Polish sausage, or beer brat, and you can build your own hot dog with a long list of toppings. On the side, pick from fries, tots, onion rings, house-made chips, and cucumber and onion salad. And if you're not feeling hot dogs at all, then you could choose an Angus burger instead. For a decadent dessert, there are deep-fried Oreos and Snickers bars.

Edley's Bar-B-Que, 2706 12th Ave. South, 12th South, Nashville, TN 37204; (615) 953-2951; edleysbbq.com; Barbecue; $. This rustic-looking spot seems to stay hopping both on the patio right off 12th Avenue South and inside where the timbers are rough and the concrete walls are the rust-red color of a well-seasoned barbecue sauce. While the ribs get rave reviews, I haven't yet been able to tear myself from the pulled pork. Moist and varied in color with black bits of bark along with chopped pieces of white and pink, it's drizzled on top with a tomato-based sauce and served either piled onto a sandwich or a plate; nearly 10 Southern-style sides are offered daily. The Brunswick stew is some of the thickest I've seen, loaded with lima beans, corn, tomato, and smoked meat. I also love the slaw, which is a crisp vinegar-based version with bits of celery seed and no mayonnaise. And then there's the cornbread, grilled rectangular slabs like slices of pound cake but with the rougher texture of cornmeal and dotted with the heat of jalapeño. You'll often hear blues on the sound system when ordering at the counter; head to the bar, if you like, where you'll find local drafts from **Yazoo** (p. 264), **Jackalope** (p. 263), and Calfkiller, among others.

Fido, 1812 21st Ave. South, Hillsboro Village, Nashville, TN 37212; (615) 777-FIDO; bongojava.com/fido.php; Cafe; $$. At first glance, you might call it a coffee shop, and indeed it's a good one. But look a bit closer and you'll find one of the best restaurants in town. Order off the specials blackboard; that's where Chef John Stephenson makes the magic happen. Committed to local, seasonal ingredients (he won't eat an out-of-season tomato), his specials have included grilled salmon with kale, grits, crispy fried onions, and feta in winter, to white peach gazpacho in summer drizzled with olive oil and loaded with a blend of seasonal fruits and vegetables. Also not to be missed is the local burger, which Stephenson will put against any other in town. Combined with a blend of local, grass-fed lamb and beef, it includes Kenny's cheddar, fried onions, fig mayo, pickles, caramelized fennel, and local lettuces. For dessert, check out the creatively named cakes such as the Red Velvet Underground or the Pink Radio Cake, which has neon-pink icing that gets its color strictly from beets. You'll see them behind the case as you line up at the counter to order. Fido's space has expanded in recent years, leaving room for students behind laptops and books, coffee drinkers over desserts, and those who come for dinner and a drink. See Chef John Stephenson and Karla Ruiz's recipe for **Empanadas** on p. 294.

Fish & Company, 2317 12th Ave. South, 12th South, Nashville TN 37204; (615) 292-2655; fishco-nashville.com; Seafood; $$$. This restaurant originally opened with the James Beard award–winning chef Louis Osteen, who made Nashville his home for a stint. And even though he has made his way back to the South Carolina coast, the restaurant has kept its focus on the fish. A seasonal raw bar is accompanied by a menu of shrimp and grits, pan-seared red grouper, or rainbow trout stuffed with crabmeat, scallions, and Benton's bacon and served alongside potatoes roasted in duck fat. Guests can request fish "simply grilled" as well by choosing a fish and a sauce like brown butter caper or New Orleans *ravigote* and a side like the "Pound Cake" Potatoes or steak-house onion rings. In the heart of the 12th South neighborhood, it can serve as a place for a drink and snack, too, as the happy hour runs daily from 4 p.m. to 7 p.m. and appetizers include crab cakes, ahi tuna lettuce wraps, a fried seafood basket, steamed mussels, and barbecue shrimp. Brunch has lots of fun options that have included—a Bacon Bloody Mary, the Hangover Burger, an egg sandwich grilled with gruyère and Benton's bacon, and bourbon-vanilla french toast with peaches, blueberries, and pistachios.

Frothy Monkey, 2509 12th Ave. South, 12th South, Nashville, TN 37204; (615) 292-1808; frothymonkey.com; Breakfast; $. A mainstay of the 12th South neighborhood, this little coffee shop stood long before the area blew up into a place for the hip to hang out. Originally opened by Miranda Whitcomb Pontes, the owner of **Burger Up** (p. 184) down the street, she sold Frothy Monkey to long-time employee and musician Ryan Pruitt in 2009. Over the years, the bungalow with all the coffee shop trademarks—worn-out sofa and Persian rug, local art, and show flyers plastered near the restrooms, has grown up a bit. With an expansion and wrap-around porch, the shop stays jammed and amped up on a caffeine buzz and creative energy. Already offering popular breakfast and lunch menus that include sandwiches and salads, Frothy Monkey also started a brilliant breakfast-for-dinner menu that includes steak and eggs with herb sweet-potato bread pudding and sautéed spinach, and chicken and waffles with sorghum bacon–herb glaze, among other options. It also serves as the model space for Urban Agrarian, a food advocacy group helping promote community gardening, as crops have been planted in small grassy strips behind the shop.

Grins, 2421 Vanderbilt Place, Vanderbilt, Nashville, TN 37212; (615) 322-8571; grinscafe.com; Cafe/Vegetarian; $. The first official vegetarian cafe in Nashville, Grins (pronounced like "greens") is located inside the Shulman Center for Jewish Life on the Vanderbilt University campus. Owned by Bob Bernstein of **Bongo Java** (p.

201) and **Fido** (p. 189) coffee shops, the cafe offers breakfast, lunch, and dinner—all vegetarian, certified kosher, and with an international flair. The menu stays simple but offers quality cafe fare. For breakfast try the Nutella panini with strawberries and banana, or the tofu rancheros wrap with veggie chorizo, avocado, grilled peppers and onions, and pico de gallo. For lunch, the wraps, panini, and salads take a more savory turn such as the "superfood wrap" with avocado, quinoa, edamame, cucumber, tomato, carrot, red cabbage, sprouts, and baby spinach with wasabi-lime mayo. Be sure to check out the vegan baked goods, too, as well as daily specials that might include chiles rellenos or Indian veggie curry.

Jackson's Bar & Bistro, 1800 21st Ave. South, Hillsboro Village, Nashville, TN 37212; (615) 385-9968; jacksonsbarandbistro.com/nashville/index.php; Bistro/Cafe; $$. Drive through Hillsboro Village on a warm afternoon and you might find Jackson's patio hard to resist. Sitting smack in the middle of the funky neighborhood near Vanderbilt University, it's a great spot for people watching and sipping on a **Yazoo** (p. 264) beer. The restaurant inside is charming, too, with its collection of fireplaces for cooler days—one even hangs from the ceiling—along with a mix of high-top, bar, and regular table seating. On the menu, I particularly like the beer cheese with sharp cheddar for sharing or the simple fish tacos—ahi tuna and pico de gallo wrapped in flour tortillas and served with sour cream and guacamole. It's easy to find a heartier meal here, though,

HOMEGROWN CHAINS: SWEET CECE'S

CeCe Moore grew up in California among the many frozen yogurt shops like Pinkberry and Red Mango. So when CeCe and her husband Brian relocated to Nashville, they opened a yogurt shop of their own in Music City in 2008—**Sweet CeCe's** (sweetceces .com). While Pinkberry and others have opened shops in Nashville after Sweet CeCe's began, CeCe in the meantime has expanded her empire from the first location in Nashville to locations in nine other states. CeCe's model is self-serve and priced by weight on a scale at the register. A few flavors always available include Original Tart, chocolate, and vanilla. Rotating flavors you might find include Can't Resist Carrot Cake, Blueberry Muffin, Cinnamon Swirl, Sweet Southern Velvet, and chocolate mint. Then after filling your cup with swirls of soft-serve, you can head to the toppings bar for snazzing up your yogurt with more options, from sprinkles to Cocoa Puffs, Golden Grahams, M&Ms, chocolate raisins, cookie dough, Butterfinger, or, of course, a selection of fresh fruit, hot fudge, caramel, and whipped toppings. One of many locations can be found at 1708 21st Ave. South, Nashville, TN 37212; many additional locations are listed on their website, sweetceces.com.

with plenty of takes on burgers, cheese steaks, panini, and BLTs, as well as entrees like steak frites or mussels and frites, and barbecue meatloaf with Parmesan mashed potatoes.

Kay Bob's, 1602 21st Ave. South, Vanderbilt, Nashville, TN 37212; (615) 321-4567; kaybobs.us; Sandwiches; $. Brothers Ali and Amir Arab who own **Pizza Perfect** (below) next door to this spot, call Kay Bob's the spot for "flatbread sandwiches with a Southern twist." Homemade dough is folded with kebab-esque ingredients to make Kay Bob sandwiches with names like the Tammie Rae, grilled chicken with barbecue sauce, coleslaw, and Jack cheese; the Aunt Kay with yogurt- and turmeric-marinated and grilled chicken with lettuce, tomato, and mango sauce; or the Uncle Bob with beef prepared like spiced *koobideh* meatballs with onion, sumac, and turmeric. There are seven sandwiches total—two of which are vegetarian—along with sides like hand-cut fries, sweet potato chips, dilled potato salad, black bean and corn salad, and two types of slaw, including the vinegar-based "signature" and a toasted sesame with almonds and ramen noodles added in a soy vinaigrette. The space is relatively no-frills, but front walls of garage doors open to bustling 21st Avenue near Vanderbilt.

Pizza Perfect, 1602 21st Ave. South, Vanderbilt, Nashville, TN 37212; (615) 329-2757; pizzaperfectonline.com; Pizza; $. Yes, it's a fairly stripped-down pizza place. But its proximity to Vanderbilt University and just really good pie make for a fantastic combination. Since 1983, patrons have been able to walk in for a slice or take a whole pizza home. First, you'll need to choose your size (medium, large, and x-large) and then type in either thin round or thick Sicilian. The menu makes some good suggestions like the BBQ chicken with barbecue sauce, cheddar, mozzarella, chicken, bacon, and onion (no red sauce), or the Perfect Pizza with pepperoni, sausage, mushrooms, onions, green peppers, and black olives. But even with lots of choices, you can build your own pizza with toppings like the standards as well as broccoli, artichokes, *salumi,* feta, and roasted garlic. There are other menu items, too, such as meatball or Italian subs, pasta dishes, and calzones, but the pizza is without a doubt the main draw. Delivery available as well. Additional location in Bellevue at 357 Clofton Dr., Nashville, TN 37221; (615) 646-7877.

PM, 2017 Belmont Blvd., Belmont, Nashville, TN 37212; (615) 297-2070; pmnashville.com; Asian/Sushi/Eclectic; $$. The most casual of the restaurants owned by Arnold Myint, PM makes for a cozy hang inside with a busy bar to the left of the front door bedecked with tiny white lights. Otherwise there's a good-size dining room and spacious porch out front. Billed as Asian-inspired cuisine with sushi, bistro fare, and bar, the menu is fairly large with a good selection of sushi and nigiri as well as small plates including dishes like Coconut Calamari, BBQ pork *bao* bun, Laotian Sausage Bites, five-spice pork ribs, and more. The salads also help showcase Arnold's international flair such as the East Meets Wedge with wasabi blue cheese, bacon, red onion, tomato, and crispy noodles. Entrees include glass noodle pad thai, green curry mussels with toast points, and peanut chicken panang. Even the burger is legendary; it's been ranked as the best in the city by the *Nashville Scene*. The beef is spiced with a hint of ginger and served with wasabi mayo.

Provence Breads & Cafe, 1705 21st Ave. South, Hillsboro Village, Nashville, TN 37212; (615) 386-0363; provencebreads.com; Cafe/Bakery; $$. This is the original Provence location, and it fits in well with the European vibe of the Hillsboro Village neighborhood. You'll find a few tables in their small space, but the main appeal is behind the cases—bowls of sides like Moroccan couscous with grape tomatoes, raisins, and mint, and rows of sandwiches like the truffled egg salad and one of my favorites, the Montecito, with white cheddar, avocado, tomato, cucumber, red onion, sprouts, and mango chutney on flaxseed bread. In the dessert case, there are fruit tarts, éclairs, and flourless chocolate cakes, and cookies along with a pastel rainbow of *macarons*. Then behind the register are rows of bread such as loaves of pumpernickel, rounds of sourdough, and long baguettes. A couple of my favorites here include the fresh hamburger buns and the beet hummus spread, irresistible with its blazing fuchsia color. And in cooler temperatures, the square home-made marshmallows—particularly the toasted coconut—make a cup of hot chocolate an even more special treat. There are additional locations at the Nashville Downtown Library, 601 Church St., Nashville, TN 37219, (615) 664-1150; and the Nashville International Airport at Terminal C. See Provence Breads & Cafe's recipe for **Buttermilk Chocolate Cake** on p. 306.

Savarino's Cucina, 2121 Belcourt Ave., Hillsboro Village, Nashville, TN 37212; (615) 460-9878; Italian; $$. As the Food

Network's Guy Fieri pointed out on a visit to this shop for the show *Diners, Drive-Ins, and Dives,* the husband-and-wife Savarino team sometimes competes to see who can roll the thinnest fettuccine. And while they do offer a hearty list of pastas with homemade sauces such as chicken parmigiana over penne, eggplant *rollatini,* stuffed peppers, and creamy risotto, locals also know the sandwiches are not to be missed. Piled onto homemade bread, they include salamis and Italian sausages and cheeses. And if you've had a sandwich named for you? Well, then, you have arrived. The restaurant is located near the Belmont Theatre, which makes it great for a predinner meal, or maybe for dessert afterward. Behind the dessert case you'll also find house-made gelato, chocolate-dipped cannoli, and cheesecake.

Sloco, 2905 12th Ave. South, 12th South, Nashville, TN 37204; (615) 499-4793; slocolocal.com; Deli; $. Author, chef, and owner Jeremy Barlow has been a vocal proponent of the local food system with his restaurant Tayst (p. 199), which received Nashville's first Green Restaurant certification. But his latest venture, Sloco, which opened in 2011, takes his cause even further by serving local and sustainable sandwiches at affordable prices. Sloco even has a Declaration of Food Independence posted in its narrow shop. In a nutshell: Make great sandwiches quickly and affordably, love the community (5 percent of profits go to Community Food Advocates), operate with a small footprint, cook responsibly, and if it's not in season, you won't find it here. And to point number one, the sandwiches are stellar. The menu changes, of course, but options might include the vegan quinoa meatball sub, a slow-roasted veggie with herbs, whole grain mustard, and tofu spread on multigrain, or the Redneck Reuben with corned pork shoulder, caraway slaw, and Dijon. See Chef-Owner Jeremy Barlow's recipe for **Veggie Meatloaf** on p. 303.

Sunset Grill, 2001 Belcourt Ave., Hillsboro Village, Nashville, TN 37212; (615) 386-3663; sunsetgrill.com; American Contemporary; $$$. Owner Randy Rayburn is like the godfather of the independent restaurant community in Nashville, having been around since the Third Coast restaurant occupied the old Rock and Roll Hotel of the 1970s and later became **Bound'ry** (p. 123). Rayburn now has three restaurants with Sunset Grill one of his most popular (others include **Midtown Cafe,** p. 219, and the trendier **Cabana,** p. 185, located across the street from Sunset Grill). At the top of the menu, Rayburn lists local producers he supports. But even with the fresh focus, a few of the entrees have been favorites for years. The Beets & Heat salad with its golden beets, arugula, fennel, goat cheese, orange segments, candied pecans, and Tabasco-honey vinaigrette, comes from the now-closed Zola run by Deb Paquette, a chef Rayburn worked with previously. Other favorites include the voodoo pasta with chicken, shrimp, andouille, and "black magic" tomato sauce over egg fettuccine, as well as the butterscotch-habanero bread pudding. The menu also includes steaks, duck, pork tenderloin, as well as dishes with Southern influence such as the shrimp and grits and free-range breast of chicken with rosemary biscuit, sorghum-seared spinach, and sawmill gravy.

Tayst, 2100 21st Ave. South, Hillsboro Village, Nashville, TN 37212; (615) 383-1953; taystrestaurant.com; Eclectic; $$$. The first green-certified restaurant in Nashville, this fine-dining restaurant just up the road from Hillsboro Village often features the farms that helped supply the menu on a blackboard just as guests enter the front door. The menu showcases Chef-Owner Jeremy Barlow's creativity and is divvied into first, second, and main taysts. The first might include Heart Beets Hash, braised heart, roasted beets, and potatoes with duck bacon and sage foam. The second often features salads and soups, and the main might include local beef with spinach bucatini pasta, smoked tomatoes, ramps, and balsamic-Parmesan whipped lardo (cured fatback). The bar includes bites at great prices, such as Sweet-Tea Pork Ribs for $4 or caramelized cheese at just $2. Or if you're feeling adventurous (and less carnivorous), ask for the chef's vegan surprise, and Barlow will wow you with what's growing from the earth at the moment in an artful way. Because even though his menu often is stacked with a variety of local meats, his wife, we hear, is a vegan after all. See Chef-Owner Jeremy Barlow's recipe for **Veggie Meatloaf** on p. 303.

12th South Taproom, 2318 12th Ave. South, 12th South, Nashville, TN 37204; (615) 463-7552; 12southtaproom.com;

American; $$. This place has become quite the hang for the hip people in the 12 South neighborhood as it has nearly 30 taps and about 70 bottled beers offering plenty to sip on at the bar or the restaurant's cozy front patio. But the menu shouldn't be overlooked either. I particularly enjoy the salmon tacos—a trio of three on corn tortillas topped with cilantro, onions, and salsa verde. But choose from other taco options like chicken, pulled pork, rib eye, or soysage if you like. Otherwise, there's a host of sandwiches, from burgers to the Nashville Cat (grilled tuna salad, roasted red pepper, black olive aioli), the Mother Clucker (chicken salad), Cuban, and Aloha Cheese Steak (rib eye, peppers, onions, pineapple salsa, and Jack cheese). You'll often find quality musicians playing the small red room later in the evenings on Monday (one wall is covered in Hatch Show Print posters, after all). Oh, and wine and sake for the nonbeer lover? They've got you covered, too.

Urban Grub, 2506 12th Ave. South, 12th South, Nashville, TN 37204; (615) 679-9342, urbangrub.net; Southern/Seafood; $$. The first time I visited Urban Grub, the hostess asked us, "Would you like to sit inside-ish or outside-ish?" It's a good way to sum up the space, as the main bar spans from an indoor area to an outdoor one, and every turned corner takes you to a different view, sometimes into rooms where large windows can be rolled up. And there's a lot of variety in the menu, too. The tagline for Urban Grub is "Fish Pit and Southern Cantina," so expect to find options from oysters on the half shell to tacos (fish or pork on tortillas) as well as hot chicken on white bread, and lobster BLT flatbread for sharing, and fuller entrees such as ribs and hearty pork chops; enchiladas stuffed with smoked chicken, brisket, or shrimp; whole fried catfish with tomatillo salsa, caper aioli, coleslaw, and fries; and shrimp and grits. Opened in 2012 by longtime restaurateur Jay Pennington and his partner William Inman, Urban Grub is an example of the growth and development of the trendy 12th South neighborhood.

Landmarks

Bongo Java, 2007 Belmont Blvd., Belmont, Nashville, TN 37212; (615) 385-5282; bongojava.com; Breakfast/Sandwiches; $. The flagship of Bob Bernstein's coffee shop collection, this funky house near Belmont University has a front deck often peppered with students hunched over their homework. But it gives the place a vibe of youth and intellectualism that goes great with a cup of organic, fair-traded coffee, and a plate of eggs. And while breakfast is served all day, the menu has more than that, such as the fancy grilled cheese, Jack with pesto and tomato on sourdough; and the black bean burrito, a grilled tortilla stuffed with beans, jalapeños, grilled onions, and cheddar, topped with salsa and sour cream. For something in between, the bagel sandwiches called "bombs" offer a good option, like the poultry bomb with roasted turkey, chipotle cream cheese, and veggies. This coffee shop does tend to shine with breakfast though, with breakfast bagels, English muffins, and burritos. For something sweet there's granola and oatmeal with fruit or french toast. Then, for something economical, go with the Bongo Basic, 2 eggs, spiced hash browns, toast, and coffee for 5 bucks.

Brown's Diner, 2102 Blair Blvd., Hillsboro Village, Nashville, TN 37212; (615) 269-5509; Burgers; $. Those lacking knowledge of Nashville's restaurants scene would probably drive right on by this old trolley car. But this dive—and no, it's not even a faux dive—is also an institution. Go for the beers and burgers, and you might find some live music happening in the small, dark front room that's a bit more "bar" than the back room, where you might find families and couples stopping in for what some consider the best burger in Nashville. I like my Brown's burger with cheese, all the way (tomato, mayonnaise, pickles), and with the onions grilled for an extra 35 cents. In addition to bottled beer, they only serve Bud on draft, which will arrive in a cold frosty mug. I also hear it's been a favorite supper spot of certain famous musicians, and well, what's good enough for John Prine is sure good for me.

MAFIAoZA's Pizzeria & Neighborhood Pub, 2400 12th Ave. South, 12th South, Nashville, TN 37204; (615) 269-4646; mafiaozas .com; Pizza; $$. This bar's two-for-Tuesday special is practically tradition in Nashville. Drinks and beer are 2-for-1, and it makes for a popular scene with students and young professionals. And what goes better with beer than pizza? Slices are 2-for-1 on Tuesday as well until 9 p.m. But even beyond Tuesday, the restaurant has happy hour Wed through Fri from 4 to 7 p.m. As for the pizza, you can build your own with toppings that range from basil and broccoli to meatballs and a vast selection of cheese. But this place also has some creative specialty options on the menu, including the Thompson, a decadent pizza with egg, sausage, and fries, as well as the Parlay topped with macaroni and cheese and Fontanini sausage. If you're not feeling pizza though, I like the Piccolo Morsi. It translates to "a few bites" and allows you to build your own antipasti from a selection of cheeses (Drunken Goat, Parmigiano-Reggiano, blueberry stilton), meats (mortadella with pistachio, Spanish chorizo, bresaola) and dips (white bean hummus, mascarpone artichoke dip, olive tapenade). The restaurant also offers a variety of pasta dishes and salads like caponata and Caprese.

Pancake Pantry, 1796 21st Ave. South, Hillsboro Village, Nashville, TN 37212; (615) 383-9333; thepancakepantry.com; Breakfast; $. Depending on your attitude, the line that snakes out the door of this Nashville landmark will either scare you off—or make you want to go there. It's indeed worth a visit though (the line moves fast, really), and it's legendary for having been family owned in Nashville since 1961. Don't expect anything fancy decorwise; it's really just a big open room with a beer-hall vibe (minus the beer). But the focus should be on the pancakes anyway. Owner David Baldwin, who has been working with his family in the kitchen since age 10, fetches flours and syrups on trips to East Tennessee to make stacks of old-fashioned buttermilk pancakes served with whipped butter and warm syrup. And the options hardly stop there. Sweet potatoes added to the batter and then topped with powdered sugar and cinnamon make a popular choice, especially when accompanied with cinnamon cream syrup. Then there are the Caribbean pancakes with banana, pecans, coconut, and powdered sugar, or the chocolate-chip pancakes, wild blueberry, and a host of others. The menu includes eggs, Tennessee country ham, and basic omelets as well as a selection of sandwiches from breakfast versions to a grilled cheese or burger.

San Antonio Taco Company, 416 21st Ave. South, Vanderbilt, Nashville, TN 37203; (615) 327-4322; thesatco.com; Taco/Tex-Mex; $. Sometimes I wonder if coeds in this town can graduate before at least one trip to San Antonio Taco Company—or SATCO as it's affectionately known. Opened in 1984 by two Vanderbilt University graduates and San Antonio natives, it does, however, draw more than students with its proximity to the hospital and Music Row.

Patrons walk in, take a pencil and mark their order on paper menus before paying at the counter. Beyond the list of tacos in options like steak, chicken, pork, and beans with cheese, you can choose the enchiladas or chili as well as a couple of salads. Don't miss the salsa bar, and regulars swear by the chile con queso with chips. When your number is called, food will be served in red plastic baskets, so the setup is certainly no-frills. But it's fun with a large deck for relaxing, and beers can be purchased iced down in buckets. An additional location of SATCO opened downtown in 1987 at 208 Commerce St., Nashville, TN 37201; (615) 259-4413.

Meat-and-Threes

At the Table, 907 12th Ave. South, 12th South, Nashville, TN 37203; (615) 242-0077; atthetablenashville.com; $. When Gwyneth Paltrow filmed *Country Strong* in Nashville, she wrote a blog post raving about the fried chicken at this meat-and-three. And while we certainly appreciate the shout-out from a big-city food lover, it's really more the *Nashville Scene*'s Best New Meat-and-Three ranking that grabs my attention. Unlike some venerable institutions in town, this soul food restaurant has only been around since 1998, but they have the right idea about using fresh vegetables from the farmers' market that go into sides like green beans, fried corn, collard greens, and mashed potatoes. You'll also find fried chicken on the menu every day, along with meatloaf and pork chops often, and the tradition of fried fish on Friday. Other down-home staples to look for include baked chicken, liver with onions, and pinto beans. And just like the variety at the steam table, you'll find all types at this establishment as it sits between the old 12th South and the more newly developed and glitzier Gulch neighborhood.

Corrieri's Formaggeria, 1110 Caruthers Ave., 12th South, Nashville, TN 37204; (615) 385-9272; cfcheese.com. Located in a little brick house behind **MAFIAoZA's Pizza** (p. 202) and Vinea Wine Shoppe, which are also operated by Brett Corrieri, this shop stocks mostly cheeses and imported products. You can stop in for conversations with staff and a block of aged Gouda to take home, or you can book catering or order trays for parties and tailgates that might including (depending on size) some Taleggio; Parmigiano-Reggiano; ricotta with honey, fig, and hazelnut spread; lavash; baguettes; and fruit. Beyond individual products, the people at Corrieri's will put them together for you on the spot in one of their sandwiches such as the Sir Signore, an Italian take on the croque monsieur; or the 10K Lira Sandwich, focaccia loaded with *prosciutto cotto, salame toscano,* mortadella, coppa, and sopressata, provolone, mozzarella, spinach, and Peppadew peppers, then drizzled with balsamic vinegar, olive oil, kosher salt, freshly cracked black pepper, and Italian seasonings.

Davis Cookware & Cutlery, 1717 21st Ave. South, Hillsboro Village, Nashville, TN 37212; (615) 298-4728. I can't imagine a more charming—or more unorganized—kitchen shop in America. It's cramped yet interesting like a great aunt's attic or an old-school hardware store. And you can rest assured that when you ask for anything—from a tiny whisk to a gigantic mortar and pestle—the father who owns this place with his two sons will make a beeline right for it. You'll find utensils of all sorts, small appliances, glassware, cutlery, and cast iron along with a selection of loose teas and coffees. The offshoot business located inside the shop and called Davis Coffee Club keeps visitors in bags of artisan beans, and also caters events with brass or copper-domed La Pavoni and La Marzocco espresso equipment. Once you visit here, sampling a sip of the coffee and catching a story from the Davises while they sharpen your knives, you may never darken the doors of a chain shop again.

Dulce Desserts, 1207 Villa Place, Edgehill Village, Nashville, TN 37212; (615) 321-8700; dulcedesserts.com. This shop is worth a visit for the fabulous cakes and cookies, and to just say hello to owner Juanita Lane. A charmer through and through, Juanita has infectious energy that she channels into her treats, which bring together a love of Southern homemade desserts with the finesse of European bakeries. Enter her funky little boutique through the front entrance beside a blue garage door in Edgehill Village and you'll find a case full of goodies such as cupcakes in flavors like *dulce de leche,* strawberry shortcake, red velvet, and chocolate as well as cookies like lime meltaways, snickerdoodles, and pecan shortbread. Juanita also makes custom cakes and desserts such as fruit tarts, coconut cream pies with macadamia nut crust, and strawberry cake layered with vanilla buttercream and fresh strawberries (add a layer of chocolate ganache or handmade lemon curd to take it up a notch). And for the bride-to-be, she'll build you an elaborate tower with cake and fillings to your liking.

Hot & Cold, 1804 21st Ave. South, Nashville, TN 37212; (615) 767-5468; bongojava.com/hot_and_cold. As owner of nearby **Fido** (p. 189) as well as two **Bongo Java** (pp. 87 and 201) locations on the east side and Belmont areas of Nashville, Bob Bernstein sells coffee. His wife Irma Paz is co-owner of **Las Paletas** (p. 209), which sells gourmet Mexican-style ice pops. So it was only a matter of time before the two joined forces under one roof to give us the yin and yang of hot and cold. In addition to Bernstein's coffee and Paz's pops with fresh ingredients and flavors like cantaloupe, plum, rose petal, avocado, and hot chocolate with peppers, the shop also offers a small case of the wildly popular **Jeni's Splendid Ice Creams** (p. 96) based in Ohio, but branching out to Nashville for its first out-of-state location. You can order Las Paletas in regular size or mini and have them dipped in local **Olive & Sinclair** (p. 97) chocolate. As for Jeni's ice cream, the creative flavors range from goat cheese and red cherries to roasted strawberries and buttermilk. The shop sits in the heart of Hillsboro Village, and though it only has a few tables inside, it draws a steady rotating crowd ordering at the counter.

International Market & Restaurant, 2010 Belmont Blvd., Belmont, Nashville, TN 37212; (615) 297-4453. Owner Patty Myint gave Nashville its first Asian restaurant, located inside this market near Belmont University in the 1970s. There are tables to the left of the front door as you walk in, but you'll have to wind your way through the market portion of this place—stacked with cans of tea, rice crackers, aloe drinks, and coconut milk—to find the steam table along the back wall. The food includes pad thai, curry tofu, pineapple chicken, and other Americanized Asian dishes that span borders, such as egg rolls, pho, dumplings, and fried rice. It's best to go for lunch as that's when the food is freshest.

Las Paletas Gourmet Popsicles, 2905 12th Ave. South, 12th South, Nashville, TN 37204; (615) 386-2101. These Mexican-style ice pops created by sisters Norma and Irma Paz have earned national acclaim; celebrity chef Bobby Flay even visited the shop during one of his Food Network throwdowns. And while there's not much to see inside the shop except for a blackboard wall with flavors scrawled upon it, it's the colorful rows of ice pops for choosing in the cases that matter most. Flavors are made with fresh fruit and ingredients including interesting options like creamy rose petal, avocado, hot chocolate with peppers, Mexican caramel, chai, pistachio, and blueberry yogurt, as well as more traditional fruit flavors without the cream, such as watermelon, pineapple chile, strawberry blackberry, and wild cards (neither creamy nor fruit) such as hibiscus. While you can find Las Paletas at **Bongo Java** (pp. 87 and 201) locations around town, the flagship store offers the best

selection, as does **Hot & Cold** (p. 208), the ice-cream and coffee shop in Hillsboro Village at 1804 21st Ave. South, Nashville, TN 37212; (615) 767-5468.

Portland Brew, 2605 12th Ave. South, 12th South, Nashville, TN 37204; (615) 292-9004; portlandbrewcoffee.com. This coffee shop might have the name of the West coast city and coffee mecca, but it's all Nashville. The owners did, however, look to Portland for inspiration. The 12th South outpost is located near **Frothy Monkey** (p. 191), yet another coffee shop in the area. Portland Brew is known for having a quieter vibe for studiers and readers while Frothy can be more about meetings and socializing. Both are great, though. While Portland Brew is a coffee shop at heart, the chocolate cookies come strongly recommended—thin, buttery, crisp, and the size of a saucer, they pull an almost fanatical following. There is an additional location at 1921 Eastland Ave., East Nashville, TN 37206; (615) 262-9088.

12th South Farmers' Market, Sevier Park, 3000 Granny White Pike, 12th South, Nashville, TN 37212; 12southfarmersmarket.com. This small market is open from May to Oct just on Tues from 3 to 6:30 p.m. But you'll see many of the faces that make all the Nashville area markets great. Managed by Mary Crimmins of Conscious Kitchen (marycrimmins.com), it often offers organic meats from West Wind Farms and nearby Triple L Ranch, which also services **Burger Up** (p. 184) restaurant in this neighborhood. Produce often comes from Delvin Farms, the largest organic farm in the area, and vendors include Alfresco Pasta and fruit pies from Papa C Pies. Other vendors might include Kenny's Farmhouse Cheese, Noble Springs Dairy, and a variety of artisan food providers. Food trucks such as **Riffs Truck** (p. 25) and the **Grilled Cheeserie** (p. 24) often pull up alongside vendors at this park where 12th Avenue South turns into Granny White Pike to give customers something to munch on while they shop.

West End, Belle Meade, Sylvan Park & West Nashville

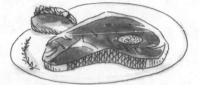

Drive down West End Avenue from downtown, and it's probably the chain restaurants you'll notice first. There are lots of them. But look a bit closer—and maybe off the main drag—and you'll see plenty of mom-and-pop establishments with independent hearts from Woodlands Indian Vegetarian Cuisine to Suzy Wong's House of Yum and the old-school comfort of Rotiers.

Keep following West End, and you'll come to the lovely Sylvan Park area on your right off Murphy Road with its fabulous neighborhood establishments like Park Cafe, Caffe Nonna, Star Bagel, Miel Restaurant, and more. Then farther down West End, you'll be in the posh Belle Meade area with the legendary Sperry's steaks and the newer spots for a fine meal like 360 Bistro.

Amerigo Italian Restaurant, 1920 West End Ave., West End, Nashville, TN 37203; (615) 320-1740; amerigo.net; Italian; $$. If you're craving a nice Italian meal somewhere between a Maggiano's and a white-tablecloth, super-stuffy affair, then Amerigo is your restaurant. Right off busy West End Avenue, it's near several hotels but also a quick skip from Music Row and West End office space. You'll certainly find favorites like chicken or veal—either piccata or Marsala—as well as pasta Bolognese, pasta di mare, and five-layer lasagna. But you can also choose filet gorgonzola and rosemary butter served with fettuccine Alfredo and green beans, or Scallops Veneto, blackened and served over polenta with lemon-basil butter sauce and grilled asparagus. For a more casual meal, you could split an appetizer of the Prince Edward Island mussels in garlic-wine broth and order from the brick-oven-pizza menu, such as the sausage with pickled red onion and smoked mozzarella. Also on the lunch menu, don't miss the Wednesday special of Nashville Hot Chicken Pasta Alfredo—hot chicken tenders over creamy pasta. End it with a scoop of local **Bravo Gelato** (p. 112) or the tiramisu, of course. Additional locations at 1656 Westgate Circle, Brentwood, TN 37027, as well as Memphis, Tennessee, and Jackson, Mississippi.

Anatolia Turkish Restaurant, 48 White Bridge Rd., West Nashville, Nashville, TN 37205; (615) 356-1556; anatolia-restaurant .com; Mediterranean; $$. Tucked in a strip mall near a Target, this

Turkish restaurant is easy to miss, but it's worth seeking out for the fresh dishes in a space that's basic in decor but warm in vibe. Owners and brothers Huseyin and Harun Ustunkaya grew up in a seaside town in the Turkish region of Anatolia, and they bring a piece of it here with their Mediterranean favorites like hummus and kebabs, but also with a menu section labeled as Classical Turkish Home Cooking. The baby eggplant, for example, is sautéed and stuffed with seasoned lamb cubes, onions, tomatoes, bell peppers, and parsley. The stew called *guvec* is cubed lamb with a host of vegetables and onion baked in a clay pot and served with rice and yogurt sauce. Don't miss dessert either—especially the *kunefe,* paper-thin layers of pastry with cheese and syrup. Just be sure to tell your server ahead of time if you're in a rush, as it takes about 20 minutes to prepare.

Caffe Nonna, 4427 Murphy Rd., Sylvan Park, Nashville, TN 37209; (615) 463-0133; caffenonna.com; Italian; $$. For more than a decade, this neighborhood restaurant has hosted cozy date nights, family meals, and friendly meet-ups. When I moved to Nashville in the early 2000s, it was one of the first places suggested to me as if it were a secret tucked into the historic neighborhood of Sylvan Park, yet the tables in this spot stay bustling with repeat business. Named for chef and owner Daniel Maggipinto's grandmother Nonna, who inspired the recipes, which are made from scratch daily. You'll find lots of comfort foods such as Nonna's White Bean Soup an herby blend of swiss chard, pesto, and Parmesan as well as mix-and-match pastas with various sauces and Lasagna Nonna, a layered stack of butternut squash, spinach, ricotta, swiss chard, and sauce between ribbons pasta. Entrees include more gussied-up options like grilled hanger steak, lamb shank, and veal roulade. Maggipinto also offers many of his sauces jarred along with his Chianti Jelly, with proceeds benefitting St. Jude Children's Research Hospital and the Zoë Marie Brain Tumor Research Fund, named for his daughter who received treatment at the hospital.

1808 Grille, 1808 West End Ave., West End, Nashville, TN 37203; (615) 340-0012; 1808grille.com; American Contemporary; $$$. It's not often that a hotel restaurant can lure the locals, but 1808 Grille at the Hutton Hotel is more than just a place for visitors to find a bite before heading out. The restaurant has a sophisticated bar area that opens into a soaring dining room that's modern but comfortable with floor to ceiling windows, a mix of tables and banquettes and centerpieces of stacked beams of amber-colored wood. The menu is billed as New American, and Chef Charles Phillips, who brings experience from Chicago, Boston, Washington, D.C., and New York, interprets it with melting-pot flair. On the menu you might find small plates that offer a trip around the world, including a sophisticated take on home: shrimp and lentil curry served with naan; herbed spaetzle and fennel-braised duck; and white cheddar grits with asparagus, fried quail egg, whiskey-spiced pecans, shaved truffle, and ancho-honey vinaigrette. Larger plates might include pork scaloppini, fennel-dusted scallops, New York strip, and even a vegan seitan "stroganoff" of portobello mushrooms and carrot pappardelle. There are breakfast, brunch, and lunch menus, too, with salads, sandwiches, and even "meat and three"—expertly prepared steak, fish, or chicken paired with three farm-to-table sides.

Kien Ghang, 5845 Charlotte Pike, West Nashville, Nashville, TN 37209; (615) 353-1250; Vietnamese; $. If you're looking to find a local chef on his night off—a Southeast Asian immigrant or a food lover of any color and stripe—this might be a good place to start. One of the first and most popular Vietnamese places in town, Kien Ghang isn't anything fancy decorwise, and it's located in a strip mall with Lucky Bamboo Chinese restaurant and the sprawling multicultural grocery **K&S International Market** (p. 180). But on the menu you'll find tasty *bahn mi,* the sandwiches stuffed into baguettes with cilantro, carrot, jalapeño, and marinated pork, as well as the egg pancakes *(banh xeo)* for scooping and dipping in sauce, and bowls of slurpy pho chock-full with cellophane noodles, seafood, vegetables, or stocked to your liking. It's often bustling and bright, but don't forget to finish with a Vietnamese coffee. One warning before you go: It's cash only.

Korea House, 6410 Charlotte Pike, West Nashville, Nashville, TN 37209; (615) 352-2790; Korean; $$. A few of my friends had been raving about Korea House's bibimbap—the famous bowl of vegetables and rice topped with fried egg—for years. But confirmation came when a Korean photographer I work with suggested I not visit because the restaurant was just too authentic. Even someone new to Korean food, though, can find plenty to love here, like the *bulgogi* (Korean barbecue), for example, and the fascinating little bowls of *banchan* or sides like kimchi. Then after reading Nicki Wood's post on the *Nashville Scene*'s *Bites* blog about the *mandu-kook,* hand-rolled noodles in homemade broth, I'm curious to give this bowl of Korean comfort food a try. Don't expect much in the way of atmosphere at this place, which is located in a strip mall off Charlotte Pike, but it's the food that will keep your interest anyway. Others items to try: the barley tea and *soondubu chigae* (a spicy tofu and seafood stew).

Local Taco, 4501 Murphy Rd., Sylvan Park, Nashville, TN 37209; (615) 891-3271; thelocaltaco.com; Mexican/Tacos; $. Can the crunchy-spicy-sweet-salty mix involved with a basket of chips, cup of salsa—plus margarita—be beat? I think not. And thankfully for west-side folk, that's what Local Taco brought to the Sylvan Park area. A bit different from the Hispanic-owned restaurants or chain Mexican-themed places, this spot has a quaint neighborhood feel with its tiny bar, cozy seating, and patio bedecked with white lights. And of course it has much more than chips and salsa. The tacos are the main draw, with options like Local BBQ, a 12-hour smoked pork butt with jalapeño coleslaw and house-made chipotle barbecue sauce; Korean BBQ, sesame-seared beef with Asian slaw; Southern Fried with buttermilk-fried chicken, honey-lime mayo, lettuce, and tomato; and Spicy Shrimp, among others. Kick it up heatwise by ordering any taco "bang-bang" to add habanero-lime sauce. You'll find enchiladas and a few fresh salads on the menu, too, and though there's a charge for chips and salsa, the options include fresh-made roja, tomatillo verde, smoked corn and black bean, and pico de gallo. There is an additional location at 146 Pewitt Drive, Brentwood, TN 37027; (615) 915-4666.

Mambu Restaurant and Bar, 1806 Hayes St., West End, Nashville, TN 37203; (615) 329-1293; mamburestaurant.com; Eclectic; $$. Maybe I'm still on board with the backlash following all those sterile-looking Miami-club-like restaurants that cropped up in the late '90s, but I've yet to find a vintage home I can't get excited about visiting to dine. Mambu has been a longtime quirky favorite in Nashville. On a side street that runs parallel to West End, it's hidden away from the hustle and bustle. And once inside, you'll find 4 rooms for dining, all decorated with a funky flair. The menu changes with the seasons, but it stays worldly and eclectic. You might find anything from seared duck breast with Gorgonzola bread pudding and locally grown green beans to paella; pork schnitzel with sweet potato hash, and wine-braised cabbage; flat iron steak; seared scallops; or pan-fried chicken. And though the inside of the restaurant is certainly charming, owner Anita Hartel, a veteran of Nashville's independent restaurant scene, has created a lovely patio space out front as well, decorated with brightly colored chairs, herbs, and greenery.

HOMEGROWN CHAINS: J. ALEXANDER'S

I once heard a high-end chef at an independent restaurant in town proclaim this local chain as one of his favorites. A bold move, I thought, but I appreciated it. **J. Alexander's** (jalexanders .com) has indeed been a favorite for Nashvillians, but it now also has locations in 13 states and cities such as Atlanta, Orlando, and Chicago. The decor and menu are classic American with an emphasis on wood-fired cuisine. Portions are generous and might include seared scallops with couscous and asparagus; swordfish steaks with Thai sauce or beurre noir; aged prime rib au jus with chive-flecked potatoes; jumbo crab cakes; fish taco; and for dessert, decadent chocolate cake with a scoop of ice cream or white chocolate cheesecake. Look for the J. ALEXANDER'S sign in red block letters at the popular location just off West End Avenue with its floor-to-ceiling glassed-in foyer. 609 West End Ave., West End, Nashville, TN 37203; (615) 340-9901. Additional locations at 73 White Bridge Rd., #130, Nashville, TN 37205, (615) 352-0981; 1721 Galleria Blvd, Franklin, TN 37067, (615) 771-7779.

Midtown Cafe, 102 19th Ave. South, West End, Nashville, TN 37203; (615) 320-7176; midtowncafe.com; Contemporary; $$$. Since 1987, this restaurant located between Music Row and West End Avenue has been offering a white-tablecloth experience for both business lunches by day and romantic date dinners by night. It has been featured in the *Wall Street Journal*'s "power lunch" listings as a place for making deals over soups and salads as well as entrees like chicken piccata, lump crab cakes, Black & Blue #1 Ahi Tuna, and the Midtown Meatloaf (which also comes in a veggie version with ground brown rice, walnuts, mushrooms, and cheeses to hold it together). While it can certainly offer a hearty meal if you'd like, the lemon-artichoke soup has earned legendary status in town, along with owner and longtime Nashville restaurateur Randy Rayburn, who also owns **Sunset Grill** (p. 198) and **Cabana** (p. 185) in Hillsboro Village. The restaurant also offers a shuttle service (with $30 minimum restaurant bill) to the Schermerhorn Symphony Center, Tennessee Performing Arts Center, Ryman Auditorium, and Bridgestone Arena.

Miel Restaurant, 343 53rd Ave. North, Sylvan Park, Nashville, TN 37209; (615) 298-3663; mielrestaurant.com; French; $$$. The name means "honey" in French, and this sleek, sophisticated space—which was once home to Johnson's Meat Market—certainly hits a sweet spot for food lovers. The restaurant has its own farm about 10 minutes away with a variety of heirloom vegetables; therefore there's a heavy farm-to-table focus as well as a French flair on the menu. You'll often find escargots, charcuterie, marinated olives, and steak tartare to start. Entrees that follow might include bouillabaisse; locally raised sirloin cooked sous vide and then pan seared with potato-celeriac gratin; or Provençal chicken, roasted in cast iron with garden vegetables. For dessert don't miss the crème brûlée served in a sugar bowl fashioned to look like amber glass. The kitchen is open, and the decor is modern with brushed concrete floors and track lighting, but as you enter, expect to be reminded of the farm not far away with jar after jar of colorful pickles and jams lining the wall.

Miss Saigon Vietnamese Cuisine, 5849 Charlotte Pike, West Nashville, Nashville, TN 37209; (615) 354-1351; misssaigontn.com; Vietnamese; $. The most you'll get from this place atmosphere-wise probably lies in the name. So go ahead and conjure up Broadway's images of Saigon in the 1970s when an American GI and Vietnamese bar girl fall in love. But at this Miss Saigon, the food is the star. Popular dishes to start include the fresh-tasting spring rolls with vermicelli and vegetables wrapped up in thin sheets with shrimp, pork, or tofu or the *banh xeo* pancake with shrimp, pork, bean sprouts, onion, served with leaves of lettuce for scooping up pancake and dipping into the sauce. You'll also find at least 10 types of warming beef pho as well as chicken noodle soups and a long list of comforting vermicelli dishes that bring together the thin noodles with vegetables and savory bites of pork, beef, and shrimp along with bits of crushed peanut on top and the rich umami that fish sauce brings. End with the coffee that's blended with condensed milk.

Park Cafe, 4403 Murphy Rd., Sylvan Park, Nashville, TN 37209; (615) 383-4409; parkcafenashville.com; Eclectic; $$$. I've been told that when you turn the corner at this little restaurant built of nooks, you just might find Dolly Parton at one of the tables. But on most nights, it's probably more likely that you'll find Sylvan Park neighborhood folk at this cozy and dimly lit spot kept bright with colored paintings on the walls and interesting food on the plates. Park Cafe has been a favorite in the area since Chef Guillermo "Willy" Thomas and his wife, Yvette, opened it in 2001. Willy moved to town from New England and worked at many of the city's best spots until opening his own place. At his restaurant you're likely to find rich, dressed-up dinner favorites like pan-roasted duck breast with blue cheese and dried-cherry risotto, snap peas, and port wine reduction, or grilled pork chop with sweet potato mash, black-eyed pea and corn salsa, and apple-cider glaze.

The Picnic Cafe & Party Catering, 4320 Harding Pike, West End, Nashville, TN 37205; (615) 297-5398; thepicniccafe.com; Cafe; $. Kathy Bonnet, recipe developer at The Picnic Cafe, once told me the place with the blue-and-white checked tablecloths is like a "free country club"—a place where ladies who lunch make repeat visits for the chicken salad, pimento cheese, egg salad, ham salad, soups like herbed tomato with homemade cheese wafers, yeast rolls, and quiche made fresh daily. The women who work at the restaurant don aprons inside this spot located at the Hill Center at Belle Meade. The Picnic has been serving its loyal clientele for three decades, with the chicken salad being the most legendary draw.

Also look for take-and-bake dinners like spinach lasagna and chicken tetrazzini as well as party trays or dessert platters with options like crescent cookies, lemon bars, and mint brownies.

For a special treat, try the Pimento Plus sandwich: pimento cheese and bacon on a toasted croissant. If you like what you try at the restaurant, you can pick up a copy of *Cherished Recipes,* The Picnic's cookbook.

Porta Via Italian Kitchen, 21 White Bridge Rd., West End, Nashville, TN 37205; (615) 356-0001; eatatportavia.com; Italian; $. Walk through the door at Porta Via and you'll likely see a rainbow of gelato flavors behind the case on your right along with espresso machine and bar. But deeper inside this Italian restaurant with clean lines and modern feel you'll find the heart of the place—the kitchen that turns out Northern Italian fare from Giovanni Giosa and the wood-fired pizza oven manned by Riccardo Bacilieri. While you'll find pasta favorites like spaghetti carbonara and penne rigate a la Bolognese, specialties include Chicken Milanese, Veal Piccata, and even the Porta Via Meatball Bolillos, stuffed french-bread sandwich. But many who frequent this open, family-friendly place go for the certified Vera Pizza Napoletana or (VPN) pizza. You'll find a long list of topping options such as fennel-peppered salami, artichoke hearts, and roasted mushroom and peppers. Ask Bacilieri how he likes his pizza and he'll say he keeps it simple with just tomatoes, garlic, and oregano. There is an additional location at 3301 Aspen Grove, Cool Springs, Franklin, TN 37067; (615) 771-7747.

Rumba Rum Bar & Satay Grill, 3009 West End Ave., West End, Nashville, TN 37203; (615) 321-1350; rumbanashville.com; Eclectic; $$. If you're craving a muddled mint drink and an exotic bite that will transport you to a faraway locale, then Rumba is your spot. Dimly lit but with a rocking vibe, this restaurant brings together Latin and Asian flavors with small plates of ginger shrimp, pork confit tacos, sesame scallops, and skewers of satay with marinated beef, chorizo, chicken, and shrimp, as well as flatbreads and larger plates of Jamaican jerk pork, shrimp masala, or Zarzuela, a mix of scallops, fish, shrimp, and mussels in a tomato-saffron broth. But really you could make an event of the drink alone with various takes on mojitos and caipirinhas for sipping inside the tropical-themed interior of the restaurant or the patio overlooking West End Avenue. For dessert, check out the tres leches, carrot cake with masala ice cream, or the piña colada (pineapple tempura, coconut jam, and rum granita).

Sitar Indian Cuisine, 116 21st Ave. North, West End, Nashville, TN 37203; (615) 321-8889; sitarnashville.com; Indian; $. For the largest variety and biggest bang for a buck, you can visit this longtime Indian cuisine favorite during the midday hours when it offers an $8 all-you-can-eat lunch buffet. Located on a side street off West End near Vanderbilt University, you're likely to see a mix of students and office workers breaking for lunch. Or visit at dinner for a more relaxed experience and to order off the menu. You'll find the rich tasty standards in chicken, lamb, or seafood such as tandoori dishes, biryanis, curries, vindaloo, and plenty of vegetarian options, of course, such as of *sag panir,* spinach with Indian cheese, or just basic lentil stews of dal. For dessert there's *gulad jamum,* the deep-fried and syrup-covered cheese balls; or rice pudding with cardamom called *kheer,* among other options. Wash it all down with a Kingfish or Taj Mahal beer, tea, sodas or a lassi, the popular Indian drink made with homemade yogurt and a touch of rosewater.

Star Bagel Cafe, 4504 Murphy Rd., Sylvan Park, Nashville, TN 37209; (615) 292-7993; starbagelcafe.com; Breakfast/Sandwiches; $. Nashville's oldest locally owned bagel shop opened in 1995, and these days it still keeps Sylvan Park families and professionals fed for breakfast and lunch. This owner started his first businesses young—collecting aluminum cans and dealing sports cards—but he decided to open a bagel shop after they kept him fueled as an avid runner, swimmer, and cyclist during college. He then took a "bagel trip" to research through Chicago, New Jersey, and New York to learn about the bread. But what started as a bagel shop has morphed into a breakfast and sandwich shop, too—with eggs and smoothies supplementing the bagels and butter, honey, jam, cream cheese, or lox. At lunch he offers soups and sandwiches like roast beef, smoked turkey, chicken salad, hot ham, and cheddar, and pizza bagels with toppings like feta, spinach, sundried tomato, pepperoni, sausage, and mushroom.

Suzy Wong's House of Yum, 1517 Church St., West End, Nashville, TN 37203; (615) 329-2913; suzywongsnashville.com; Asian; $$. Chef Arnold Myint opened this restaurant—his third after **PM** (p. 195) and **Cha Chah** (p. 186) both in the Belmont area—in Nashville's trendiest alternative nightlife scene, and it's his biggest party yet. The restaurant is located among the popular clubs on this street, and even opens into Tribe nightclub. Suzy Wong's could pass for a club with its low lights and cocktail seating along exposed brick walls all under a brightly colored, Asian-style dragon painted on panels of fabric. The name of the restaurant refers to the 1950s novel, *The World of Suzie Wong,* about an Asian "lady of the evening" who falls in love with an American diplomat. And the menu is mostly split between a long list of shared plates and "Yum bowls." Snack on whimsical Asian wonton nachos, red curry queso dip, coconut-Thai chile chicken wings, BBQ braised pork ribs, Spicy Tuna & Cucumber Napolean Roll, and more. The Yum bowls, including the pineapple red-curry shrimp, green curry mussels, and peanut chicken panang, come with side of white or brown rice and offer a large portion.

360 Wine Bar & Bistro, 6000 Tennessee 100, Belle Meade, Nashville, TN 37205; (615) 353-5604; 360bistro.com; Bistro/Wine Bar; $$$. Located in a posh mall (of sorts) called Spaces, this Belle Meade wine bar and bistro originally began as The Grape, a small chain of wine bars out of Atlanta. But owner Nick Jacobson made a break for it in 2007 to open an independent restaurant with more freedom in the kitchen and bar. Wine lovers relish the options, and food lovers have a menu that freshens up regularly with the seasons. In spring you might find dry-aged New York strip with

whipped potatoes, sautéed wild mushrooms or pan-seared diver scallops with shaved brussels spouts, fennel salad, blood orange segments, shaved red onion, and a saffron tarragon aioli. And even though the restaurant is a white-tablecloth and votive affair, you can find a more casual bite here, too, such as the thoughtfully constructed grass-fed burger on Silke's rosemary bun with heirloom tomato, local lettuces, onions, bacon, and garlic aioli.

Tin Angel, 3201 West End Ave., West End, Nashville, TN 37203; (615) 298-3444; tinangel.net; Contemporary; $$. Like so many people in this town, Tin Angel owner Rick Bolsom followed the music when he came to Nashville in the 1970s as a journalist. But he eventually found his calling in food as a longtime supporter of independent restaurants in town. The building that houses Tin Angel used to host the likes of singer/songwriter Rodney Crowell when it was a burgers-and-beers bar. Bolsom lived in the apartment building across the street in those days, but after involvement with other restaurants in town, he opened Tin Angel with his wife Vicki in 1993. The exposed brick, white lights, and votives on pub tables that Bolsom refurbished himself give the room a warm vibe along with the circular brick fireplace near the front door and bar. The restaurant offers comfortable but creative food without pretension and a touch of international flair. You might find steak frites, chicken schnitzel, sauteed rainbow trout, and *codillio,* smoked pork shanks with red current glaze. At lunch the Med Salad, with its grilled shrimp, chickpeas, artichokes, roasted red bell peppers, orzo, feta, and toasted pumpkin seeds, has been a favorite for years.

West End Cafe, 1720 West End Ave., West End, Nashville, TN 37203; (615) 321-2209; westendcafenashville.com; Breakfast/ Cafe; $. A relative newcomer on West End, this breakfast spot and cafe that opened in 2011 sits between the Hutton Hotel and Hotel Indigo, as well as local office buildings, which brings a steady flow in to its modern gray-and-black decor. Breakfast begins at 6:30 every morning with solid options like omelets of ham and cheese, the veggie-packed garden option, as well as chorizo and manchego, and salmon and egg white. Belgium waffles, breakfast sandwiches, and coffee drinks with Drew's Brews locally roasted beans also help start the day. Lunch offers a roster of sandwiches and salads such as chicken salad on cranberry pecan bread, pimento cheese on jalapeño cheddar bread, Thai chopped chicken salad with sesame vinaigrette, and cobb salad with grilled chicken, bacon, boiled egg, white cheddar, and chipotle ranch dressing. The dinner menu served from 5 p.m. to 9 p.m. adds grilled steaks, fish, and pork tenderloin, as well as a variety of burger options.

The Wild Hare, 316 White Bridge Rd., West Nashville, Nashville, TN 37209; (615) 818-0219; thewildharenashville.com; Cafe; $. Maybe it was the family-friendly atmosphere, location in a stretch of White Bridge Road that called for an independent restaurant, or the affordable creative mix of pizzas and full entrees, but this place opened to rave reviews in 2011. Between the charming red walls and black-and-white checkerboard floors, diners dig into deviled eggs, pimento cheese, burgers, fried fish- and avocado-stuffed tacos, filet mignon, cornmeal-crusted catfish, roast chicken, and pizzas like the Wild Hare version topped with caramelized onions, herbed ricotta, Benton's bacon, roasted garlic, and charred scallions. Other pizza pulled from the wood-burning oven include fig and prosciutto as well as Moroccan pizza piled with roasted red peppers, curry-rubbed chicken, mozzarella, and a Moroccan spice blend all piled on top of butter- and honey-brushed crust. And when the kids get restless, you can send them to the blackboard wall to make chalk art.

Woodlands, 3415 West End Ave., West End, Nashville, TN 37203; (615) 463-3005; woodlandstennessee.com; Indian; $. This wholly vegetarian Indian restaurant is one of the few restaurants in town that completely omits meat, but you won't miss it for a minute as the entrees here are packed with flavor and spice. In fact, many consider it to be the best Indian restaurant in town. Located in the bottom of a mid-rise off West End Avenue, it's easy to drive right by, and once inside the decor doesn't get much better. But under the fluorescent lights, the food on the plate keeps it interesting. A good way to sample many of the flavors is the economical lunch buffet. Otherwise, you can't really go wrong off the menu. You'll find it divided into sections including the *dosa,* rice, and lentil crepes; *uthappa,* rice and lentil pancakes; curries like channa masala (chickpeas with spices), *mutter panir* (peas with cheese, onion, and bell peppers in tomato sauce), vegetable korma in coconut sauce; and Indo-Chinese offerings. And I haven't even gotten to appetizers, sides, breads, and dessert. There's lot on this menu to travel through and explore.

Landmarks

Bobbie's Dairy Dip, 5301 Charlotte Ave., Sylvan Park, Nashville, TN 37209; (615) 463-8088; Burgers; $. It looks like something out of a movie—and almost too adorable to be real—with its retro, cartoonish pink sign and row of colored lights ringing this little box of a place. For more than 50 years, it's been the place for families and friends to steer the car when craving an ice cream twirled into a cone soft-serve style and, if you'd like, dipped in chocolate. The sweet potato fries also bring repeat business served with hand-formed burgers along with an updated vegetarian option made with black beans. And rather than an ice-cream cone, you can also take the milk shake route, with classic flavors as well as more advanced options like the Memphis Mafia with peanut butter, banana, and bacon. You might have to wait on summer nights while you take in the tunes that match the decor, and then order at the window

Homegrown Chains: Cracker Barrel Old Country Store and Restaurant

When it comes to homegrown chains, this one certainly has become legendary.

Founder Dan Evins worked in the family petroleum-sales business until he noticed an unmet need for gasoline at the intersection of Highway TN 109 and I-40 in Lebanon, Tennessee, about 30 miles outside of Nashville. He added a gift shop and restaurant to the gas station, and in 1969, **Cracker Barrel** (crackerbarrel.com) was born.

The country cooking of Cracker Barrel—along with nostalgic snacks, gifts, and even audio books for the road trip—can now be found in more than 600 locations in 42 states. With white rockers and checkers on the front porch, and a menu of favorites like chicken and dumplings, meatloaf, pinto beans, turnip greens, stacks of pancakes, eggs, country ham, warm biscuits, and hot coffee, this chain manages to keep it real in the face of its growth. And Cracker Barrel now has a place along America's highways, giving those of us on the road a little consistency and the taste of comfort.

before taking a seat at one of the brightly colored picnic tables around the side of this beloved Nashville classic.

Cafe Coco, 210 Louise Ave., West End, Nashville, TN 37203; (615) 321-2626; cafecoco.com; Breakfast/Sandwiches; $. Visit this place at 2 a.m. and you'll find a mix of students behind laptops and partiers behind beer-bleary eyes. One of the few 24-hour places to grab a bite, Cafe Coco is near Vanderbilt University and the Rock Block, an area that holds the legendary Exit/In live music venue. It's partly a coffee shop—local art on the walls, show posters tacked on various surfaces, and counter service—but after ordering you can find a spot to park it among the nooks and crannies of the building or on the spacious patio. There's also an area in the back that hosts live music and regular songwriter nights. Visit in the morning for breakfast fare, or later in the day you can choose a hummus platter with pita and cucumber slices, spinach artichoke dip, quesadillas, burgers, sandwiches, and pastas, including a create-your-own option. Cafe Coco delivers as well.

✓ **Elliston Place Soda Shop,** 2111 Elliston Place, West End, Nashville, TN 37203; (615) 327-1090; Burgers/Meat-and-Three; $. Nashville's oldest continuously operating restaurant has been at the same location where it opened in 1939, and it has endured as a relic of a simple and more innocent time, even in the heart of Nashville's legendary "rock block," an area that has catered to a bit more of a rock and roll crowd than a country one. Elliston Place Soda Shop also nearly caused citywide panic when owners almost shut the doors for good in 2011 over a lease and rent issue. Thankfully both parties made concessions to keep the doors open. This is a "shotgun" space (narrow in width but long in depth) with a red awning and neon sign, and inside you'll find chrome booths along the bar, tiny tiles on the floor, and a mini jukebox at every booth. On the menu, there are home-style breakfast offerings like country ham, biscuits, eggs, and grits. And for lunch its burgers, fries, shakes, malts, and sundaes as well as meat-and-three offer-  ings such as fried chicken, pork chops, liver and onions, with sides like turnip greens, mashed potatoes, fried okra, congealed (Jell-O) salad, and homemade banana pudding.

The Gold Rush Restaurant & Bar, 2205 Elliston Place, West End, Nashville, TN 37203; (615) 321-1160; Pub Food; $. Definitely don't go here looking for fancy food, but the "if these walls could talk" factor certainly applies. It's a Nashville landmark in the heart of the Rock Block just across the street from **Exit/In** (p. 273), the live music venue where Jimmy Buffett is rumored to have found his first major music break. So since 1974, the Gold Rush has been feeding the rock and rollers with drinks and dinners. The most leg- endary item on the menu is the bean roll, essentially a bean burrito with refried beans and cheese wrapped up in 10-inch tortilla and topped with secret red sauce, cheese, lettuce, tomato, sour cream, and jalapeño. There are several variations, too, adding stuffings like chicken or steak, or even barbecued pork and onions to the traditional version. Beyond bean rolls, you can choose from a list of sandwiches, burgers, salads, and bar food like nachos (I especially get a kick out of the Gold Rush Diet Plate with grilled chicken or hamburger patty, cottage cheese, tomato, and pineapple). The interior of the Gold Rush is dark, with pool tables in between two bars, which makes it the perfect place to visit before or after a show.

Jimmy Kelly's Steakhouse Restaurant, 217 Louise Ave., West End, Nashville, TN 37203; (615) 329-4349; jimmykellys.com; Steak House; $$$. It's the oldest school of steak houses in Nashville, and visiting this place feels like walking into someone's grand old home for dinner. Enter through the foyer and take a seat in the dining room near the fireplace or take the staircase to the cozy dining rooms on the second level. Open since 1934, the restaurant is in its third generation of family ownership. The walls are paneled in dark wood, and the tablecloths are red-and-white checked. The menu keeps it fairly simple with crab cakes, oysters, shrimp, mussels, and calamari to start. I recommend the Original Faucon Salad as well, which has been on the menu for decades with its bacon, hard-boiled eggs, and blue cheese on iceberg lettuce. As for the main course, it's what you'd expect from a classic steak house—filet mignon, chateaubriand, New York strip, a 20-ounce bone-in rib eye, a Bootlegger's Ribeye that's cooked in an iron skillet with

Creole spices, as well as rack of lamb, lobster, fish of the day, simply grilled salmon, and shrimp and grits.

McCabe Pub Restaurant & Lounge, 4410 Murphy Rd., Sylvan Park, Nashville, TN 37209; (615) 269-9406; mccabepub.com; American/Pub Food; $. Like the neighborhood golf clubhouse—but without the golf course—this restaurant paneled in light wood is an everyone-knows-your-name type of place where the bartender, James, will put your drink in front of you (once he learns it) before you can utter your order. As for the food, McCabe pub is known for a few things in particular—the squash casserole, broccoli casserole, and sweet potato casserole as side dishes with main courses of fried fish, chicken livers, pork chop, or meatloaf. The Best Bacon Cheeseburger in Town, as it's called on the menu, also gets rave reviews along with the other burger selections with chili or various kinds of cheese. Otherwise, the menu options are pretty vast, with a long list of sandwiches including homemade pimento cheese and open-faced roast beef with gravy. But no matter your dinner choice, be sure to save room for a slice of the coconut cake.

Sperry's Restaurant, 5109 Harding Pike, Belle Meade, Nashville, TN 37205; (615) 353-0809; sperrys.com; Steak House; $$$. This is a place where certain dishes have become tradition. People go gaga for the green goddess dressing at Sperry's, which has been open in Nashville for nearly 40 years. And while it's dimly lit with dark-paneled walls, and escargots and steaks are on the menu, it still has a walk-up salad bar that regular customers love. It was opened by high school sweethearts, and the proof is on the tree with their names carved on it at the back of the building. You'll find classic steak house fare like New York strip, rib eye, prime rib, and the filet Oskar with crabmeat, asparagus, and béarnaise, but there also are several seafood options such as Alaskan king crab legs, barbecued shrimp and grits, lobster tails, and rainbow trout almondine. You'll also find a few favorites as sides, too, such as the grilled artichoke and lobster-truffle mac and cheese, and the famous brandy Alexanders and bananas Foster for 2 also keep the regulars coming back. There is a second location at 650 Frazier Dr., Cool Springs, Franklin, TN 37067; (615) 778-9950.

Sportsman's Grill, 5405 Harding Pike, Belle Meade, Nashville, TN 37205; (615) 356-6206; sportsmansgrille.com; Steak House / Barbecue; $$. For more than two decades, this restaurant has been helping Nashville gets its carnivorous fix with smoked ribs, barbecued pulled pork shoulder on the famous Cajun cornbread, catfish, and steaks. But even with the lodge-like focus, the restaurant also has a list of burgers, sandwiches, and entree salads with housemade dressings such as a cobb, classic-style Caesar, Greek, and Santa Fe chicken with ranch, tortilla strips, salsa, sour cream, and guacamole. This is the original location of the three restaurants in town, and while they all have their own unique vibe (the Hillsboro Village location has live music, for example) there's something about this one that feels original and uniquely Nashville. There are additional locations at 1601 21st Ave. South, Hillsboro Village, Nashville, TN 37212, (615) 320-1633; and 1640 West Gate Circle, Brentwood, TN 37027, (615) 373-1070.

Valentino's, 1907 West End Ave., West End, Nashville, TN 37203; (615) 327-0148; valentinosnashville.com; Italian; $$$. It's the sort of place you're likely to find music execs making deals or unwinding after work, but it's also appropriate for date night with live music offered Wednesday through Saturday nights. Located in an old townhome, the inside decor is white tablecloths and exposed brick. Beginning with antipasto, you'll find options like carpaccio on arugula with citronette dressing and Parmesan cheese, and the traditional Caesar salad is worth ordering as it serves 2 and comes prepared tableside. Pastas and risottos are grouped together on the menu and include handmade gnocchi and options such as pappardelle with sweet Italian sausage meatballs, roasted peppers, tomato sauce, and Pecorino Romano. Finally the main course thankfully eschews chicken parmigiana for grilled lobster, scallops, and fish of the day simply prepared with olive oil, garlic, lemon, and herbs as well as veal scaloppini Marsala or osso bucco Milanese. Visit during happy hour, Mon through Fri from 5 to 7 p.m., for $5 house wines, well drinks, and $1 dollar–off beers as well as $7 appetizers (or 3 for $20) including smoked salmon, grilled Italian sausage, stuffed eggplant, bruschetta, and cheese plate.

Rotiers, 2413 Elliston Place, West End, Nashville, TN 37203; (615) 327-9892; $. This dark little cottage of a restaurant near Vanderbilt serves meat-and-three fare to hipster students sipping Miller High Lifes in booths and to blue-haired grannies who have been coming in every week for years. But in addition to the plate lunches of fried chicken and mashed potatoes, squash casserole, okra, and hash brown casserole, Rotiers is known for the burgers. Served on french bread if you like (and I recommend it this way), the secret to the great taste, I've been told, might be more the ancient griddle in the back. Look for the green-and-white awning and neon sign, but on busy days, you might have to take a number, literally, and stand at the small bar near the cluttered cash register where the cooks pop their heads out on occasion to check Titans or Predators scores on the TV. The milk shake, though not officially on the menu, is strongly recommended.

Sylvan Park Restaurant, 4502 Murphy Rd., Sylvan Park, Nashville, TN 37209; (615) 292-9275; $. One of the oldest meat-and-threes in town, this simple white dining room in the Sylvan Park neighborhood treats Nashvillians to the finest in plate lunches from servers who have been working this room for many moons. Favorites include the pork chops, fried chicken, and chicken fried steak with a host of sides—fresh fried corn, collard greens, stewed tomatoes, okra, and stewed apples—served in separate bowls. Definitely save room for dessert choices of cobblers or banana pudding, or the trademark pies such as the chess, sweet potato, caramel, coconut, or chocolate meringue. Breakfast also is served Wednesday through Saturday; the fried bologna is a favorite. And just a warning (and maybe more of a reason to go)—you'll have to go through the kitchen to get to the bathroom. There is a second location at 2330 Franklin Pike, Nashville, TN 37204; (615) 269-9716.

Wendell Smith Restaurant, 407 53rd Ave. North, West Nashville, Nashville, TN 37209; (615) 383-7114; $. They call it Biscuits and Booze, as the owners of this meat-and-three also have a liquor store at the front of the building. It opened in the 1950s under a man everyone called Big Wendell, and the restaurant is still in the family with hardly a thing changed in the dining room. Beginning with breakfast, you'll find country ham and a variety of egg and pancake dishes. But the main draw is the meat-and-three fare of roast beef, pork chops, fried chicken, fried catfish, chicken, and dressing as well as turnip greens, fried corn, white beans, broccoli casserole, mac and cheese, and desserts of pecan pie and caramel pie. If you'd rather go a different route, though, there's a fried bologna sandwich offered here, and when I spot one of those on a menu, I find them hard to resist.

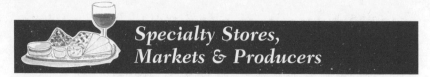

Specialty Stores, Markets & Producers

Dose Coffee & Tea, 3431 Murphy Rd., Sylvan Park, Nashville, TN 37203; (615) 457-1300; dosecoffeeandtea.com. Residents of Sylvan Park heading toward West End Avenue or the junctions of major highways at the corner pass right by this coffee shop, which makes it a perfect stopping point to fuel up on caffeine. The small booths along one wall also make for a good place to meet a friend or discuss business. The shop has an espresso bar and brew bar and serves milk from a local dairy, JD Country Milk. While coffee might come from artisan roasters such as Madcap, a selection of teas come from SerendipiTea and TeaSource. You'll also find a selection of single-origin chocolates such as Ritual Chocolate, Askinosie, and the beautifully packaged Mast Brothers.

The Produce Place, 4000 Murphy Rd., Sylvan Park, Nashville, TN 37209; (615) 383-2664; produceplace.com. When Barry Burnett opened this neighborhood market more than 20 years ago, he said he struggled through the winters waiting eagerly for peach season, which he knew would bring him business. It was a cash-only business in the early days, just bringing farm food to West Nashville. But these days, The Produce Place thrives not only with locally raised peaches, cartons of strawberries and other fruits and vegetables, but it also serves as a gourmet market with milk in glass containers from a local dairy, jars of *kombucha*, organic versions of cereals and crackers, and gourmet packaged foods. The market fits right into the Sylvan Park neighborhood where the clientele appreciates having a spot to stop in on the way home without having to trek to Whole Foods.

West Nashville Farmers' Market, 385 46th Ave. North, West Nashville, Nashville, TN 37209; (615) 585-1294. This market held on Saturday from spring through fall at the Richland Park off Charlotte Pike is only open for a few hours each week, but it's a popular stop for residents on the west side of town. The market is sponsored by Good Food for Good People, a local food advocacy group, and all the vendors are local—from area farms to candle makers, bakers, pie makers, and food truck vendors. You could also catch a free yoga class, live music, or a free massage to get your busy Saturday started off right. Expect to find farm-fresh produce from growers like the popular and organic Delvin Farms, milk from producers like Hatcher Family Dairy, eggs, cheeses, local honey, flowers, seasonal fruits, breads, and more, such as fresh juices from Juice Nashville and locally produced soaps.

Franklin, Brentwood & Cool Springs

This section of town could have a book of its own. But the restaurants mentioned here offer a greatest hits of sorts for this area south of Nashville.

Driving on I-65 from downtown, you'll first pass through Brentwood and then Cool Springs, home to Cool Springs Galleria mall and a host of chain restaurants as well as the Nashville area's second Whole Food Market location.

Driving a bit farther, about 20 miles from downtown Nashville, you'll find the heart of Franklin proper. It has been called the Beverly Hills of Nashville as it is home to many country stars, and the historic downtown area is as picturesque as a postcard with its small town vibe and attractions like the recently refurbished Franklin Theatre built in 1937. I especially recommend spending an afternoon shopping and snacking along Main Street in Franklin or visiting the lively Franklin Farmers' Market on Saturday at The Factory. Nearly 100 local vendors set up at the old brick plant, refurbished into an art, shopping, and dining space. If you don't fill up on samples of jams, honeys, cheeses, and breads, Saffire is a popular choice at The Factory for both lunch and dinner.

Foodie Faves

Basil Asian Bistro, 9040 Carothers Pkwy., Franklin, TN 37067; (615) 771-0999; basilasianbistro.com; Thai/Sushi; $$. This place goes beyond the typical pad thai, and red or green Thai curries (though, yes, they've got those, too). On the menu you'll find soft-shell crab in either panang curry or chile garlic sauce as well as frog legs in garlic or basil sauce. There's lobster tail in ginger sauce, roasted duck, and whole fried snapper with ginger or chile garlic sauce as well. The decor takes on a more modern and updated vibe, too, with clean lines and sleek lighting. And for a change from the typical ting of Asian music, you can hear live jazz on Thursday evenings beginning around 6:30 p.m. You'll also find three pages of sushi selections to choose from as well as favorite Thai dishes like green papaya salad with shrimp, chicken coconut *(tom kha kai)*, and chicken lemongrass *(tom yum kai)* soups, and several stir-fry, noodle, and fried-rice dishes that include several vegetarian options.

Bombay Bistro, 9040 Carothers Pkwy., Franklin, TN 37067; (615) 771-9105; bombaybistrotn.com; Indian; $. The clean brick exterior might not suggest much in the way of exoticism, but inside, the menu and flavorful food say otherwise. Visit at lunch for a vast sampling of dishes at just $8.99 on weekdays and $9.99 on weekends. Or order the Northern Indian cuisine here off the menu including samosas, a selection of *chat* (sort of like an Indian version of nachos) and poori (a puffed fried dough with filling like potato and chutney), and a long list of vegetarian, chicken, and lamb dishes from Chef Krishna Ganatra, a native of northern India who came to the United States in 1998. The space has a clean, minimalist feel in decor, which keeps the focus on the food. You'll also find a long list of beers on the menu, including Taj Mahal and local **Yazoo** (p. 264) and cocktails such as the Chai Tini with Stolichnaya Vanil, Voyant Chai liqueur, and coconut milk.

Boxwood Bistro, 230 Franklin Rd., Franklin, TN 37064; (615) 791-9411; boxwoodbistro.com; Contemporary; $$. Located in the old payroll office of a historic cluster of brick buildings known as The Factory, this restaurant manages to feel both relaxed with its warm lighting and elegant with its white tablecloths. Live music on weekends and an outdoor, rooftop patio also make for a social environment at pre- and post-dinner times. Owner John Franks has a section of the menu called "Hickory Smoked Competition 'Q'," and he smokes whole roasts of prime rib in a pit as well as baby back ribs at 205 degrees for 4 hours, and pork shoulder for pulled pork slider sandwiches at 195 degrees for 15 hours. The menu also offers grilled meats—rib eye with wine demi-glace, filet, lamb chops, salmon, and more—as well as a separate steak menu with even more options like porterhouse and cowboy rib eye. Specialties include shrimp and grits, herb-crusted pork tenderloin, lobster ravioli, and Southern fried chicken. You'll find sumptuous sides and salads, too, like the spiced maple-pear salad with mixed greens, maple-Dijon vinaigrette, red grapes, blue cheese, red onion, candied pecans, and Chardonnay-poached pears, as well as sandwiches and salads for lunch, and a brunch on Sunday.

Cool Cafe/Mangia, 1110 Hillsboro Rd.; Franklin, TN 37064; (615) 599-0338 for Cool Cafe; (615) 538-7456 for Mangia; cool cafefranklin.com; facebook.com/mangianashville; Meat-and-Three/ Italian; $ for Cool Cafe and $$$ for Mangia. It's a meat-and-three by day and an Italian pop-up restaurant by weekend. Visit Monday through Friday, and you'll be treated to daily plate specials that might include meatloaf and ham with scalloped potatoes as well as green beans, fried okra, turnip greens, broccoli salad, coleslaw, and deviled eggs. Then on Friday at 8 p.m. and again on Saturday at 6 p.m., the cafe morphs into Mangia, a New York–style Italian family dinner experience. As guests arrive, and throughout the 5-course meal, tunes by Frank Sinatra and Dean Martin drift from the sound system as Chef Nick Pellegrino ducks out of the kitchen to lead diners in sing-alongs. Meals served family style might include antipasti of bruschetta with Tuscan white-bean dip along with fried green olives stuffed with cheese; classic Caesar salad; rigatoni with beef short rib Bolognese, veal osso bucco, rosemary lemon chicken; and dessert of cannoli and *zeppole*. Though that might seem like a hearty lot (especially for the $45 prix fixe and $5 BYOB corkage fee), I've hardly listed a full-night's menu. And thankfully, Pellegrino works it like a true Italian and spreads the meal out to last all night. Reservations only for Mangia.

55 South, 403 Main St., Franklin, TN 37064; (615) 538-6001; eat55.com; Southern; $$. The name *55 South* refers to the interstate highway that runs from Memphis to New Orleans—a trek Chef-Owner Jason McConnell made many times when the West Tennessee native attended college in Oxford, Mississippi. The stretch of terrain also covers some pretty good eating, which McConnell captures at this downtown Franklin restaurant. You'll find oysters served on ice, roasted or char-grilled; Delta-style beef tamales; fried quail and biscuits with peach butter; seafood gumbo; chicken and sausage gumbo; shrimp and grits; po' boys made with baguettes brought in from New Orleans; Memphis-style barbecue spaghetti; and chicken and sausage jambalaya. But there's also a nod to Music City, where McConnell worked for several years at **F. Scott's** (p. 108), with a fiery Nashville-style hot chicken sandwich served as it should be with white bread and dill pickles. All of these find their home in the exposed-brick space with weathered wood and reclaimed materials on historic Main Street.

Judge Bean's BBQ, 7022 Church St., Brentwood, TN 37027; (615) 823-2280; judgebeans.com; Barbecue; $$. Aubrey "Judge" Bean has been a fixture among the barbecue crowd of Nashville, opening and closing restaurants throughout the city. Bean also took some time off to recuperate from heart bypass surgery, but he's back, and this location seems to be the one that will stick. Though it sits in the heart of the suburb strip malls, this spot has walls of rough wood decorated with license plates, strings of Christmas lights overhead, and a stage for bands. Bean's style is rooted in Texas, too, so brisket lies at the heart of this place, but in addition to the slices of beef, you'll find chopped pork, smoked sausage, baby back ribs and smoked chicken with a rather long list of sides as barbecue joints go, including barbecue beans, fries, slaw, potato salad, fried okra, corn on the cob, and even tamales. Indeed, you'll find some Tex-Mex

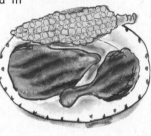

influences also in the corn tortilla tacos stuffed with brisket, catfish, or pork and topped with salsa and guacamole. In 2011, Bean opened a location in West Nashville called The Judge's Vinegarroon at 1805 Church St., Nashville, TN 37203; (615) 678-7116; thejudges vinegarroon.com.

Mack and Kate's, 3078 Maddux Way, Ste. 100, Franklin, TN 37064; (615) 591-4104; mackandkatescafe.com; Southern; $$. These days it seems an "Old School" Deviled Egg can be hard to find. But not at Mack and Kate's. That's how they name them on the menu. Yet Mack and Kate's blends the old with the new and offers a sophisticated take on the Southern cuisine. For example, the fried green tomatoes are served with homemade chowchow and pimento cheese that is made with goat cheese. The menu at this restaurant—named for the owners' daughters MacKenzie and Kathleen—changes regularly to reflect the local and seasonal produce, but you might find shrimp and grits, too, and entree of cast-iron-seared beef tenderloin; hash brown potato cake, grilled asparagus, fried egg, and jalapeño hollandaise. Visit for lunch and you can check out the 8 options under $8 that mostly bring together sandwiches and salads or maybe a half macaroni and cheese with bacon topping. Brunch happens on Sunday, but one benefit that happens regardless of when you visit: Black-pepper biscuits hit the table soon after you do.

McCreary's Irish Pub, 414 Main St., Franklin, TN 37064; (615) 591-3197; mccrearyspub.com; Irish; $. Walk through the door of this downtown Franklin pub and you'll find it smells just as it should—like fish-and-chips. With exposed brick and natural-colored wood tables and chairs, it's a lively, narrow room that serves breakfast, lunch, and dinner. To begin the day, the Ulster Fry packs a Northern Ireland wallop with 3 banger sausages, 3 slices bacon, sliced corned beef, 2 eggs, grilled tomato, potatoes, and black-and-tan bread. Or later there's a menu of corned beef and cabbage; fried cod and fries; shepherd's pie; salmon with brown sugar–whiskey glaze; and Dublin Pot Pie, a creamy blend of shredded chicken, peas, carrots, corn, and potatoes underneath a flaky blanket of crust. On tap is Guinness, of course, as well as Smithwick's, Harp's, Woodchuck Apple Cider, a beer of the month, and a variety of bottled beers and wine. There are also a few tables out front on the sidewalk for a view of picturesque downtown Franklin and the restored Franklin Theatre across the street.

Meridee's Breadbasket, 110 4th Ave. South, Franklin, TN 37064; (615) 790-3755; merridees.com; Bakery/Cafe; $. Right in the heart of downtown Franklin, you'll find this bakery and cafe in a former hardware-store warehouse with its creaky wooden floors and blue-and-white checked tablecloths. Order at the counter where breads and pastries keep guests tempted, and where it feels like a restaurant gone back in time. Opening at 7 a.m., Meridee's breakfast includes scratch-made biscuits (and gravy if you like), almonds swirls, cinnamon rolls, and sticky buns as well as omelets and the breakfast braid, a popular item for business meetings. Then for lunch the salads are the big draw—chicken salad, egg salad, tuna salad, pimento cheese, and curried chicken between slices of fresh bread. The baked crescents, dough wrapped around a filling such as turkey and honey Dijon on oatmeal, also bring repeat business as do daily soups, casseroles, and quiches. To drink, try the homemade lemonade or raspberry fruit tea. Though the restaurant opened in the early 1980s, it really dates back to the 1800s. Merridee Erickson (who passed away in 1994) moved to Tennessee with culinary knowledge from her grandmother, Anna Maria Faust, who came to the United States from Sweden and even worked as head cook to the Pillsbury family.

Puffy Muffin Dessert Bakery & Restaurant, 229 Franklin Rd., Brentwood, TN 37027; (615) 373-2741; puffymuffin.com; Bakery/ Cafe; $. For more than 25 years, the Puffy Muffin has offered its home-style casseroles and baked goods, but it all began at Lynda Stone's home when she made bread and rolls for friends and family. After years of rave reviews for her baking, she started a home-based business and then grew the business, renting commercial bakery space at a local grocery. In 1992, she opened her own place, and it continues to be popular with a loyal local following. For a taste of the tradition, try the poppy-seed chicken casserole with shredded chicken in a Parmesan cream sauce with a buttery poppy-seed crumb on top. It's served over rice with cranberry salad and a freshly baked roll. You'll also find a quiche plate as well as popular old-school salads like ambrosia or shredded carrot and spreads like pimento cheese. Bakery items include brownies, pies (fruit, chess, fudge, pecan, Boston cream) and cakes (carrot, Italian cream, German chocolate, red velvet, caramel, chocolate amaretto bundt, and the list goes on). Additional location in Cool Springs at 91 Seaboard Ln., Brentwood, TN 37027; (615) 309-0703.

Red Pony, 408 Main St., Franklin, TN 37064; (615) 595-7669; red ponyrestaurant.com; Southern; $$$. When it comes to dining in downtown Franklin, Jason McConnell is pretty much the man.

Homegrown Chains: Pie in the Sky

From their Franklin home and test kitchen, Kelly and Caroline Black wanted to create a "Nashville-style" pizza. Focusing on fresh ingredients and freshly made dough, the Blacks opened their first **Pie in the Sky** (pieintheskypizza.com) location in 2001. A few of the specialty pizzas include steak & blue with tenderloin, mushroom caps, red onion, and Gorgonzola; teriyaki chicken with pineapple; shrimp scampi with garlic in white-wine reduction, olive oil, Romano, and mozzarella and served with fresh lemon wedges; as well as the cheeseburger pizza with cheddar, ground beef, and topped with mustard, mayo, ketchup, chopped lettuce, onion, tomatoes, and pickles. But guests can also build their own with more than 55 topping choices and crust style—signature, thin, ultra-thin, and gluten-free. And while the pizza remains the main draw, the menu has a host of other items including sandwiches, salads, calzones, pastas, and entrees like chicken Parmesan and shrimp scampi. Locations include 1770 Galleria Blvd., Cool Springs, (615) 778-0988; 6917 Lenox Village Dr., Lenox Village, (615) 837-9500; 110 Lyle Ave., Midtown/Vanderbilt, (615) 321-1223.

Though he now owns **55 South** (p. 246), **Sol** (p. 253), and a private event space called McConnell House, it all started with the Red Pony. The restaurant along Main Street in historic downtown Franklin has exposed brick walls and hardwood floors that offer a warm glow. Take a seat on one of the tall red bar stools, head to the dining rooms, or climb the stairs to the lounge. I love that the menu fits on one page, and though it might change with the seasons, examples from it include a roasted beet salad, a Boston lettuce salad with buttermilk blue cheese panna cotta and candied bacon *gastrique,* and grilled grouper with skillet spoon bread made of sweet corn, buttermilk, and chives, with asparagus and tomato butter. I also like that McConnell infuses his restaurant with bits of himself and his past that have taken him from Tennessee to Mississippi, New Orleans, New York (for the Culinary Institute of America), and back to Tennessee again.

Saffire, 230 Franklin Rd., Franklin, TN 37064; (615) 599-4995; saffirerestaurant.com; American; $$$. Housed inside The Factory, a 12-building space and former stove factory transformed into a shopping, art gallery, theater, and dining space, Saffire Restaurant offers rustic sophistication with its exposed brick walls, worn table-tops, and mismatched chairs. Upon entering, you'll find an old fac-tory windowpane-turned-art piece with blue glass in place of clear panes and single blue lightbulbs hanging over the bar. Much of the cooking happens over Tennessee hickory in an open kitchen at the back of the room. On the menu, you'll find a strong representa-tion of seafood including oysters on the half shell and favorites like the grilled or blackened fish of the day over grits and topped with tasso meunière or the pan-seared salmon with Jones Mill Farm lemon marmalade and farmers' market vegetables. Open for nearly a decade, this restaurant is owned by TomKats, the company that caters movie sets and also owns **The Southern Steak & Oyster**

(p. 43) in downtown Nashville. On Tuesday and Sunday nights, bottles of wine are half off.

Sol, 403 Main St., Franklin, TN 37064; (615) 538-6021; solonmain .com; Mexican; $$. One of the most refreshing aspects of this restaurant is a menu that doesn't overwhelm with too many choices. Expect fresh ingredients and authentic flavors such as the simple but genuine guacamole prepared tableside with avocado, serrano chile, lime, and cilantro. Look for the handmade beef tamales in tomato sauce as well as empanadas with mushrooms, cheese, and Guajillo sauce. As for entrees there's Lomito en Mole Poblano, a

grilled pork tenderloin with a sauce of 32 ingredients; scallops with mango salad and avocado rice; *cochinita pibil,* pork roasted for 8 hours in Yucatán spices served with sour-orange *mojo,* poblano rice, and fresh tortillas; and several salads such as the *tres colores* salad with Oaxacan cheese, tomato, avocado, cilantro, and balsamic chimichurri. The restaurant shares space with Chef-Owner Jason McConnell's **55 South** (p. 246) restaurant in the warm vibe of an exposed-brick building in Franklin's historic downtown. And while you'll find margaritas, of course, the bartenders here can also help you choose among more than 100 tequilas for sipping.

Sopapilla's, 1109 Davenport Blvd., Franklin, TN 37064; (615) 794-9989; sopapillas.com; New Mexican; $$. Owner Steve Dale grew up in Phoenix and Albuquerque but came to Nashville in the 1990s for music. He spent months perfecting his salsa that he would take on tour when he played bass with artists like Carrie Underwood and Little Big Town. He also threw "fiestas" after shows for his band-mates, and the concept for his Franklin restaurant developed over about a 3-year period in the back of a tour bus. Dale considers himself somewhat of an educator on New Mexican cuisine with his restaurant. The namesake sopapillas, for example, often arrive midmeal in New Mexico, like we might have biscuits in the South. He serves them gratis here after the meal with honey for drizzling. Another authentic dish on the menu includes the blue-corn chicken enchiladas with a fried egg on top. You'll also find green-corn tamales, huevos rancheros, grilled mahimahi, and New York strip seasoned with Hatch green chile and served with black beans, rice, cara-melized onions, and a grilled poblano chile. As for the restau-rant, it's located in a neighborhoody work-live-play development and has popular front-patio seating as well as a relaxed modern vibe inside the restaurant.

Wild Ginger, 101 Market Exchange Ct., Cool Springs, Franklin, TN 37067; (615) 778-0081; dinewildginger.com; Asian/Fusion; $$$. Wild Ginger thankfully brings a bit of independence to a sea of chain restaurants in the Cool Springs area. The contemporary fusion restaurant has floor-to-ceiling windows in the front room that give it an open feel and allow for lots of natural light, as does the open kitchen and sushi bar. Co-owned by Andrew Siao and John Chen, former owner of Grand China, and with Malaysian chef Ken Teoh in the kitchen, you can find miso seabass, braised short ribs, and the "crazy cow" sushi roll—a tempura shrimp roll topped with filet mignon. The food comes divided among the lunch, dinner, and sushi menu, and it does bring together a worldly mix from tandoori halibut with brussels sprouts, purple cauliflower, melon chutney, and butter-caper beurre blanc as well as Caribbean lamb rack with jerk marinade, tempura yam, and jalapeño-corn slaw. You'll even find an Asian Smoked Reuben made of Szechuan-smoked corned beef, spicy kraut, swiss cheese, grilled pineapple, pickled cucumbers, tomatoes, and Sriracha Russian dressing. Brunch is served on Sunday, and the outdoor patio often hosts live bands.

Wild Iris, 127 Franklin Rd., Brentwood, TN 37027; (615) 370-0871; wildirisrestaurant.com; Bistro; $$. A favorite neighborhood restaurant in Brentwood, Wild Iris is a sister restaurant to **The Yellow Porch** (p. 176) in Berry Hill. Both spots have an independent vibe with fresh food. At Wild Iris, choose the outdoor patio or dine inside over sophisticated but casual black tablecloths or at the bar with its walls of wine behind it like artwork. The menu offers bistro fare with a few nods to the South like the fried green tomatoes with goat cheese, pepper jelly, and arugula or the spiced, brown sugar–glazed pork chop with sweet chile fried rice cake, Szechuan green beans, and mango ponzu sauce. But it's also a place to grab a lighter bite at lunch or dinner such as the homemade daily soups or the arugula salad

with sorghum-Tabasco vinaigrette, orange-scented beet and carrot relish, mandarin oranges, sage goat cheese, and candied pecans.

Landmarks

Mere Bulles, 5201 Maryland Way, Brentwood, TN 37027; (615) 467-1945; merebulles.com; American/Southern; $$$. Mere Bulles, translated as "Mother Bubbles," is the nickname of Michele Bouvier, a French woman who had a fondness for champagne and ran a popular restaurant in Charleston after becoming widowed during the Civil War. Today Mere Bulles, opened by the great-great-niece of Mother Bubbles, lives on as a restaurant in a historic plantation-style home in Brentwood wedged among the more modern Maryland Farms development. Out front the home has white columns, brick walls, and black shutters around the windows. Diners can be seated on the 2nd level veranda or inside among a varied collection of dining rooms—some of which are divided by french doors. The menu is sophisticated but comfortable with options like Charleston she-crab bisque, filet mignon, rack of lamb, prime rib, seared scallops, herb-crusted salmon, and shrimp and grits with buttermilk and goat cheese grits creamed with country ham and fresh spinach. The property is a popular spot for wedding parties.

Meat-and-Threes

City Cafe, 330 Franklin Rd., #250, Brentwood, TN 37027; (615) 373-5555; $. Longtime meat-and-three legend Hap Townes, of the Hap Townes restaurant, started in the restaurant business as a young boy when his father ran a pie-wagon food cart that began in the 1920s. So when the current owner of City Cafe, Jerry Cunningham, asked his advice about opening a meat-and-three, Hap did his best to talk him out of it. Cunningham wouldn't hear of it though, and so with Hap's advice—after all—he serves meat-and-three food every weekday to the folks of Brentwood at City Cafe. The menu changes regularly but might include catfish, fried chicken, meatloaf, and vegetables such as greens, fried okra, carrot raisin salad, and the sides that sort of qualify as vegetables, such as mashed potatoes and macaroni and cheese. Sit at the community table if you'd like to make a new friend. And as often the case with meat-and-threes, you never know who you might meet—from politicians to truck drivers to musicians.

The Daily Dish, 2205 Hillsboro Rd., Franklin, TN 37069; (615) 791-1255; dailydishtn.com; $. Though it's under the meat-and-three category this restaurant spruces up the steam table with a sophisticated and contemporary flair. While you'll find standbys like country fried steak, pot roast, meatloaf, and chicken and dumplings, you'll also find pecan- or coconut-encrusted fried chicken, tilapia, roast pork loin, and gourmet sandwiches and salads like the roasted turkey breast salad with pecan-encrusted sweet potato cake on mixed greens with apple-cranberry chutney, bacon, and maple-cider vinaigrette. The menu changes regularly, but the options just go on and on including green bean casserole as well as brussels sprouts or traditional cold-salad side dishes like ambrosia and broccoli salads. Chef Sean Begin has a commitment to fresh ingredients with down-home style, but he also has a background that includes the **Capitol Grille** (p. 28) at the Hermitage Hotel downtown and the **Copper Kettle** (p. 55), which he opened, making for a fabulous combination. Sunday brunch and catering are also available.

Dotson's Restaurant, 99 E. Main St., Franklin, TN 37064; (615) 794-2805; $. They say you can't judge a book by its cover, but I think it's probably safe to judge Dotson's by its sign. The neon sign is as old-school as the menu with its fried chicken, meatloaf, chicken and dumplings, and barbecued chicken and pork. Sides? They got 'em, and it might be hard to pick just three—turnip greens, fried okra, green beans, white beans, baked apples, and mashed potatoes to name a few as well as retro choices like Jell-O. You'll have your choice of biscuits or cornbread, but try to save room for dessert, too, including the scratch-made banana pudding, cobblers, and pies like coconut, chocolate, caramel, and chess. The atmosphere feels old-school, too, with a drop ceiling and paneling bedecked in menus and headshots signed by country stars. Cash only (and I couldn't imagine it any other way).

Specialty Stores, Markets & Producers

Franklin Farmers' Market, 230 Franklin Rd., Franklin, TN 37064; franklinfarmersmarket.com. What started as just a handful of farmers gathering on Saturday to sell their wares has grown to about 100 vendors—70 percent of them farmers and all of them local—in just 10 years. This market takes place at The Factory, a collection of historic brick buildings that once housed a packaged foods facility, and it draws a loyal crowd to this bustling spot with live music and plenty of sampling. You'll find seasonal crops like fragrant peaches in the summertime and bins of tomatoes, stalks of corn, and lettuces as well as cheeses, eggs, meats, flowers, and natural products. The market is open year-round but with limited hours during the winter months. A smaller branch of the Franklin Farmers' Market also takes place on Tuesday across from The Factory at the Park at Harlinsdale Farm.

Nashville Drink Culture

I once spotted these words scrawled onto a blackboard sandwich sign outside Robert's Western World on Lower Broadway: "Welcome to Nashville, y'all. It's time to drink!" But even beyond the honkytonks, where you'll certainly hear lots of clanking beer bottles between songs, this city has a burgeoning craft beer scene (and several beer festivals to celebrate it), several new distilleries, and creative cocktail bars that keep the libations flowing. In 2009, Tennessee state laws were changed, allowing distilleries (which includes breweries by definition) to operate in counties with liquor by the drink. Since then, at least 12 applications have been filed. At the time of this writing, for example, a couple of breweries remain in the works including Broadcast Brewing Company and Fat Bottom Brewery as well as the first Nashville Whiskey Festival.

Breweries & Distilleries

Blackstone Restaurant & Brewery, 1918 West End Ave., Nashville, TN 37203; (615) 327-9969; blackstonebrewery.com. This brewery and pub has been a fixture along West End Avenue for nearly 20 years. Inside the bar area, the dark wood and votives on tables give it a pub vibe, and the back nook—with its comfortable chairs, bookshelves, and chessboard—is the best spot in the house to settle in with a flight of beers. Behind the bar you'll see the stainless-steel vats where the beer is brewed, and the arched brick doorways on either side of the room open up into more of a rustic beer-hall feel with tiled floors and high ceilings of exposed ductwork. Ask for a tour of the brewery if you'd like, and for food, you can expect burgers, sandwiches, wood-fired brick-oven pizzas, and entrees like steaks, grilled salmon, and Cajun pasta. Blackstone opened a new brewing and bottling facility in the summer of 2011. Bottled beers now available at bars and stores throughout Middle Tennessee include the Nut Brown Ale, St. Charles Porter, the A.P.A. (American-style Pale Ale), and the Chaser Pale.

Collier and McKeel/SPEAKeasy Spirits, 900 44th Ave. North, Nashville, TN 37212; collierandmckeel.com; speakeasy-spirits.com. Mike Williams's family came to Tennessee in the 1790s after the Whiskey Rebellion, and his family is steeped in the whiskey-making business. It had long been a dream of Mike's to someday make whiskey, too, and so when he mentioned it (again) on his 50th birthday, his wife turned to him and said, "Either do it or shut up." Five years later, you can visit Mike at his small-batch distillery in West Nashville where he makes Tennessee whiskey the traditional way with a sour mash that goes through a charcoal mellowing—or Lincoln County process—before aging in small barrels. He shares space at the open no-frills warehouse with Speakeasy, a marketing company and makers of Whisper Creek, a Tennessee sipping cream that blends Collier & McKeel whiskey with cream, sugar, and flavors of sorghum and pawpaw. One sip of Whisper Creek over ice or in a cup of coffee and you may never drink Bailey's again. Tours of the facility and both processes are available.

Corsair Artisan Distillery, 1200 Clinton St., Nashville, TN 37203; (615) 321-9109; corsairartisan.com. Located in Marathon Village, the historic collection of brick buildings that once housed an automobile plant, Corsair brings to Nashville an alternative craft spirits micro-distillery with products such as Rasputin Hopped Whiskey, Triple Smoke Whiskey, Pumpkin Spice Moonshine, Red Absinthe, Quinoa Whiskey, and Barrel-Aged Gin. At Corsair, which means "pirate gentleman," you can sample spirits in the sophisticated tasting room with its black-and-white bar or enjoy a pint of locally brewed beer from **Yazoo** (p. 264) or **Jackalope** (opposite) across the hall. In between the two, you'll find an outdoor courtyard with tables under strings of white lightbulbs for hanging out. Take a tour of the facility (check the website for availability first), and you'll learn about the process involved in making spirits, including Corsair's stainless-steel vats, but you'll also see the copper still that operated legally pre-Prohibition, then almost fell to the ax of a revenuer, then operated illegally on a farmer's property, and finally fell into the hands of Corsair owners rather than a moonshine museum. And now who wouldn't want to drink from that?

Jackalope Brewing Company, 701 8th Ave. South, Nashville, TN 37203; (615) 873-4313; jackalopebrew.com. Perhaps it's apropos that the women behind this brewery met over a drinking game. They were headed for careers in law and business, but the bond over beer pong lasted, and the pair started a brewery after relocating from the Northeast to Nashville. The taproom is open Thurs through Sat only from 4 to 8 p.m., but it's decorated like a kitschy hunting lodge and draws a mix of interesting folks looking for a fun place to have a couple beers during the happy hours. For a snack, order one of the cheese plates that pairs artisan cheeses put together by local cheesemonger Kathleen Cotter of **The Bloomy Rind** (p. 99) with jam or other accoutrements like locally made Bathtub  Gin marmalade. Or grab a bite from one of the food trucks that usually park outside the taproom on the days that it's open. As of 2012, Jackalope's beers like Thunder Road, an ale named for Davy Crockett's fictional wife, also are available in several local bars and restaurants.

Yazoo Brewing Company, 910 Division St., Nashville, TN 37203; (615) 891-4649; yazoobrew.com. When Linus Hall came to Nashville from Mississippi in 1996, most of the tire engineer's beer experience came out of his basement homebrew operation. But after craft-brewing education through the American Brewer's Guild and an internship at Brooklyn Brewery, Hall opened Yazoo Brewing Company in 2003. Community support poured in as his Pale Ale poured into pub glasses. The darker Dos Perros, with its caramel flavor, and the banana-citrus flavor of his Hefeweizen also gained fame. And Hall and company continue to experiment, giving us options like the beer named Sue with a black label (just like Johnny Cash); the full-bodied smoked imperial porter has a slight cherry finish. Yazoo's beers are now widely available at bars and restaurants across Nashville, and the taproom is open Thurs through Sat, limited hours. Brewery tours also are available on Sat beginning at 2:30 p.m. and running every hour until 6:30 p.m. The $7 cost will get you a guided look at how the beers are made as well as a Yazoo pint glass and samples of the beers during the tour.

Craft Cocktails

Holland House Bar & Refuge, 935 W. Eastland Ave., Nashville, TN 37206; (615) 262-4190; hollandhousebarandrefuge.com. It's a gorgeous spot for a cocktail, with chandeliers hanging from exposed ductwork. And handsome bartenders in suspenders will make you a drink behind the square bar that sits like a centerpiece in the front room. But the creativity in these cocktails is gorgeous, too. The menu changes regularly, but you might find it divided into sections: House Classics, Old School, Beer, Wine, and Spirits. The Old Schools might include pisco sour, mai tai, and Dark & Stormy, but rather than typical tequila and grapefruit in La Paloma, for example, the version here is made with tequila reposado, smashed lime, cinnamon-infused St. Germain liqueur, and grapefruit soda. As for Holland House classics, the Black Lemon Old-Fashioned brings together bourbon, smashed lemon and blackberry with honey syrup, and lemon bitters. And if you really want to get the party started, try a $45 Knockout Punch for the table, including the Haymaker #2 with Weller 107 Bourbon, strawberry-chocolate tea, fresh lemonade, and phosphated citrus soda. (For information on Holland House as a restaurant, see p. 73)

No. 308, 407 Gallatin Ave., Nashville, TN 37206; (615) 650-7344; bar308.com. Bartenders Alexis Soler and Ben Clemons met at the Tales of the Cocktail convention in New Orleans, and not long after, Alexis proposed to Ben in room number 308 of the Ace Hotel in New York City. They moved to Nashville and opened Bar 308 after working at clubs in New York City and Miami. But rather than a speakeasy, Clemons once called it a speakhard, because while there are expertly made cocktails on the menu with fresh juices and house-made soda, it's also the type of place where you can order a can of beer or a Writer's Block shot like the Tom Robbins, a shot of mescal, or the Richard Brautigan, a shot of whiskey with a sugared watermelon chaser. The dark space with banquettes along the walls of the room, a long elevated bar in the center, and a well-edited collection of mismatched furniture draws a crowd that might draw East Nashville neighbors to Dan Auerbach of The Black Keys. The menu changes with the seasons, but look for classic cocktails as well as specialties like the Mickey Fin (gin, cardamom, grapefruit, and maple syrup).

The Patterson House, 1711 Division St., Nashville, TN 37203; (615) 636-7724; thepattersonnashville.com. Maybe it's the scent of the house-made bitters that mixologists in dapper speakeasy style drip into drinks like chemists, or a server who will seat you in this space—with a square bar as focal point in the middle of the room. But make no mistake: Even though it has sophistication, 7 types of twice-filtered ice, and fresh ingredients, it is still a bar. The menu

is divided according to spirit, and while it changes, you'll find creative options as well as perfectly made standards. One to look for is the Juliet & Romeo; created by consultant Toby Maloney of The Violet Hour in Chicago it brings together gin, cucumber, lime, rosewater, and a smack of mint in a dainty *coupe* glass. Though the cocktails are the main draw, the snacks on the menu are worth checking out as well (see The Patterson House entry in the Gulch/Midtown section of this book, p. 128, for more information about the food.)

Classic Honky-Tonks

Robert's Western World, 416 Broadway, Nashville, TN 37203; (615) 244-9552; robertswesternworld.com. This narrow bar with shelves of boots lining one wall is without a doubt one of the best honky-tonks in town. It's where you might find the house band led by bolero-wearing bar owner Jesse Lee Jones and his Brazil Billy Band blazing through traditional country tunes by the likes of Johnny Cash, Hank Sr., and Marty Robbins rather than newer country. Jesse, who came to the United States from Brazil without knowing a word of English, eventually bought the bar from longtime owner Robert Moore in 1999. There's a dance floor up front and a balcony level with a great overall view of the place on the second floor. If you're hungry, order the Recession Special—a fried bologna sandwich, bag of chips, moon pie, and can of PBR for $5. And on busy weekends when there's a line in front, do like the locals and enter through the back door on the second level that opens into the alley between the bar and the Ryman Auditorium.

The Station Inn, 402 12th Ave. South, Nashville, TN 37203; (615) 255-3307; stationinn.com. This plain gray cinder-block building sits like a bastion of a different era smack in the heart of the hip Gulch. But here, under the low drop ceiling, you'll hear some of the best bluegrass in the city. The Station Inn opened in 1974, and it continues to welcome guests through its red front door 7 nights a week. There's no charge on Sunday for the Bluegrass Jam—literally an open jam session, but on Tuesday, make a reservation (it sells out regularly) to the acclaimed Doyle & Debbie Show, a parody duet that both idolizes and makes fun of country music. Other nights, longtime visitor Vince Gill has been known to jump on stage with the Time Jumpers, and Dolly Parton even joined Nickel Creek's Chris Thile. The space is small and dark and the chairs mismatched, but the music makes up for all else.

Tootsie's Orchid Lounge, 422 Broadway, Nashville, TN 37203; (615) 726-0463; tootsies.net. Long before Kid Rock and Pamela Anderson were married on the stage here, Willie Nelson and Kris Kristofferson wrote songs in this lilac-colored building on Lower Broadway. Other early visitors include Patsy Cline, Mel Tillis, and Waylon Jennings. Loretta Lynn once said her husband would hang out at Tootsie's when she performed at the **Grand Ole Opry** (p. 275). Indeed, it was like tradition to sneak across the alley and through the back door for a drink during breaks. Originally called Mom's, Tootsie Bess opened this bar in 1960 and changed the name when it was painted purple. These days there are two stages—one downstairs and another stage upstairs where musicians perform covers of popular country music. And if you miss the original Tootsie's on Lower Broadway, you'll have one last chance at its outpost at the airport. Just don't expect it to have quite the character of the original.

Watering Holes & Dive Bars

The Red Door Saloon, 1010 Forrest Ave., Nashville, TN 37206; (615) 226-7660; thereddoorsaloon.com. The mix of company at this busy East Nashville bar is as eclectic as the decor. A few of the walls are lined in leftover wine corks, for example, and there's also a photo of Marilyn Monroe among the bric-a-brac, flying skeletons, and a bike hanging upside down from the ceiling. You'll find east-side hipsters, bikers, day regulars who have lasted into the night, and students crossing the river for something different—all swilling some beers in this little house trimmed in purple and lit inside with red light. The patio out front  with its high-top tables fills up on warmer days and for 2-for-1 specials (on Sunday and Tuesday). The Red Door also is right in the heart of East Nashville's Five Points and within walking distance of many other bars and restaurants. The original location has a different atmosphere being wedged between Music Row and Vanderbilt University on the west side of town at 1816 Division St., Nashville, TN 37203; (615) 320-6525.

The Springwater Supper Club and Lounge, 115 27th Ave. North, Nashville, TN 37203; (615) 320-0345. Well, there's not much "supper" about it—in a sophisticated sense at least. This is the dive-iest of dive bars in town. Barbecue is sold next door, and it's located behind a McDonald's off West End Avenue and near Centennial Park. But the music is often stellar and eclectic, from indie to hard-core to spoken word. Bands play before a fringe of red Mylar curtain on a low stage. In the room where the main bar keeps eclectic groups of folks entertained, there's a pool table and jukebox and screened in porch off of the room with picnic tables. The place has a past as a speakeasy in the 1920s and a rumored gambling spot for Jimmy Hoffa. More recently Wayne Cohen of the Flaming Lips was spotted with Ke$ha when he was in town working with the Nashville pop singer on her new album. You never know what might happen here. But bring dollar bills, y'all. It's cash only.

3 Crow Bar, 1024 Woodland St., Nashville, TN 37206; (615) 262-3345; 3crowbar.com. It's been a watering hole for neighborhood folks in the heart of East Nashville's Five Points since 1949, but it's had many names and makeovers before 3 Crow, and it stays steadily busy drawing a mix of regulars, sports fans watching big games on the TVs, and neighborhood hipsters. You'll find darts and foosball as well as two patios—one enclosed and another on a raised porch that is shaded with trees. In the main room of the bar, the windows roll up on warmer days. And even though it stays busy, the bartenders serve drinks quickly from a wall of taps, coolers of bottles, and a frosty machine for bushwackers, a favorite and rather

legendary alcoholic chocolate milk shake of sorts. It's a dark, smoky bar setting for sure, but if you're hungry try the burgers made with free-range, grass-fed, local beef braised in Yuengling lager, topped with artisanal Kenny's Farmhouse Cheese and served on locally made **Provence** (p. 196) brioche rolls. There's live trivia every Thurs at 8 p.m. and 2-for-1 on Sunday and Wednesday when you might see members of the East Nasty running club as they often end their weekly runs here for a beer.

Villager Tavern, 1719 21st Ave. South, Nashville, TN 37212; (615) 298-3020. This is where you might find some serious dart nerds—not that there's anything wrong with that. Several dart boards line the wall of the backroom, which makes it a good spot for tournaments. Elsewhere the walls are plastered with photos of people who have visited the place. The bar in the front part of the room stays busy, too, as it's located near Vanderbilt and sits in the heart of Hillsboro Village. If it's your birthday, you can have a free drink (at your own risk) out of a dog bowl big enough to quench the thirst of three Great Danes. The Villager hosts a motley mix of regulars with the students and darts sportsmen or locals waiting for their movie time at the nearby Belcourt Theatre. But if you don't like smoke with your pint of Guinness, you might want to pick another bar.

The Barn at the Loveless Cafe, 8400 Highway TN 100, Nashville, TN 37221; (615) 724-7991; lovelessbarn.com; music cityroots.com. The barn out behind the **Loveless Cafe** (p. 283) off Highway TN 100 is spanking new compared to the namesake restaurant in front of it. While the Loveless opened about 60 years ago, the barn threw open its doors in 2009. Still it hosts one of the highest quality weekly music experiences in the Nashville area. The live radio show broadcast every Wednesday from the barn—called *Music City Roots*—often has a more organic feel than other parts of commercial country Nashville. Recent acts have included David Mead, Kim Richey, Ben Sollee, Alejandro Escovedo & The Sensitive Boys, Tristen, and the Martin Family Circus. But like the Opry, it offers you short sets by each performer, giving you just enough to whet your appetite for more. And speaking of appetites, you can purchase fried chicken, biscuits, barbecue, and moonshine drinks (as well as beer, of course) during the *Music City Roots* shows. The atmosphere is stellar, too—you'll sit in folding chairs under dripping lights as if you've been invited to a really cool wedding reception, as the barn sometimes hosts those too.

The Bluebird Cafe, 4104 Hillsboro Pike, Nashville, TN 37215; (615) 383-1461; bluebirdcafe.com. This world-famous listening room holds down an unassuming spot in a Green Hills strip mall. Just look for the blue awning among the brick and you'll find the 100-seat venue that has launched the careers of many, including Kathy Mattea and Garth Brooks. Most nights at the Bluebird feature three or four songwriters taking turns playing and accompanying one another in front of twinkling white Christmas lights and photos of the many musicians who come through the place in all manner of genres. Reservations are strongly recommended, though a few seats are kept open as first-come-first-served for the early shows. Also know there is a $7 food and beverage minimum per seat, but the menu is fairly varied, from baked brie and hummus and edamame to sandwiches like smoked pork with pickled green tomato, Jack Daniel's barbecue sauce and house-made chips. Only serious listeners should apply. Talk during a song at this spot, and you will definitely get shushed.

Exit/In, 2208 Elliston Place, Nashville, TN 37203; (615) 321-3340; exitin.com. The Exit/In has been hosting bands since 1971, and many of the visitors have had their names scrawled on walls both inside and out—The Allman Brothers, The Police, R.E.M., Johnny Cash, The Ramones, The Kings of Leon, Lyle Lovett, and many more. Sitting in the midst of a section of town near Vanderbilt University dubbed the Rock Block, the venue holds about 500, and is absolutely no-frills. Painted solid black, it's hard to miss, and if you check the FAQs section of the website, you'll find this answer regarding its paint: "It is a more slimming color, and we have put on a little weight over the years." Don't expect to find a meal at the Exit/In either unless you have a hankering for a microwaved Hot Pocket. But you will, however, be treated to fine music in a legendary venue with stellar sound.

The Family Wash, 2038 Greenwood Ave., Nashville, TN 37206; (615) 226-6070; familywash.com. This spot also has a mention in the East Nashville section of this book (p. 69), because it's nearly as much a restaurant as a live music venue. And I say "nearly," because even though the shepherd's pie is worth a trip alone, the music is even more so. It's a tiny room at a quiet corner of East Nashville with just a few seats at low tables, high-tops, and along the bar, but it hosts some of Nashville's best talents. There's often a Jazz Diner Series on Saturday nights as well as the Sons of Zevon, a group of musicians and guests vocalists choosing a year of focus in the 1970s. And beyond all of that, it's just a gorgeous, interesting, funky little room with a folk art American flag on the wall as backdrop. Underneath exposed duct work, bulbs of drooping lights and hanging paper lanterns, it's one of the most romantic and rock and roll combinations in Nashville.

The 5 Spot, 1006 Forrest Ave., Nashville, TN 37206; (615) 650-9333; the5spotlive.com. Located in the midst of East Nashville's Five Points, this little box of a club offers plenty of character in its lineup before a red-curtained stage. *GQ* magazine, for example, called its Monday Night "Keep on Movin' Dance Party," a mix of old-school rockabilly and R & B, the most stylish party in America. The monthly Boom Bap also draws a packed house for its hip-hop. Then other nights it might be country, singer-songwriters, punk, hipster square dances, or just straight-up rock and roll. Other themed nights include a $2 Tuesday, which features $2 **Yazoo** (p. 264) beers, $2 hot dogs, and a $2 cover to hear a group of bands and musicians. On Wednesday there's the Old Time Jam, which brings pickers out of the woodwork to literally stand in little groups throughout the room. And if you need a break from the live music, there are plenty of other watering holes in the neighborhood including the **Red Door Saloon** (p. 269) next door.

The Grand Ole Opry, 2804 Opryland Dr., Nashville, TN 37214; (615) 871-OPRY; opry.com. It's the world's longest-running live radio program, and even if you don't like country music, this show is a treat. You might also hear bluegrass, comedy, gospel, and more by cast members as well as guests. I like that the 2-hour show mixes up the talent into segments, so you might—depending on the night and the lineup—see up to 13 performers include Rascal Flatts, Kellie Pickler, Ronnie Milsap, Ricky Skaggs, Jimmy Dickens, and the Opry Square Dancers, to name a few. While the Opry began in the 1920s, it made its home at the Ryman Auditorium downtown in 1943, and then moved to the Opry House in 1974. Located near the Gaylord Opryland Hotel complex, there's plenty to eat, see, and do in the area about 10 miles from Nashville. But the show is so steeped in tradition that even in its more modern digs it's as if you can still smell the fried chicken that guests used to pack and bring with them to enjoy as they listened and watched.

The Listening Room Cafe, 209 10th Ave. South, Ste. 200, Nashville, TN 37203; (615) 259-3600; listeningroomcafe.com. Singer-songwriter Chris Blair opened The Listening Room Cafe in 2008, and though it draws a crowd at lunch for its menu, the heart of this place is its music. The venue sits inside Cummins Station, a large, redbrick building that dates back to 1907 and now hosts a variety of offices and restaurants. With its 5,200 square feet, The Listening Room Cafe keeps a busy calendar of up-and-coming local acts as well as more established ones. The venue also hosts CD 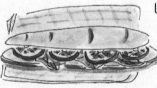 release parties and catered events and offers live, studio-quality audio and visual recordings. It's similar to venues like **The Bluebird Cafe** (p. 272), where there is a $7 food-and-drink minimum purchase per person. But with a menu of specialties like Yazoo Taco Chili made with local beer, gourmet burgers, and pulled pork hoagie topped with slaw and house-made Jack Daniel's barbecue sauce and pickles, you probably won't have any problem reaching that amount. Lounge and couch seating have no minimum purchase.

Mercy Lounge/Cannery Ballroom/The High Watt, 1 Cannery Row, Nashville, TN 37203; (615) 251-3020; mercylounge.com; thehighwatt.com; thecanneryballroom.com. This industrial-looking brick building off 8th Avenue South holds three of Nashville's most popular clubs. The Cannery building, as it's called, operated as a flour mill in the late 1800s and then became a food-processing plant for condiments and jams in the late 1950s. It later became a restaurant before it was transformed yet again to a music venue in the 1980s. The Mercy Lounge area of the building holds about 500 in a room decorated in sultry red and black. A bar in back has pool tables, and a second stage in this building is called The High Watt, the newest of the group having come to pass in 2012. The Cannery, a larger open room (and with less character, in my opinion) holds about 1,000. Recent acts have included singer-songwriter Joe Purdy to indie darling St. Vincent, pop star Uncle Kracker, and smooth R & B operator Mayer Hawthorne.

The Ryman Auditorium, 116 5th Ave. North, Nashville, TN 37219; (615) 889-3060; ryman.com. They call it the "Mother Church of Country Music" and the "Carnegie Hall of the South" as it hosted the **Grand Ole Opry** (p. 275) performers ranging from Houdini to Dolly. Built as an actual church in 1890, they say it has acoustics second only to the Mormon Tabernacle Church in Salt Lake City, Utah. It's where a rambunctious Johnny Cash kicked out the foot lights, and today it hosts everyone from Aretha Franklin to Arcade Fire, The Flaming Lips, Old Crow Medicine Show, The Kings of Leon, and Primus. There's not a bad seat in the house; you'll sit in wooden pews before arched panes of colored glass, and you can bet that performers here will bring their A game. The first time I visited the Ryman, before I lived in Nashville, I stopped to take the tour. But

I worried about the $13 self-guided ticket as I was traveling on budget. The attendant noticed my concern and gave me a friendly Nashville welcome, because when I gave her my money, she just slid a ticket back to me along with my $20 bill and said, "Have a good time, honey."

3rd & Lindsley, 818 3rd Ave. South, Nashville, TN 37210; (615) 259-9891; 3rdandlindsley.com. Named for its location at the cross section of 3rd and Lindsley, this nearly 20-year-old venue looks unassuming in its strip mall space just outside of downtown. And up until 2011, it was a rather small space in which to see live music at mostly high-top tables 7 days a week. After a renovation to expand its capacity, it has hosted the likes of Sheryl Crow, pop-indie acts like Paper Route and First Aid Kit to the Western swing of The Time Jumpers and successful professional songwriters for major acts like Jeffery Steele. The lineup ranges from Nashville acts to more national. Full lunch and dinner menu offers steak, pork chops, fish of the day, spaghetti, and stir-fry as well as sandwiches like meatball subs, Reubens, and burgers. Happy hour is daily until 6 p.m.—$2 longnecks and 2-for-1 well drinks.

Worth the Drive

It would be a big job to include all the restaurants worth driving to from Nashville (and it ultimately depends on how far you're willing to go). But these are some of my favorites both relatively near to town and up to an hour and half away from downtown—Lynchburg, Tennessee, the home of Jack Daniel's distillery.

In this list you'll find meat-and-three fare and barbecue to fine dining, Mediterranean, and tiki-style Polynesian in the heart of Smyrna, Tennessee.

The Beacon Light Tea Room, 6276 Highway TN 100, Bon Aqua, TN 37025; (931) 670-3880; beaconlighttearoom.com; Southern; $. Open since 1936, this restaurant along Highway TN 100 draws regulars for its breakfast, lunch, and dinners of country cooking, such as fried chicken, country ham, green beans, mashed potatoes, fried okra, and redeye and brown gravies. But if anything should encourage you to visit this roadside spot, it's the biscuits. Rather than fat, over-size versions, these biscuits look and taste like something you'd find from home—small enough to warrant more than two, made with lard rather than butter, and served with homemade blackberry and peach preserves. And the atmosphere—though dark and lived-in—feels almost like a trip to church. A painting of Jesus hangs over the coffeemaker, as well as other places throughout the room, and on each table you'll find a plastic loaf of bread holding strips of scripture to read as you wait for your order. Man cannot live on bread alone, you might read, but at the Beacon Light, I wouldn't mind trying.

Cafe Rakka, 71 New Shackle Island Rd., Hendersonville, TN 37075; (615) 824-6264; caferakka.com; Middle Eastern; $$. While Hendersonville offers many reasons to visit (it was Johnny Cash's home after all), Cafe Rakka offers a fresh bite to eat. Riyad Al-Kasem, or Chef Rakka, learned family recipes from his grandmother while growing up in Syria. Check out the hummus bar with toppings for the chickpea-tahini mixture that include garlic, eggplant, and pine nuts, for example, as well as the freshly baked pita bread, homemade yogurt sauce, saffron rice, and marinated beef, lamb, or chicken prepared in the *sajj*, a type of Mediterranean wok. Don't miss the kebab halabi, a mixture of seasoned and grilled ground lamb and beef that Rakka says was his father's favorite. Many other Mediterranean favorites can be had as well from falafel, tabouli, baba ghanoush to shrimp *jalfrezi* cooked with tomato, onion, herbs, and a sauce of citrus, herbs, and olive oil. Chef Rakka often makes appearances on local television as well as the Food Network's *Diners, Drive-Ins, and Dives* with Guy Fieri.

Five Senses, 1602 W. Northfield Blvd., Murfreesboro, TN 37129; (615) 867-4155; fivesensesdining.com; Contemporary; $$$. Culinary Institute of America graduate Mitchell Murphree opened Five Senses with his sister Mollie in 2004, and he blends his culinary-school technique with fresh Southern ingredients. The siblings' grandfather founded a country ham business, so they have Southern food business in their blood. But the room also offers a sophisticated place to dine in Murfreesboro, which holds the campus of Middle Tennessee State University. Though the menu changes regularly, entrees might include braised lamb shank with smashed potatoes, spring vegetables, and mint and lemon gremolata, or pan-roasted organic chicken spiced with cumin and coriander and served with falafel, cucumber yogurt, spinach, roasted red pepper, and tahini drizzle. Lighter bites include grilled whole wheat pizzas with smoked Gouda and bacon, or mozzarella, grilled onions, garlic, and balsamic. The menu at lunch offers more Southern country-cooking options like buttermilk fried chicken with honey mustard, and blackened tilapia with remoulade along with sides like pickled beets, green bean casserole, brussels sprouts with bacon, peppers, and onions. To be closer to the action, ask for a seat at the open kitchen-bar.

Hachland Hill Countryside Retreat, 5396 Rawlings Road, Joelton, TN 37080; (615) 876-1500; hachlandhill.com. Contemporary/Southern; $$$. This retreat has cozy log walls, stone fireplaces and quilts on the beds at its main house and offers additional space at the Tobacco Barn and Springcreek Inn, a separate home down by a brook. But even with the homespun charm, it's the vivacious proprietor, now in her 80s, who really makes it special. Innkeeper Phila Hach hosted the first television cooking show in the South (before Julia Child even) with guests like June Carter and Duncan Hines. Hach's mother, a home demonstrator, taught her about food from an early age, but Hach picked up more worldly knowledge while working as a flight attendant when she asked chefs in the Savoy in London or the George V in Paris if she could cook with them. "How many times did you get turned down?" I once asked her. "Never," she said. She also once cooked for the entire delegation of the United Nations (and later wrote one of her 17 cookbooks from the experience). Today her food continues to have international flair. She might serve you sushi or dainty European-inspired vegetable creations—but she'll also serve you fried chicken, biscuits, and slices of chess pie.

Kleer-Vu Lunchroom, 226 S. Highland Ave., Murfreesboro, TN 37130; (615) 896-0520; Meat-and-Three; $. When the subject of meat-and-threes comes up in this area—as it often does with most of us staking a claim on a favorite—Kleer-Vu almost always makes it into the mix. Located in a plain white building and former neighborhood grocery, it has held three generations of family members making soulful food like fried chicken, turnip greens, mac and cheese, chicken and dressing, barbecue, and hot water corn-bread with each plate. For dessert you might choose a fruit cobbler or chess pie. You'll need to take a tray (some inscribed with the Decherd Elementary School 1974–75 insignia) and take a place in line at the steam table. Kleer-Vu draws a diverse mix of people, as meat-and-threes tend to do, from Middle Tennessee State University college students to professionals, blue-collar folk, and celebrities like Rubin "Hurricane" Carter.

Loveless Cafe, 8400 TN 100, Nashville, TN 37221; (615) 646-9700; lovelesscafe.com; Southern; $. This place is just about as famous as any restaurant can be in the Nashville area. For more than 60 years, it has offered travelers a home-style meal along TN 100 (it used to be a hotel as well) and at one end of the Natchez Trace Parkway that goes straight down to the Mississippi coast. The food and vibe remain largely the same with a menu of famous fried chicken, turnip greens, meatloaf, mac and cheese, mashed potatoes, creamed corn, barbecue from the nearby smokehouse, and, of course, the famous biscuits served with house-made preserves and, upon request, a side of sorghum. Open for breakfast, too, the country ham with eggs, or fried chicken and eggs are legendary along with specialties like redeye gravy and hash brown casserole. Also don't miss the desserts by Alisa Huntsman—banana pudding (she makes her own vanilla wafers), fruit cobblers, and pies, including the Key lime, which has a crust that involves baking sheets of chocolate and almond biscotti to combine with more nuts and butter. Enter from the front porch bedecked with hanging plants into a hardwood-floored foyer with walls covered in signed celebrity headshots. See the recipe for **Loveless Cafe's Meatloaf** on p. 297.

Martin's Bar-B-Que Joint, 7238 Nolensville Rd., Nolensville, TN 37135; (615) 776-1856; martinsbbqjoint.com; Barbecue; $. When visitors ask me where to find the best barbecue in Nashville, I suggest they go ahead and drive just a bit farther to Nolensville. Pat Martin, a former bonds trader but country boy through and through, learned the art of whole hog barbecue during his college years from elders in West Tennessee. These days, he's often nationally recognized in magazines or receiving regular invitations to New York City's Big Apple Barbecue Block Party and hosting Guy Fieri of *Diners, Drive-Ins, and Dives*. But Martin keeps it real at this simple barbecue joint with Jimmy Buffett and Waylon Jennings on the sound system and walls chock-full with posters of everyone from Daisy Duke to the cast of *Lonesome Dove*. The Redneck Taco is famous—a peppery corn cake piled with pulled pork, sauce, and slaw.  But really you can't go wrong from ribs to brisket, smoked turkey, and wings with Alabama white sauce. Check the restaurant's Facebook or Twitter to hear when the whole hog hits the smoker for a more than 20-hour turn over low heat and hickory smoke. Then head down to watch and drink beer around the pit.

Miss Mary Bobo's Boarding House, 295 Main St., Lynchburg, TN 37352; (931) 759-7394; Southern; $$$. Located in a grand old home near the main square of Lynchburg, Tennessee, and the home of Jack Daniel's distillery, this restaurant opened as a traveler's hotel in 1867. Jack Daniel himself was a regular. Then Miss Mary Bobo ran the place until her death in 1983, one month shy of her 102nd birthday; these days the woman in charge is Lynne Tolley, a descendant of Jack. The restaurant offers two or three seatings a day, depending on demand, and reservations are required. Guests gather in the foyer and parlors of the old home until the dinner bell rings, and then diners are seated at communal tables for family-style meals of fried chicken, meatloaf, green beans, mashed potatoes, fried okra, macaroni and cheese, apples drunken with local product, and for dessert, pies such as chess pie with cream whipped with more local product. A hostess seated at each table keeps conversation going and shares history about the restaurant.

Omni Hut, 618 S. Lowry St., Smyrna, TN 37167; (615) 459-4870; omnihut.com; Polynesian; $$. Who needs Trader Vic's when you've got this mom-and-pop tiki hut? Situated in Smyrna, about 25 miles from Nashville, it's been a fixture since 1960. It was founded by the late Maj. Jim Walls, who worked in the kitchen of a local Chinese restaurant while stationed in Hawaii. Walls joined the Army Air Corps at age 20 and was stationed at Pearl Harbor in 1941 when the base was attacked by the Japanese. He opened the Omni Hut after retiring from Smyrna's Sewart Air Base. Bedecked in rattan and bamboo, the Omni Hut offers the complete experience with a menu that includes full luau dinners. Choose the Tahitian

Feast, for example, and you'll be treated to egg flower soup, Bora Bora (bacon-wrapped pineapple), wonton soup, crab rangoon, egg roll, rumaki (bacon-wrapped chicken livers and water chestnuts), Polynesian Pit Ribs, beef teriyaki, shrimp Panamanian, Tahitian Tid Bits, sweet-and-pungent pork, chicken chow mein, and shrimp fried rice. Hawaiian, Hong Kong, and Samoan luau dinners are available as well as steaks and kebabs and seafood dishes. And the teriyaki sauce on these dishes isn't store-bought; it's made from fresh ginger and honey, and you can buy it by the bottle.

Recipes

Celery & Blue Cheese Soup

Guerry McComas's Celery & Blue Cheese soup has earned a following at The Yellow Porch restaurant over the years for its blend of rich cheese with fresh, light celery flavor. But then again, much of McComas's food has a following at the quaint little restaurant behind the garden in the eclectic Berry Hill.

Makes about 2 quarts

2 cups chopped celery
1 cup chopped onion
1 tablespoon butter
Dash of salt
2 cups water
2 cups milk

1 cup heavy cream
4 ounces blue cheese
8 ounces cream cheese
1½ teaspoons celery salt
Salt and black pepper to taste

Sweat the celery and onion with the butter. Sprinkle a dash of salt on the vegetables, cover and cook over low heat until the vegetables are translucent.

Add the water, milk, and cream and bring to a simmer.

Add the cheeses and process in a blender. It may be best to allow the soup to cool a bit before blending or the heat can cause pressure to build up and blow the top off the blender, sending hot soup all over your kitchen and yourself.

Strain the soup through a large mesh strainer, and add the celery salt and seasonings to taste.

Courtesy of Executive Chef Guerry McComas Jr. of The Yellow Porch (p. 176)

Butternut Squash Soup with Coconut Milk, Curry, Chantilly, Toasted Almonds & Chives

Foodies throughout Nashville patiently set their oven timers in anticipation of Hal Holden-Bache's Lockeland Table Community Kitchen & Bar, which opened in August 2012. The former chef at Eastland Cafe (p. 68), Holden-Bache has earned a following for his honest, fresh bistro cuisine. He also has taken top honors repeatedly at the Our Kids Soup Sunday chef competition, and here he gives one of his winning recipes.

Makes 8 to 12 servings

1 small onion, diced small

2 cloves garlic, roughly chopped

1 shallot, roughly chopped

2 large butternut squash, peeled, seeded, and diced large

3 tablespoons grapeseed oil

Kosher salt and white pepper to taste

½ cup white wine

1 quart vegetable stock, plus additional for thinning if necessary

1 (14-ounce) can coconut milk

10 dashes Tabasco sauce

Chantilly (as garnish, see recipe below)

Toasted sliced almonds (as garnish)

Thinly slices chives (as garnish)

Over medium heat, sweat the onion, garlic, shallot, and squash with the grapeseed oil. Stir and cook for at least 5 minutes; season with salt and pepper as you cook.

Deglaze the pot with white wine and reduce for 1 minute. Add vegetable stock and allow to simmer for 15–20 minutes. Squash should be soft.

Puree soup with blender or stick blender.

Put soup back in the pot and add coconut milk. Bring to simmer, add Tabasco; taste and adjust seasoning. If soup is too thick, add more warm vegetable stock. You may need to adjust seasoning again.

Garnish with chantilly, almonds, and chives.

Chantilly

8 ounces heavy cream	**2 tablespoons yellow curry powder, or more to taste**

Whip cream to stiff peaks. Gently fold in curry powder. Store in airtight container.

Courtesy of Hal Holden-Bache,
Chef and Owner of Lockeland Table Community Kitchen & Bar (p. 75)

Chicken Tortilla Soup

Behind the wheel of a 1970s Winnebago, Teresa Mason started one of the first mobile food trucks in our city. But beyond her groovy DIY style, she makes some of the best food in town from her cozy brick-and-mortar space that opened in East Nashville. This chicken tortilla soup, for example, comes loaded with comfort yet stays bright with lime and fresh ingredients. And as for the Winnebago, it still makes cameo appearances around town.

Makes 8 servings

1 (4-pound) chicken

1 onion, quartered

5 garlic cloves, smashed

1 or 2 habanero chile peppers

1 or 2 jalapeños (with seeds), halved lengthwise

7 cilantro sprigs

3 tablespoons (or more) fresh lime juice

Kosher salt and freshly ground black pepper

Vegetable oil (for frying)

5 corn tortillas, cut in ½-inch-thick strips

2 ears husked corn, grilled and cut off cob

Fresh cilantro, halved cherry tomatoes, avocado wedges, and queso fresco

Bring chicken, onion, garlic, peppers, and 16 cups water to a boil in a large pot; skim foam from surface. Reduce heat to medium and simmer, skimming the surface frequently, until chicken is cooked through, about 1 hour.

Transfer chicken to a plate. Strain broth into another large pot. Return chiles to broth and discard remaining solids. Shred chicken meat; discard skin and bones. Transfer chicken meat to a medium bowl and set aside.

Meanwhile, set pot with strained broth over medium heat and add cilantro sprigs. Bring broth to a simmer; cook until reduced to 8 cups, about 1 hour. Discard cilantro sprigs. Stir in 3 tablespoons lime juice. Season with salt, pepper, and more lime juice, if desired. Add shredded chicken to broth.

Attach a deep-fry thermometer to the side of a large cast-iron skillet or other heavy skillet. Pour oil into the skillet to a depth of 1 inch. Heat over medium heat until thermometer registers 350°F–360°F. Working in batches, fry tortilla strips, turning occasionally, until crisp and golden brown, 2–3 minutes per batch. Using a slotted spoon, transfer to paper towels to drain. Season with salt.

Divide soup among bowls. Top generously with corn, tortilla strips, cilantro, tomatoes, avocado, and crumbled queso fresco.

Courtesy of Teresa Mason, Owner of Mas Tacos Por Favor (pp. 25 and 78)

Roasted Cauliflower
with Turmeric, Peanuts & Raisins

Laura Wilson is a superwoman in the Nashville culinary scene. You might see her whip up meals on the fly from a Community Supported Agriculture box at a makeshift kitchen at the farmers' markets, or you could see her kicking tails at the Nashville Scene's Iron Fork competition. She's consulted in kitchens all over town, but these days, Laura most often can be found educating Nashvillians through cooking classes, demonstrations, and programs she organizes at Grow Local Kitchen at the Nashville Farmers' Market (p. 145).

Makes 8 servings

- 3 heads cauliflower, cut into florets
- 2 tablespoons olive oil
- 1 teaspoon turmeric
- Salt and pepper to taste
- ½ cup peanuts
- ½ cup golden raisins

Preheat oven to 375°F. Toss cauliflower florets with olive oil, turmeric, salt, and pepper. Roast on a sheet pan for 30 minutes. Retoss with peanuts and raisins. Roast for 10 minutes. Serve warm.

Courtesy of Laura Wilson of Grow Local Kitchen at the Nashville Farmers' Market (p. 145)

Empanadas

Back in the kitchen of Fido, a lively Hillsboro Village gem often jammed with students peering into laptops, you'll find some of my favorite chefs in town. Check out John Stephenson's daily blackboard specials for inventive dishes using only the best seasonal ingredients he can find. John also prepares this empanadas recipe by sous chef and Mexico City native Karla Ruiz.

Makes 12 empanadas

Tortillas

2 cups masa harina
½ teaspoon iodized salt

1⅓ cups warm water

Makes 12 tortillas

In a bowl, place masa harina, salt, and water. Mix together well until it forms a dough, adding more water if necessary. Keep a clean damp cloth or rag over the dough to keep it from drying out. Using a spoon, make small balls of the dough (approximately 1½ ounces or a ball of dough the size of a ping pong ball), using your damp hands to make them smooth and round. Keep covered with damp cloth.

Place a ball of dough between two pieces of waxed paper inside of a tortilla press. Press the dough out, and set aside under the damp towel. Repeat with the rest of the dough.

The tortillas are now ready to use in empanadas, or they can be cooked in a pan with about a teaspoon of oil for 1½ minutes per side and used for soft tacos. After cooking, they can also be cut into strips and fried for use in Chicken Tortilla Soup (p. 291).

Empanadas

12 fresh, uncooked corn tortillas

Filling for Tortillas

½ cup chorizo
½ cup roasted cubed potatoes

½ cup shredded Jack and cheddar cheese

Making the Tortillas

3 cups vegetable or canola oil

Curtido, avocado, sour cream, crumbled white cheese, and hot sauce for serving

Place a tortilla on the work surface and put 1 tablespoon filling in the middle. Fold the tortilla over the filling and press down on the edges to make a half-moon shape. Crimp the edges to seal and repeat with rest of the dough.

Let rest for 10–15 minutes in the refrigerator.

In a deep pot, add 3 cups vegetable or canola oil and heat until it reaches 325°F. Add two or three tortillas at a time and fry until golden brown, turning several times during cooking.

Drain on paper towel, then transfer to a plate and serve with curtido (an El Salvadorian slaw), avocado, sour cream, crumbled white cheese (queso fresco or feta), and hot sauce!

Courtesy of Chef John Stephenson and Karla Ruiz of Fido (p. 189)

Brunswick Stew

These days James Beard–award nominee Tyler Brown of The Hermitage Hotel often trades his chef's coat for farmer's clothes as he tends to the garden at Glen Leven, a 66-acre historic site he cares for in partnership with the Land Trust for Tennessee. And the relationship shows in his menus, with heirloom vegetables and locally raised beef prepared with care, sophistication, and Southern grace. Guests of the hotel with its Capitol Grille dining room and Oak Bar might be treated to fresh produce from the harvest at checkout for taking home to enjoy.

Makes 6 to 8 servings

- 5 slices applewood-smoked bacon, diced
- 1 large onion, cut into medium dice
- 4 cups fresh corn (5 to 6 ears)
- 3 cups fresh baby lima beans
- 5 tomatoes, blanched, peeled, and diced
- ⅓ cup fresh thyme, picked from stem
- 1½ quarts chicken broth
- ½ pound pulled pork
- ½ pound roasted and pulled chicken
- Salt and pepper to taste

In medium stockpot, cook the bacon over low heat until crisp. Add onion and cook until translucent.

Add corn, lima beans, tomatoes, thyme, chicken broth, pork, and chicken. Cook over medium heat until beans are tender, then adjust seasonings as desired. There should not be an abundance of excess broth.

Courtesy of Executive Chef Tyler Brown of Capitol Grille (p. 28) and the Oak Bar at The Hermitage Hotel (p. 37)

Loveless Cafe's Meatloaf

The legendary Loveless Cafe now serves country cooking—and those famous homemade biscuits and jams—to nearly half a million people a year. And Jesse Goldstein is the man who keeps this ship sailing smoothly while also helping to preserve the culture and tradition of what made it great in the first place. This recipe for meatloaf uses oatmeal in the mix as opposed to bread crumbs.

Makes 4 to 6 servings

2 ounces butter

1 medium onion, chopped

1½ pounds ground chuck or ground round

1 egg

½ green pepper, chopped

½ cup uncooked rolled oats

1 (16-ounce) can crushed tomatoes

Salt and pepper to taste

1 strip Loveless Cafe bacon

Heat skillet over medium heat, add butter, and sauté onions until they are clear.

Combine beef, egg, sautéed onion, green pepper, oats, and half the tomatoes and mix well. Season with salt and pepper and, in a glass baking dish, shape the mixture into a loaf.

Place the strip of bacon lengthwise on top of the loaf and bake, covered, at 350°F for 45 minutes.

Remove meatloaf from the oven, pour remaining tomatoes over the top, return to oven, and bake uncovered for 30–45 minutes until cooked through.

Courtesy of Jesse Goldstein, Brand Manager of Loveless Cafe (p. 283)

Elevated Hot Chicken

Nashville-style hot chicken has become our culinary claim to fame, and one of my favorite versions of the dish to prepare at home comes from Toby Willis, formerly of the Nashville City Club. Granted, Willis's version comes baked, not fried. But to me, that's all the more reason to enjoy it as often as possible.

Makes 2 servings

Brine

1 quart water
1 quart buttermilk
½ cup salt
½ cup sugar
½ cup hot sauce of choice

2 airline chicken breasts,* split in half (Chef Willis uses Springer Mountain Farms brand)

Coating

½ cup vegetable oil, plus 2–3 tablespoons for searing
7 tablespoons cayenne
1½ teaspoons sugar
2 teaspoons dry mustard

1 teaspoon paprika
2 teaspoons kosher salt
½ teaspoon garlic powder
1 teaspoon white pepper

Sliced white bread and pickles for serving

*What is an airline chicken breast? According to Toby Willis, "Most generally agree that a modern 'airline chicken' descends from traditional European cuts, most notably, 'hotel cut,' 'french cut,' and 'supreme.' The airline version leaves the meat on the first joint of the wing. Traditional European cuts are bone only. All versions are skin on."

Combine the first five ingredients for the brine—water through hot sauce.

Submerge chicken in the brine and refrigerate, covered, overnight.

Heat ½ cup oil in small saucepan over medium heat until shimmering. Add other ingredients and cook until fragrant, about 30 seconds. Divide oil between two bowls.

Rinse brine off chicken and marinate in one bowl of oil for a couple of hours.

Preheat oven to 400°F. Heat 2–3 tablespoons oil in a sauté pan. Sear breasts on each side. Finish in the preheated oven for 18–20 minutes, until cooked through. With a clean brush, brush the chicken again with second bowl of spiced oil. Serve on top of sliced white bread and top with pickles.

Courtesy of Toby Willis, Former Executive Chef of Nashville City Club (p. 52)

Grilled Trout with Bacon, Red Onion & Tomato Butter

Long before East Nashville became a happening neighborhood, Margot McCormack recognized potential in a run-down gas station and transformed it into one of the best and most stylish restaurants in town. She's known for her country French and Italian cuisine at Margot Cafe & Bar, such as pan-roasted duck breast, asparagus, and ricotta crepes, or linguine with tuna confit. This simple trout dish with a bacon, red onion, and tomato butter works well for summer outdoor grilling, with a relish that's easy to prepare as well.

Makes 4 servings

4 (8–10 ounce) trout fillets	**Sprig of fresh thyme**
Olive oil	**1 basket cherry tomatoes**
Salt and pepper to taste	**Splash of white wine**
8 slices bacon, chopped	**⅓ cup chicken stock or water**
¼ cup diced red onion	**2 tablespoons butter**
1 teaspoon chopped garlic	

Grill trout fillets using just a little bit of olive oil and salt and pepper on the inside flesh. They retain their moisture if you grill them whole instead of opening them up in a butterflied fashion.

Either before or while the trout is cooking you may prepare the sauce by rendering chopped bacon in a sauté pan.

Once the bacon is crispy, drain off most of the fat and add the red onion, garlic, and sprig of fresh thyme and cook until golden brown. This should only take a *couple of minutes. Then add the cherry tomatoes. They will blister quickly in the heat of the pan.*

Add a splash of white wine and ⅓ cup chicken stock or water. Bring to a quick boil, mound in the butter, and stir to make a sauce-like consistency. Season to taste with salt and pepper.

Pour over trout fillets right off the grill when they finish cooking. Eat immediately.

Courtesy of Margot McCormack, Chef and Owner of Margot Cafe & Bar (p. 77)

Orange & Fennel Roasted Pork Butt

He's no doubt one of the best chefs in town, but more often than not, you'll spot him in a Piggly Wiggly T-shirt with a pencil behind his ear rather than in a stuffy chef's coat. Tandy Wilson is the James Beard–nominated chef and owner of City House, the hip but laid-back restaurant that he opened in 2007. A Nashville native, Wilson spent time in California and Italy before returning home, where he had also worked as sous chef in Margot McCormack's kitchen. He's racked up accolades in many issues of national food magazines, and he draws a celebrity—and just plain loyal—clientele for his wood-fired, brick-oven pizzas and his inventive cuisine that brings us Italian through a home-style Southern lens. This recipe for roasted pork is something he would make for holidays at home.

Makes 4 to 6 servings

1 (2-pound) boneless pork butt
Salt and pepper to taste
⅓ cup fennel seeds

Zest and juice of 3 oranges, separately set aside
3 cups dry white wine
Extra-virgin olive oil (optional)

Season the pork butt liberally with salt and pepper and set aside.

Lightly toast the fennel seeds in an ungreased sauté pan for 3 to 4 minutes or until fragrant, and then grind them. (A coffee grinder will work.)

Combine zest and toasted fennel seeds and rub onto the roast. Place pork in a roasting pan and roast at 325°F 4–4½ hours, or until fork tender.

Pour wine and juice from oranges over pork. Roast an additional 15 minutes. Remove from oven and let the meat rest. The juice and drippings will serve as sauce with a drizzle of olive oil, if desired.

Courtesy of Tandy Wilson, Chef and Owner of City House (p. 144)

Veggie Meatloaf

I can't imagine a chef in town more committed to making a difference in our food system than Jeremy Barlow. He's written a book, after all, called Chefs Can Change the World, *and his fine dining restaurant Tayst became the first in the city to obtain green certification. Most recently, he opened Sloco, a sandwich shop with a Declaration of Food Independence on the walls and a dedication to serving all-local, sustainable sandwiches at an affordable price. And when he's not in a chef's coat, you might find him helping in a school garden, working to give our children better options for fresh healthy food.*

Makes 8 servings

2 carrots

1 celeriac

2 turnips

1 rutabaga

2 beets

2 taro roots

½ cup sherry vinegar

1½ tablespoons Dijon mustard

1 cup olive oil

Salt and pepper to taste

1 large yellow onion, minced

4 shallots, minced

½ cup garlic cloves,

¼ cup garlic oil

8–10 cups vegetable stock

1 cup crimson lentils

1 cup white lentils

1 cup black lentils

Gravy or tomato sauce for
    serving

Crispy onion rings for serving

Cut all vegetables into ½-inch thick slices.

Combine sherry vinegar and mustard and whisk olive oil into it, making a vinaigrette.

Marinate vegetables in the vinaigrette for about an hour, season with salt and pepper, drain the vegetables, and then throw them on the grill to cook. Leave them on until just before they are done. They should be cooked but have a little bite to them. Be careful not to burn or char; black marks make the finished product bitter.

Dice veggies into ½-inch cubes and combine, setting aside in a large bowl. (If you don't want pink vegetables, you may choose to keep the beets separate until the end of the recipe.)

Roast garlic cloves in oil at 350°F until soft and just starting to brown. Cool, strain, and reserve garlic and oil separately.

Combine minced onions and shallots. Separate into three equal piles.

Using three saucepans, sweat onion mixture, covered, in roasted garlic oil. When onions are translucent, add roasted garlic and beat up with a spoon.

In one saucepan, put 2 cups of stock, and put 3 cups into each of the remaining pots. Bring all three to a boil. Reserve the remaining stock to use if needed.

Put the crimson lentils into the pot with 2 cups stock; follow with the white and the black lentils in the other pots. Turn all pots down to a low simmer and cook until the lentils are soft. They must be cooked separately because they all cook at different times. The crimson lentils will be very mushy when they are finished; this will act as your binder for the finished product. The white and black lentils may need additional stock; the lentils must remain covered with liquid while cooking and evaporation will vary from stove to stove and day to day. If you need to add more stock, just add reserved liquid to cover the lentils. When they are soft but still hold their shape, they are done. Strain them and pour them into the bowl with the vegetables.

Mix lentils and vegetables well and season to your taste. Make sure product is still warm.

Fill a parchment-lined 9 x 5-inch loaf pan lined with the mixture, cover with another piece or parchment, and press down with another pan or a piece of cardboard cut to fit inside rim of pan. Weigh it down with a brick or some cans or anything with weight and put in fridge to set overnight.

Pull from the fridge and remove from the pan. Cut into desired size and heat in a 375°F oven until warm throughout.

Top with gravy or tomato sauce and crispy onion rings.

Courtesy of Jeremy Barlow, Chef and Owner of Tayst (p. 199) and Sloco (p. 197)

Buttermilk Chocolate Cake

Chef Kim Totzke has worked all over Nashville, including the kitchen of beloved chef Deb Paquette before her restaurant Zola closed on West End. Totzke later worked with Laura Wilson as co-chef of Ombi on Elliston Place. But these days, Totzke is in charge as director of operations at Provence Breads & Cafe. This recipe comes from Totzke and executive pastry chef Joshua Pion.

Makes 1 (8-inch) round cake

10½ ounces sugar

5½ ounces flour

3¼ ounces cocoa powder

½ teaspoon baking soda

¼ teaspoon baking powder

Pinch of salt

1 egg yolk

2 eggs

6 ounces buttermilk

¾ teaspoon vanilla

3 ounces melted butter

6 ounces hot water

Sift all dry ingredients together. Combine yolk, eggs, buttermilk, and vanilla. Combine melted butter and water.

Add all liquids to dry ingredients and mix by hand with a whisk until just combined.

Pour batter into a parchment-lined, greased 8-inch round baking pan. Bake at 325°F for about 40–50 minutes or until toothpick comes out clean.

Cool completely and remove from pan. Prepare frosting recipe (opposite).

Chocolate Italian Buttercream Frosting

5 ¼ ounces egg whites

13 ounces sugar, divided

2 ounces water

1 pound butter

4 ounces cocoa powder

Combine egg whites and 2½ ounces sugar and whip to soft peaks.

Cook 10½ ounces sugar and water to 238°F. Pour hot sugar into whipped whites. Continue to whip until cool and then add butter and cocoa powder slowly. Continue whipping until smooth and fluffy.

Use immediately to frost the cake and/or refrigerate any leftovers.

Courtesy of Provence Breads & Cafe (p. 196)

Appendices

Appendix A: Eateries by Cuisine

American
Holland House Bar & Refuge, 73
McCabe Pub Restaurant & Lounge, 235
Mere Bulles, 256
M. L. Rose Craft Beer & Burgers, 171
Patterson House, The, 128
Saffire, 252
Silo, 150
Tavern, 129
12th South Taproom, 199
Whiskey Kitchen, 131

American Contemporary
Arpeggio, 27
Bound'ry, 123
1808 Grille, 215
Ellendale's, 167
Sunset Grill, 198
YOLOS Restaurant and Bar, 116

Asian
PM, 195
Suzy Wong's House of Yum, 226
Wild Ginger, 254

Barbecue
B&C Market BBQ, 142
Corner Pub Midtown, 124
Drifters, 67
Edley's Bar-B-Que, 188
Jack's Bar-B-Que, 51
Judge Bean's BBQ, 246
Martin's Bar-B-Que Joint, 284
Roosters Texas Style BBQ, 42
South Street Original Smokehouse, Crab Shack & Authentic Dive Bar, 134
Sportsman's Grill, 236

Bistro
AM@FM, 141
Eastland Cafe, 68
Firefly Grille, 109
Germantown Cafe, 146
Germantown Cafe East, 72
Jackson's Bar & Bistro, 192
Lockeland Table Community Kitchen & Bar, 75
Macke's, 111
Marche Artisan Foods, 76
Margot Cafe & Bar, 77
360 Wine Bar & Bistro, 226
Wild Iris, 255

Breakfast
Athens Family Restaurant, 164
Bongo Java, 201
Bongo Java East, 87
Cafe Coco, 232

MAFIAoZIA's Pizzeria
and Neighborhood
Pub, 202
Manny's House of
Pizza, 34
Pizza Perfect, 194
Porta Via Italian
Kitchen, 223
The Wild Hare, 229

Polynesian
Omni Hut, 285

Pub Food
Batter'd & Fried / Wave
Sushi Bar, 64
Beyond the Edge, 65
Broadway Brewhouse &
Mojo Grill, 132
Crow's Nest Restaurant,
107
Family Wash, The, 69
Gold Rush Restaurant &
Bar, The, 233
McCabe Pub Restaurant &
Lounge, 235
Past Perfect, 38
Riverfront Tavern, 41
Tin Roof, 129
Village Pub & Beer Garden,
The, 85

Sandwiches
Bongo Java, 201
Bongo Java East, 87
Cafe Coco, 232
The Food Company, 118
Kay Bob's, 194
Piranha's Bar & Grill, 39
Sam & Zoe's Coffee House
and Cafe, 174
Savarino's Cucina, 196
Sloco, 197
Star Bagel Cafe, 225

Seafood
Batter'd & Fried / Wave
Sushi Bar, 64
Eastside Fish, 69
Fish & Company, 190
South Street Original
Smokehouse, Crab
Shack & Authentic
Dive Bar, 134
Urban Grub, 200

Southern
B&C Market BBQ, 142
Beacon Light Tea
Room, 279
Cabana, 185
City House, 257
Corner Pub Midtown, 124
55 South, 246

Hachland Hill Countryside
Retreat, 281
Loveless Cafe, 283
Mack and Kate's, 247
Macke's, 111
Mere Bulles, 256
Miss Mary Bobo's
Boarding House, 284
Puckett's Grocery &
Restaurant, 250
Red Pony, 250
Silo, 150
South Street Original
Smokehouse, Crab
Shack & Authentic
Dive Bar, 134
Southern Steak & Oyster,
The, 43
Urban Grub, 200

Steak House
Demos' Restaurant, 48
Jimmy Kelly's Steakhouse
Restaurant, 234
Kayne Prime, 125
Nero's Grill, 113
Old Hickory Steakhouse
Restaurant, 157
Prime 108, 39
Sperry's Restaurant, 235
Sportsman's Grill, 236
Stock-Yard Restaurant, 54

Appendix B: Dishes, Specialties & Specialty Foods

Bagels
Bagel Face Bakery, 93

Bakery
Bagel Face Bakery, 93
Bread & Company, 105
Dozen—A Nashville Sweet
    Shop, 156
Dulce Desserts, 207
Fox's Donut Den, 117
Foxy Baking Co., 95
Geraldine's Pies, 159
Merridee's Breadbasket,
    249
Provence Breads &
    Cafe, 196
Puffy Muffin Dessert
    Bakery & Restaurant,
    250
Sweet Betweens, 100

Sweet 16th Bakery, 101
Sweet Stash, The, 161

Bread
Bread & Company, 105
Provence Breads &
    Cafe, 196

Breweries
Blackstone Restaurant &
    Brewery, 261
Jackalope Brewing
    Company, 263
Yazoo Brewing Company,
    264

Candy
Bang Candy Company, 58
Diana's Sweet Shoppe, 60
Peanut Shop, The, 62

Cheese
Bloomy Rind, The, 99
Corrieri's Formaggeria, 206
East Nashville Farmers'
    Market, 95
Franklin Farmers'
    Market, 259
Nashville Farmers'
    Market, 145
Turnip Truck, The, 101
Turnip Truck Urban Fare,
    The, 139
12th South Farmers'
    Market, 210
West Nashville Farmers'
    Market, 241

Chocolate
Olive & Sinclair Chocolate
    Company, 97

Coffee

Barista Parlour, 94
Bongo Java, 201
Bongo Java East, 87
Cafe Coco, 232
Casablanca Coffee, 137
Crema, 58
Dose Coffee & Tea, 240
Drinkhaus Espresso &
    Tea, 240
Fido, 189
Frothy Monkey, 191
Hot & Cold, 208
J&J's Market, 138
Phat Bites Deli &
    Coffeeshop, 173
Portland Brew, 210
Sam & Zoey's Coffee
    House and Cafe, 174
Sip Cafe, 99
Ugly Mugs Coffee &
    Tea, 102

Cookies

Bread & Company, 105
Christie Cookies, 112
Dozen—A Nashville Sweet
    Shop, 156
Marche Artisan Foods, 76
Sweet Betweens, 100
Sweet Stash, The, 161
Table 3 Market, 120

Craft Cocktails

Holland House Bar &
    Refuge, 264
No. 308, 265
Patterson House, 266

Cupcakes

Cupcake Collection, The,
    24, 155
Dulce Desserts, 207
Gigi's Cupcakes, 127
The Painted Cupcake, 119

Distilleries

Collier and
    McKeel/SPEAKeasy
    Spirits, 261
Corsair Artisan
    Distillery, 262

Farmers' Markets

East Nashville Farmers'
    Market, 95
Franklin Farmers'
    Market, 259
Nashville Farmers'
    Market, 145
12th South Farmers'
    Market, 210
West Nashville Farmers'
    Market, 241

Honky-Tonks

Robert's Western
    World, 267
Station Inn, The, 267
Tootsie's Orchid Lounge,
    268

Ice Cream/
   Gelato/Ice Pops

Bobbie's Dairy Dip, 230
Bravo Gelato, 112
Hot & Cold, 208
Jeni's Splendid Ice
    Creams, 96
Las Paletas Gourmet
    Popsicles, 209
Mike's Ice Cream, 61
Pied Piper Creamery, 98
Sip Cafe, 99
Sweet CeCe's, 193

Live Music

Barn at the Loveless Cafe,
    The, 272
Bluebird Cafe, The, 272
Exit/In, 273
Family Wash, The, 274
5 Spot, The, 274
Grand Ole Opry, The, 275
Listening Room Cafe,
    The, 276

Index